SIEGE

SIEGE
Malta
1940 - 1943

ERNLE BRADFORD

WILLIAM MORROW AND COMPANY, INC.

New York

Grateful acknowledgment is made for permission to quote from "The Hollow Men" in *Four Quartets* by T. S. Eliot, copyright 1943 by T. S. Eliot; copyright renewed © 1971 by Esme Valerie Eliot. Reprinted by permission of Harcourt Brace Jovanovich, Inc.

Library of Congress Cataloging-in-Publication Data

Bradford, Ernle Dusgate Selby.
Siege: Malta, 1940–1943.

Bibliography: p.
Includes index.
1. Malta—History—Siege, 1940–1943.   I. Title.
D763.M3B73   1986   940.54′21   85-21503
ISBN 0-688-04781-5

Printed in the United States of America

First Edition

1   2   3   4   5   6   7   8   9   10

BOOK DESIGN BY MARY CREGAN

Foreword

I first saw Malta as navigating officer of a British destroyer in July 1943. I was on the bridge at dawn, and I remember how, when the sun rose, the low tawny coast showed up on our port bow as we made our landfall, slightly to the south of Grand Harbour and the island's capital, Valletta. Six months after the siege had ended, the waters around the island were still dangerous from mines of every type, and we were very careful to stay well within the swept channel as we made our approach to the harbor entrance.

Malta had haunted me—and I suppose all others in the Mediterranean fleet—ever since I had first arrived in this sea at the age of nineteen in 1941. It was a name not only famous in the world but also of ill-omen and foreboding. How often had I seen merchant ships loading in Alexandria, destroyers alongside jetties taking on stores, and barges going out to capital ships deep-laden with ammunition and stores of every kind—all for Malta. Twice I had been destined for the island myself on what was euphemistically called "the Malta run." Once the ship on which I was serving was torpedoed; the second time, in another ship, our convoy was turned back to Alexandria because too many merchantmen had been lost to make it worthwhile proceeding any farther. In any case, we were less than halfway there, and most of the escorting ships had almost run out of antiaircraft ammunition. The violence of the action during that convoy, in the sinister area south of Crete known as "Bomb Alley," had stayed in my mind as nightmarishly as the Battle of Crete itself. So, to see Malta at long last from a destroyer's bridge, unbombed and untorpedoed, seemed a kind of achievement.

To enter Grand Harbour, with the long defenses of Fort Ricasoli on the port hand and bomb-battered Fort St. Elmo (a legend in itself) to starboard, was to sail into history. Some of my friends and many wartime acquaintances had died in or off this island, and many more had failed to reach it or never succeeded in getting back to Alexandria. Malta was no enchanted place that lured men toward it with siren voices but, rather, a Medusa that killed with a glance. I was vaguely aware that the island had an ancient and remarkable history, but young men who are in the thick of modern history have little or no time for the past. In any case, as I saw from the moment we entered Grand Harbour, a new part of Malta's amazing story was unfolding.

That great inlet had probably never before been so full of ships in all its long maritime life: battleships, aircraft carriers, and cruisers were almost commonplace, and as for destroyers, minesweepers, and lesser fry, their masts, guns, and radar antennas bristled above every dusty stretch of quayside or landing stage. Hardly had we ourselves secured in our appointed berth—outboard of two others—than an American destroyer came in alongside us. (I have long forgotten her name or number, but I remember that her first lieutenant was one of President Roosevelt's sons, for we became acquainted later over a drink in our wardroom.) Every one of the harbors and creeks of Malta—even those rarely used—was as thick with ships as Grand Harbour itself. Operation Husky, the assault on Sicily, was due to start in three days' time.

To say I saw nothing of Malta during the war may sound absurd, since I revisited the island on at least a dozen occasions, but all I remember is trudging ashore occasionally through dust and ruined buildings on some official business connected with the ship. There was little enough to go ashore for "on pleasure bent," and the war in the Mediterranean was moving elsewhere: first Sicily, then Italy and the Salerno landings, and finally Anzio. Our ship returned to Malta to revictual, reammunition, refuel, and on one occasion to have some shell damage repaired—from, of all unlikely things, a German Tiger tank in Sicily's Augusta harbor. A friend who was in Hal

Far for over a year during the siege remembers nothing but his flying operations and a few parties in the mess; another who was in one of the cruisers of Force H remembers, apart from the air raids, the joy of coming back after one successful operation and finding the whole of Grand Harbour lined with cheering people. For myself, when I finally left, posted to the Home Fleet and Russian convoys, I neither expected nor particularly wanted to see the island again.

I returned to Malta, this time of my own volition, in 1951 at the helm of my own small sailing boat. During the following three years I used Malta as my base for expeditions to Greece and the Aegean islands and as many other places in the central and eastern Mediterranean as I could find time for. It was during the months spent in Malta, wintering or refitting after some cruise, that I really got to know something of its people and the strange, intense quality of the island. By that time most of the damage from the war had been made good, although work would go on for years. The authorities were being wise enough in almost all places to restore rather than rebuild in the usual postwar fashion. I spent one whole winter in the small boat harbor originally designed for the galleys of the Knights of St. John that lies between Fort St. Angelo and the old city of Vittoriosa. In the narrow, twisting alleys—heavily bombed during the war but now vivid with life, where carved coats-of-arms in stone and elaborate windows and doorways still spoke of the sixteenth century, I did my daily shopping. Boat trips by *dghaisa* across Grand Harbour brought me to the restored grandeur of Valletta, and many expeditions into the countryside began to uncover for me something of the extraordinary complexity of this island. Smaller than Britain's Isle of Wight, Malta contains in its onionskin towns and villages layer upon layer of ancient life and cultures, while parts of the barren and scarcely visited ridgeland to the west speak of an unfathomable past, older even than the great Neolithic and Copper Age temples that are one of Malta's great gifts to the world.

During those years and subsequently I have been to most of the islands in the Mediterranean, from the Balearics in the west to Cyprus in the east, to the far north of the Aegean and to sun-blinded Jerba in the south, yet for some curious reason I have found nowhere that detained me as did Malta and its smaller sister island, Gozo. They held me so much indeed that I lived there for more than ten years. And yet the islands have none of the conventional beauty that draws visitors to so many others in this sea. Perhaps it was the rich layers of visible history, going back over thousands of years, attracted me, but even more than that it was the nature of the people. They had an outward warmth that was not unusual in the Mediterranean, but their friendship once given was totally enduring, and they were endowed with a rocklike strength of character. Something of this I have attempted to show under the terrible conditions of adversity during the siege of 1940–1943.

Curiously enough, I went back to the island in 1960 intent on writing a history of that other siege—by the Ottomans in 1565—of which Voltaire said, "Nothing is better known than the siege of Malta," but of which practically nothing had been written in English. It was while I was working on this book that a friend who had been in the island throughout the Second World War, and had married and settled there, remarked that he thought my subject had been much written about during the war itself. I realized we were talking at cross-purposes and explained that the siege I was trying to explore and describe was not the recent one. Thinking about it, I reckoned I was lucky to be dealing with such old material, since reputations were inviolate and even the effects of the whole action had long since ceased to have much bearing on modern times. The recent siege would, I thought, prove much more difficult—overdocumented and laden with pitfalls.

I considered then that fifty years would need to pass before enough dust had settled for the Second World War "Great Siege of Malta" to be viewed in anything like perspective. It is a few years less than that now, but I have now attempted it. The survivors, even on the island, are relatively few, for many Maltese have emigrated in the past forty years, and the passions and sadnesses of those days have largely faded or been burned away by many subsequent summer suns. The ships are all gone under the sea, and most of the men with them. Grand Harbour, though merchantmen still call and cruise liners visit, is largely a place of peace and silence now. Manoel Island in Marsamuscetto, the former submarine headquarters, provides berths for a multitude of yachts of all shapes and sizes under the flags of all nations. Luqa Airport, vastly extended since those days, roars only with jet airliners full of businessmen and tourists, coming and going. (They provide those peaceful flashes in the sky.) Malta has been an independent republic since 1964, although its flag is still the same half-white, half-red symbol that has flown for centuries, and English is still the second language.

After so many years living on the island, ten of them in a house on Kalkara Creek, seeing Grand Harbour under my eyes every day, I found that the second siege would not leave me alone. I had written about the first, in addition to a history of the Knights, but the ghosts of my contemporaries encountered on early morning or evening walks beside the still waters of the harbor seemed to represent something of a reproach. How distant does history have to be before you can write about it? It has not been any easier than I estimated it would be, over a quarter of a century ago.

—E.B.
1985

Contents

CONTENTS

List of Maps

13

If the Turks should prevail against the Isle of Malta it is uncertain what further peril might follow to the rest of Christendom.

QUEEN ELIZABETH I, 1565

To Honour her brave people I award the George Cross to the Island Fortress of Malta to bear witness to a Heroism and Devotion that will long be famous in History.

KING GEORGE VI, 1942

Bay of Biscay

FRANCE

SWITZ⁰

AUSTRIA HUNGARY

YUGOSLAVIA

RUMANIA

Black Sea

BULGARIA

TURKEY

Dardanelles

Aleppo

Haifa

CYPRUS

Port Said

Suez

Alexandria

Cairo

El Alamein

Mersa Matruh

Sidi Barrani

Rhodes

Aegean Sea

Athens

Piraeus

MOREA

C. Matapan

Navarino

Maleme

CRETE

'BOMB ALLEY'

Bardia

Tobruk

Bomba

Gazala

Derna

CYRENAICA

Benghazi

G. of Sirte

El Agheila

ALBANIA

Valona

Ionian Sea

Taranto

Adriatic Sea

ITALY

Naples

Tyrrhenian Sea

Messina

Reggio

Palermo

Catania

Trapani

SICILY

Syracuse

The Narrows

MALTA

Pantellaria

Lampedusa

Kerkenah Is.

Buerat

LIBYA

Tripoli

Sfax

TRIPOLITANIA

TUNISIA

C. Bon

Tunis

Bizerta

Bone

Skerki Bank

Cagliari

Decimomannu

SARDINIA

CORSICA

La Maddalena

G. of Genoa

BALEARIC IS.

SPAIN

Algiers

Oran

ALGERIA

Gibraltar

MOROCCO

M.K.

EGYPT

0   100   200   300   400   500 Miles

1

A Distant Day

Over dinner on June 11, 1940, Hitler heard that the Italians had just bombed the British colony of Malta. He was at his temporary headquarters in a deserted village in southern Belgium, and the second half of his campaign against France, Operation Red, was proceeding smoothly. France, weak within and without, was collapsing according to plan and almost on schedule—something that had never been achieved by the invading armies of the kaiser in the First World War. These were the golden hours of Hitler's life, and it might have been expected that his Italian partner would manage to inject the only note of discord.

Mussolini had served a formal declaration of war on Britain and France the previous day, provoking his ally's contempt. Hitler held that such formalities belonged to the Middle Ages and were no more than a hypocritical pretense that the age of chivalry was not dead. He believed in striking first and letting the scream of the dive-bombers and the grinding clatter of the tanks be the declaration of war. Over dinner the select group of a dozen or so who attended on the Führer discussed the Italian action in the Mediterranean. The Germans agreed it was no more than a gesture, for it was no secret that the British Mediterranean fleet had withdrawn from Malta to Alexandria: With Latin grandiosity Mussolini was attacking nothing of importance. It was over an empty harbor, decrepit buildings, and sun-stunned peasants that the Regia Aeronautica triumphantly rode through the sky. The Germans doubted whether the Italian fleet would do the same upon the sea. If Mussolini really meant business, why were the Italians not already bombarding Malta's Grand Harbour prior to a seaborne invasion? It should have been possible, for the modern Caesar had laid claim to the Middle Sea in true Roman fashion as *Mare Nostrum.*

Embittered by the fact that Italy had not clearly associated herself with Germany in the autumn of the previous year, Hitler (who had known about this impending declaration of war for several days) was not prepared to pull the Italian chestnuts out of the fire—and they were already asking for help. They urgently needed formations from the Luftwaffe to assist their drive into France through the Alps, but none could be spared until the battle for France was over. Hitler had tried to persuade the Duce to withhold entry into the war at this moment, but the Italian leader was eager to lay his hands upon the spoils of war and had determined to rush in as soon as it was clear that France was falling.[1]

Hitler little knew at that time how often over the years to come he would be called to the assistance of his ally in the south, nor how much the weaknesses in that quarter would later distract him from other important theaters of the war. While the British mocked and compared the Italian dictator's activities to a jackal's, the Germans cynically nicknamed their allies "the harvest hands" for their entry upon the field at such a moment. Over the Mediterranean, which had hardly yet become a theater of war, the seeds of distrust between the Axis partners were already sown.

It was at five minutes to seven on that blue June morning when the first air raid siren of the thousands that were to follow sounded over the island of Malta. The raid had long been expected; indeed, Malta had held practice blackouts years before they became a part of life in the Western world, for the island had been anticipating war ever since the Italian-Abyssinian crisis of 1935. A shadow of terror, arising from the First World War, was the expectation that in any subsequent conflict poison gas would be used—dropped from aircraft this time and not, as before, released from canisters on the ground. Although it was highly unlikely that gas would be effective on a small island where, even in an apparent calm, some light airs are always stirring, almost the only preparations for war that had been made, and instructions given to the civilian population, were antigas. High-explosive and incendiary bombs had hardly been taken into account. As early as October 1935 the first mock air raid had been carried out on Malta's capital, Valletta, with dummy explosions, church bells ringing as a warning, and public utilities turned off. The explosions, very similar to the petards that the Maltese loved to fire during their many religious *festas,* had brought cheering people out onto the streets.[2] It was very different in 1940, and it would be years before the bells would call to church or the fireworks of peace explode.

Even without the early radar that had been installed on Malta, the enemy raiders would soon have been spotted in that clear summer sky. Two small groups—ten planes in all—of Savoia Marchetti trimotor bombers were escorted by nine Macchi fighters. Few enough for the first raid of the war, they were more like the gauntlet flung down to confirm the high words of their leader on the previous day. All nineteen aircraft were from the great island of Sicily, only sixty miles to the north. They came over at about twenty thousand feet in the conventional high-level bombing technique of the time—one that the Germans had already discounted, having proved over Europe that it was low-level dive-bombing tactics that were accurate and at the same time instilled the maximum amount of terror.

The flashes of sun on their silver fuselages and the mumbling rumble of their engines inspired an unknown fear among the watching population. Like so many in those distant days, the Maltese who looked skyward knew only by picture and report of the devastation caused by bombing in countries that seemed to them very far away. Anticipation of pain, injury, loss, or death is often worse than the reality, which, when it occurs, must be somehow or other endured. Then, from far up, the high-whistling, thin-screaming of the falling bombs began, and the sound of the antiaircraft barrage—mute indeed to what it would become—reinforced by the guns of the old monitor, *Terror,* and two "China river gunboats," the *Aphis* and *Lady Bird,* moored in the harbor to aid the shore defenses, thundered on eardrums accustomed only to the sounds of island life. The war had begun. Like random dabs of shaving soap the first shells burst against the sky below the high-flying silver fish that seemed so inhuman, but in which young Italians were enduring their baptism of fire and feeling for the first time the great life of bursting air below them that told of a fearful hostility equal to their own.[3]

An island is always besieged by the surrounding sea. Its inhabitants throw up their defenses of breakwaters and harbor walls, which must constantly be repaired, while in the surge and thunder of bad weather the natural defenses of cliff and headland are always under assault. Islanders are accustomed to the feeling of being on their own—they are independent people whose only connection with the outside world is through the estranging sea, which only unites through boat or ship. The intensification of this eternal siege by an act of war is not, then, so grave a shock as is similar violence to the inhabitants of an inland city. The islanders are accustomed to foreign intrusion—commercial, friendly, or hostile. Deep in their racial memory lie the necessary responses designed to cope with the arrival of strangers by sea, a different language used by visiting traders, along with the knowledge that some alteration in the balance of power among the distant, invisible nations may mean a change in their own lives. People who live in small islands do not expect to be able to alter things; theirs is the acceptance world.

On that first day of their war there were eight air raids on the Maltese homeland. In the later raids, during the afternoon and early evening, thirty-eight bombers escorted by twelve fighters invaded the sky that those beneath the bombs felt was Maltese.[4] The last raid was the most unpleasant, but all of them were designed primarily to demoralize the population as well as cause damage to the dockyard installations and the airbases. That there was no strong force of fighters to rise to meet the raiders, or to be destroyed on the ground, was the result of a decision taken long ago by the Royal Air Force that Malta was indefensible in the event of war. Only four old Gloster Gladiator fighters, obsolescent if not obsolete, had clattered up from Hal Far airstrip—to the surprise of the islanders, most of whom did not even know of their existence, and to the alarm of the attackers, who had been incorrectly informed that no fighters were to be expected.

The last raid, at nightfall, was the heaviest and caused the most casualties, almost all civilians. Indeed, throughout the day's raids only a few soldiers were killed at their posts, and no guns were knocked out. The casualties were mostly among the families living in the small cube-shaped houses around the dockyard where they earned their bread. This was inevitable under high-level bombing attack—inaccurate as it was at that time—and because Malta, particularly its dockyard area, was one of the most densely populated areas in the whole of Europe.

No islander had quite expected that civilian men, women, and children would die under bomb blast or be razored by flying glass or be crushed under falling walls. Violent death was something that was associated on the island principally with sailors in the great warships, with airmen up in the remote sky, or perhaps with gunners at their posts, and very few Maltese had any comprehension of what it meant. Even the warships with their ominous long guns that had slept like peaceful whales in Grand Harbour and the adjacent creeks of the island throughout the interwar years had principally been regarded with affection, as the source of money and prosperity. Their function was hidden so far away as to be invisible. The distant thunder of the guns on practice shoots off the island had been no more disturbing than the familiar rumble of electric storms over the Mediterranean—it was part of the pattern of life. Their real purpose and that of the aircraft, hitherto regarded as eccentric new toys of the island's rulers, was now fully revealed—Death.

Things can be anticipated but not really understood, and certainly the reality of unknown things can never be fully imagined. The cold fact that about thirty civilians were killed and more were wounded was immediately felt throughout a population of 250,000 of close-knit families, where it often seemed that everyone was related to everyone else.[5] It was quickly established in those first raids that the solid limestone blocks with which most of the houses were built, combined with their flat roofs of stone, made them almost impervious to incendiary bombs and highly resistant even to high explosives. The island itself was little more than a huge block of limestone rising out of the sea, and it was this geological fact that was to contribute to its defensibility under later horrific bombardment, heavier and more intense than ever imagined. That the stone could be quarried easily meant that hundreds of tunnels would soon shelter its people, resulting in a casualty rate almost unbelievably low when measured against the thousands of tons of explosives rained down upon the island.

The Mediterranean has witnessed innumerable sieges as the races, nations, and empires have swayed back and forth in the pendulumstruggles for power. There is hardly a city on a headland, hardly an island out of the hundreds in the sea, that at some time or other has not been the subject of a siege, great or small.

Standing at the crossroads of the sea, Malta had inevitably been involved in previous sieges. Indeed, the Great Siege of Malta in 1565 is one of the most famous in recorded history. Then, the Ottoman Empire under Suleiman the Magnificent had attacked this outlying bastion of Christendom—and been defeated. Of this savage epic Voltaire had said "Nothing is better known than the siege of Malta." In the Wars of Religion Malta, as the fortress-home of the Knights of St. John, had played a major part in the Marches of the West. So famous had the island become after 1565 that the Knights, the oldest order of chivalry in existence and the third oldest religious order in Christendom, had become known throughout the world as the Knights of Malta.[6] In the many accounts in almost every known European language of the Knights and their deeds—particularly during that Great Siege—the role of the people of Malta themselves had largely escaped the attention of biographers and historians. Now, after the first day of the siege that was to eclipse all others, the Maltese entered a new phase of their lives—most in their familiar small homes near the harbors but many, resuming a trek that had begun with the outbreak of war, with friends, relatives, or acquaintances in outlying villages.

On the following day, June 12, 1940, one Italian reconnaissance aircraft flew over from Sicily to assess the damage caused by the first acts of war. It was shot down.

2

Islanded in Time

At the crossroads of the Mediterranean, almost equidistant from Gibraltar on the one hand and Cyprus on the other, the small Maltese archipelago commands the trade routes not only between east and west but also between north and south. Sicily lies sixty miles to the north, and Tripoli in Africa is just over two hundred miles to the south. Gibraltar and Cyprus (or Port Said for the Suez Canal) are each about a thousand miles away. In the siege of 1565 the Sultan Suleiman was interested in Malta as a stepping-stone to Sicily and Italy for the expansion of his empire into Europe. Over two centuries later Napoleon seized the island in 1798 on his way from Europe for the conquest of Egypt and the East. In this new siege that was beginning it was the north-south axis that interested Italy's Duce, since this was the main sea route between Italy and Sicily and the Italian colony of Tripolitania to the south.

Malta possessed in its Grand Harbour and other ancillary harbors and anchorages the finest fleet base in the central Mediterranean. It could give secure refuge and watering and fueling facilities to the largest fleets in the world. The accident of nature that had carved Grand Harbour with its attendant creeks out of Malta's northeastern coast into a deep-water basin that could easily accommodate the drafts of modern battleships and aircraft carriers and their attendant deep-laden tankers had made its acquisition important even in the

days of comparatively shallow-draft warships and merchantmen. A natural harbor standing in the center of the sea, it was unique.

It was small wonder that Malta had been important in Mediterranean history long before history was even written. Neolithic and Copper Age temples are found there in greater profusion and sophistication than anywhere else in the world. Their giant pillars, lintels, and altars, washed by the sea air, still breathed the peace of the Great Earth-Mother and made the island unique. After these unknown temple-builders died out or departed, the Phoenicians trading with Spain in the far west for tin and other metals were the first to use the island's harbors. Since they had no need for deep water but only a place to drag their boats ashore for repair and security, they made their settlement at Marsaxlokk, the shallow southern harbor. Their descendants, the Carthaginians, who found the island a useful stepping-stone to their colonies in western Sicily, colonized Malta and its sister island to the north, Ghaudex, or Gozo. Greeks also came there in the way of trade but left little imprint, whereas their Semitic rivals left not only their tombs but also their language. When Carthage fell and the island came within the Roman Empire, the inhabitants were found to be speaking a Semitic dialect, which was to lead the chronicler of the Acts of the Apostles to refer to them as *barbaroi,* barbarians, meaning those who spoke a language other than Greek or Latin. The shipwreck of St. Paul (traditionally in the bay that bears his name) produced Malta's first Christian church leader, or bishop, in Publius, the head man of the island.

The Christian faith, by tradition at least, can thus be said to have existed in Malta longer than almost anywhere else in the world. However much it may have been overlaid by Islam in the centuries when Malta, like Sicily, was subject to Moslem rule, Christianity has never been extinguished on the island since the visit of the Apostle. This fact is neither obscure nor irrelevant to the history of the twentieth-century siege, for the attitude and behavior of the islanders can be attributed at least to some certain degree to their deep faith and their belief that from the time of St. Paul's visit they have come under special protection. The Maltese have a more real and traceable link with the founder of Christianity than any of the subsequent nobles who have ruled them have had with their so-called blue-blooded ancestors.

Malta is a slate upon which has been written and overwritten the whole history of the Mediterranean.[1] After the Romans came the Byzantines, and after them the Arabs. The latter in their two centuries of occupation left the most significant imprint of all, their language. Finding a population who already spoke some old version of a Semitic tongue, it was not difficult to impress their Islamic Arabic upon the Maltese, whose modern language, despite all its borrowings from Italian, Spanish, French, and English, is still an Arabic language in grammar and construction and in all its basic words. The possession of this tongue, now recognized as a distinct language, different to a degree from all others, has served throughout the centuries to give this small people a national character. It is this that has sustained them throughout the centuries and has given this small people a national character. It is this, too, that has sustained them throughout all occupations and colonization—this and their attachment to the Catholic Church.

Like every other Western country in the decades subsequent to the Second World War, Malta has been changed by the internationalization of the world. Despite this and some decline in the simple religious beliefs that previously sustained its people, the Maltese still keep their almost private language and their somewhat medieval attachment to the Church, giving them a character that is different from all their Mediterranean neighbors. Seeing that Malta is only seventeen miles long and nine miles across at its widest point, with a population that in 1939 was a little over a quarter of a million, it is close to miraculous that the island has retained its identity through all the vicissitudes of political, military, and cultural invasions. The Maltese are indeed a nation. The key to this independent and individual survival is to be found not only in Malta's language and churches but also in its villages and countryside. Many British servicemen billeted in remote parts of the island during the twentieth-century siege stumbled upon this secret Malta with some surprise. It might have been with Malta in mind that Virginia Woolf wrote: "The peasants are the great sanctuary of sanity, the country the last stronghold of happiness. When they disappear there is no hope for the race."

After the Arabic centuries came the Norman conquest, restoring the Church, which had greatly declined in the years when those who did not accept Islam paid a heavy tax for the privilege. Although rulers rather than colonizers, the Normans brought the island back once again within the European fold. This process was further strengthened by the Aragonese, who also controlled Sicily. They introduced some aspects of Spanish life and culture as well as reinforcing Malta's Catholic ties. When the island was finally given by the Emperor Charles V to the homeless Knights of St. John in 1530, the period of its greatest fame and prosperity was at hand. The Knights were members of the oldest and richest families in Europe, and the fame that Malta acquired in the Great Siege of 1565 not only brought an influx of money but also made the island from then on a focus of international interest. During the centuries to come, through their organized and "official" piracy of the Moslem shipping lanes, the Order and with it the island prospered. From this period date the innumerable fortifications that protect and embellish Malta's rocky shores as well as the magnificent palaces, churches, and the great cathedral of St. John—so many of the buildings that were to be badly damaged or destroyed in the Second World War.

By the end of the eighteenth century the Order had become an anachronism in the new nationalistic Europe, and its rule over Malta collapsed with hardly a sigh before the armada of Napoleon, which was then pursuing his imperialistic ambitions in the East. It was now that the Maltese, not for the first time in their long history, displayed the dogged and resolute character that was to be so marked a feature of the years between 1940 and 1943. They may well have been tired of the Order, which had become not only decadent but inefficient in its later years, but they were not prepared to accept the arrogance and the atheism of the revolutionary French. More than anything else it was the wanton defacement and vandalizing of their beloved churches—the heart of every village—that drove the Maltese to revolt against the French garrison imposed upon them by the departing Napoleon.

This spirited reaction of an illiterate peasant people, led by their priests and a handful of the educated, against the conquerors of Europe, the all-powerful French, was significant. At that time no country except Britain had withstood the triumphant armies of Napoleon, yet now, in the middle of the Mediterranean, the people of a little island had had the temerity to reject him, his soldiers, and his revolutionary doctrines. With the assistance of British troops and the Royal Navy the Maltese proceeded to conduct a siege of their own capital, Valletta, where the French had taken refuge. By the autumn of 1800, after an occupation of just over two years, the French were forced to capitulate and leave the island. "Brave Maltese," said a British colonel who had served with the Anglo-Maltese land forces, "you have rendered yourselves interesting and conspicuous to the world. History affords no more striking example."

In the maelstrom of the war that engulfed Europe the Maltese now sought protection within the British Empire. Curiously enough, the British were reluctant at this time to add the island to their many other charges. Even Nelson, whose victory at the Battle of the Nile had largely led to the French capitulation in Valletta, did not at first see the importance of Malta's position. Napoleon, on the other hand, had never been in any doubt, declaring: "Peace or war depends upon Malta. . . . I would put you in possession of the Faubourg Saint Antoine rather than of Malta."

By the time the long Anglo-Napoleonic war ended, the British had come to realize the significant role that Malta played in the control and administration of the Mediterranean as well as in commanding the sea route to the East. In 1814, and confirmed a year later at the Congress of Vienna, the Maltese islands came under the British Crown. Below the Royal Arms on the main guard in the Palace Square of Valletta are engraved in Latin the words: "To Great and Unconquered Britain the Love of the Maltese and the Voice of Europe Confirms These Islands A.D. 1814."

Malta, then, was a colony unusual among all the many in the British Empire in that the protection of Great Britain had been sought by the inhabitants at all levels, and that Maltese and British had fought together to restore the island's freedom against an unwanted conquering power. The intervening century and more had cemented this strange union between a small island race of basically Semitic blood, situated between the two worlds of Europe and Africa, and the northern island race whose Mediterranean fleet came to form the mainstay of Malta's economy. The island had always been dependent upon grain imports, especially since the great expansion in population from the nineteenth century onward. At all levels there had been much intermarriage, and although there had been a number of differences on matters of internal politics, the soldiers and sailors of all ranks and classes had got on well with the Maltese islanders, above all perhaps because they shared a coarse and earthy sense of humor—something rather rare in the Mediterranean.

Despite the Great Depression of the 1930s, Malta was affluent compared to most Mediterranean countries. Visitors during the interwar years might have echoed the remarks of the eighteenth-century traveler Patrick Brydone,[2] who visited Sicily and Malta in 1770: "On getting on shore [Valletta] we found ourselves in a new world indeed. The streets crowded with well-dressed people, who have all the appearance of health and affluence; whereas at Syracuse there was scarce a creature to be seen; and even those few had the appearance of disease and wretchedness. . . . [We found] an inn, which had more the appearance of a palace. We have had an excellent supper, and good Burgundy. . . . We are now going into clean, comfortable beds, in expectation of the sweetest of slumbers."

Malta's sister island Gozo lies across a narrow strait a few miles to the northwest. About half the size of Malta and without any similar harbors, Gozo was untouched by the Great Siege of 1565 (and relatively little affected during the siege of 1940–1943). True, a few Axis bombers out of weariness or spite would off-load unused bombs on Gozo while fleeing back to the north, or machine-gun fishing boats or errant country people on the roads, but Gozo remained, as it had always been, the farm and vegetable garden for the larger island. In the channel between the two was the small island of Comino, inhabited by a few peasant families, and an uninhabited islet, Cominotto. Just off the south coast of Malta was Filfla, another uninhabited islet, and there was yet another on the east coast, surmounted by a statue of St. Paul, marking the entrance to the bay where the Apostle was reputed to have been shipwrecked. Such was the totality of the Maltese archipelago upon which all the efforts of the Axis partners, Germany and Italy, the rulers of modern Europe in 1940, were to be directed in an attempt to neutralize it by siege. Although predominantly carried out by air, the siege would also entail the mining by submarine and surface craft of all the approaches to Malta, along with the destruction by submarine, surface warships, and bombers of any convoy that endeavored to break a blockade that for long periods, not of weeks but of months, surrounded the island with what seemed to be a ring of steel.

It was this potential isolation of Malta in the event of a war involving Italy that had led the British Army and particularly the Royal Air Force to conclude that, in view of the proximity of seemingly overwhelming air power that could be deployed by Italy's

Regia Aeronautica from its bases in Sicily, Malta would be untenable. The Navy did not share this opinion. That the British Mediterranean fleet had now withdrawn to Alexandria in Egypt, and that the Italian fleet could match it ship for ship and with a greater number of submarines, and that most of the Italian battlefleet was completely modern as compared with the aging British Capital ships, all seemed to argue that the pessimistic view of Malta's future was the correct one.

3

The Divided Sea

In the early summer of 1940 the Mediterranean seemed relatively quiet. The eastern end was dominated by the British from their fleet base at Alexandria, while the western basin was in the hands of the French from their harbors in North Africa and the south of France. In the center, however, the young but powerful Italian Navy posed a threat to both the older established powers. Then, with the fall of France, the whole balance of the sea was suddenly and drastically altered.

"Graver and graver became the news from France," wrote Admiral Cunningham, recalling those days when he was commander-in-chief of the British Mediterranean fleet, "until, on June 24th, we heard that she had capitulated to Germany and Italy." He himself had never been in any doubt about the importance of Malta to the control of the Mediterranean. It was he who had given the authority for the four Gloster Gladiators to be uncrated from boxes where they had been found on the island—these planes were to provide the only fighter coverage in those early days.[1] One of them was destroyed in the first day's engagement, but for some time to come the other three were to furnish a morale booster to the islanders and to the men on the guns. There were few enough of the latter: There was sufficient weaponry for shore defense against the anticipated landings that never came, but there was a great shortage of antiaircraft

31

guns. There would be just enough to keep the Regia Aeronautica on high and imperfect courses for the moment, during which time convoys would bring to the island sufficient guns of heavy and light caliber to stand up under the thunderous Wagnerian onslaught that was to come.

With the fall of France the whole basin of the Mediterranean was left in a state of vacuum—one that, by reason of their geographical position, the Italian Navy should have found it easy to fill. Their fast, modern ships, their preponderance of submarines, and their recently modernized harbors and port installations—at Taranto on the heel of Italy, in Sicily, and on the coast of the Italian peninsula—in theory should have enabled them to dominate all but the eastern Mediterranean now that the French fleet was out of the war. Many factors, however, militated against the triumph that should have been theirs. It was not lack of courage, as British propaganda was to maintain at the time, for courage—particularly of an individual character—was something that this nation was to display at sea over and over again during the war.

Morale was another matter. At a lower-deck level, among sailors less well-educated and less well-trained than their British counterparts, this essential canvas of a navy was too light to withstand the storm of war. Sailors likely to be of use in a modern battlefleet were hardly to be found among the fishermen and merchant seamen raised in the waters of the Mediterranean. Underpaid and poorly educated, coming from bad housing, they were often regarded by their superior officers as little more than seagoing peasants. If officers were something of a superior class in the British Navy, they were a whole breed apart from their sailors in the Italian. The officers in the imposing *Marine Militare* were, as they demonstrated in small-boat exploits and in minisubmarines, capable of that passionate bravery—especially of a quixotic kind—that is almost a hallmark of the Latin people. The long and boring endurance of modern warfare, however, calls for a slower and more dour kind of courage. Among many Italian officers, moreover, and particularly the more senior, there was always a feeling that their loyalties were to old-fashioned values, to noble blood, and to the royal family. The Duce, it could not be disguised, was a very common fellow. (Many German officers felt this about their Führer, too, but he at least had proved his brilliance and had shown a grasp of strategy far in advance of anything that the well-bred military ancien régime of Germany had demonstrated in the Kaiser's war.)

The Italian Navy had good ships, good guns, good torpedoes, and flashless ammunition, but they lacked radar. (Indeed, this was as yet far from universal throughout the British fleet.) At all levels, however, and this of course mattered most at the top, they lacked confidence. The age-old reputation of the Royal Navy overawed them, and they lived and they fought in the sea over which the shadow of Nelson lay like a great cloak. An anecdote in Admiral Cunningham's autobiography points this up in his pawky Scots way.[2] In 1938 two Italian battleships, *Giulio Cesare* and *Conte di Cavour,* had paid a courtesy visit to Malta. Admiral Riccardi, who became chief of the Italian Naval Staff, had entertained Cunningham on board: "We lunched on board the *Conte di Cavour* with Admiral Riccardi, and came to the conclusion that he must have embarked the whole catering staff and band from one of the best hotels in Rome, so distinguished was his entertainment. Afterwards he took us round his palatial and highly decorated private apartments, and took some pride in pointing out a book, *The Life of Nelson,* which always lay on a table by his bedside. His subsequent actions during the war showed that he had not greatly profited by his nightly reading."

Throughout the war the Italian Navy also suffered from the most crippling of constraints—shortage of fuel. Whereas the British had full access to the oil of the Persian Gulf, Italy was dependent upon the generosity of her German partner and the oil fields of the Balkans. As the Nazis' fortunes waxed or waned in later years during their drive into Russia and their pursuit of oil in the east, so did their controlling hands upon the levers that could release oil from Rumania to the fleet of their Italian ally. Without oil and without coal, Italy was condemned to the role of jackal while her German partner carved up the feast of Europe.

Another major failing in the Italian fleet, accounting to some degree for its indifferent showing during the war, was its complete lack of battle experience. This is not only an acquired but also an inherited characteristic. Lacking a tradition of naval warfare (and few but Genoese could point back to Andrea Doria with any real confidence), their senior officers could only be fired by the feeling that the Mediterranean was justifiably *their* sea upon which the Anglo-Saxons were trespassing. But these sentiments were not enough to produce a necessary fire in the belly. There were other practical matters, such as their complete lack of training and, therefore, skill in the difficult technique of nightfighting. "They had not," wrote Cunningham, "visualised a night action between heavy ships and did not keep their heavy guns manned [during the dark hours]. . . . They were no further advanced than we had been at Jutland twenty-five years before."[3] These were but some of the reasons why the Italians, with what was on the surface a superb navy, could not keep the British with their fleet of aging capital ships bottled up in Alexandria—if not destroyed in one great action.

Early sweeps carried out by Cunningham from Alexandria served to confirm the Italian naval command in its sense of inferiority and to increase in the British an inherited self-confidence, which was soon to be eroded when it became evident that the power of shore-based aircraft was to dominate the actions at sea. At first both fleets were ill-served by their long-range reconnaissance air arms, the Italians being dependent upon single-engined Cant seaplanes that came under their Air Force command, and the British on a handful of flying boats totally incapable of operating within range of shore-based fighter aircraft. Admiral Cunningham had, however, one asset that was never available to the Italians—an aircraft carrier. This was the *Eagle,* originally a battleship built for the Chilean Navy, and converted shortly after the 1914–1918 war to be one of the first aircraft carriers in the world. Until finally sunk on one of her many runs to Malta, she carried seventeen Swordfish biplanes, which were designed for reconnaissance and torpedo-carrying. Slow though they were, these planes proved themselves time and again incomparable in their dual role. As torpedo-carriers they were to inflict a strike upon the Italian fleet that changed not only the balance of power in the Mediterranean but the whole history of warfare at sea. Flying out of Malta in the years to come, Swordfish aircraft were also to inflict grave losses on the Italian shipping fleet as it moved its cargoes of men and matériel between Europe and North Africa. The Swordfish was highly maneuverable but very slow, though this latter characteristic was sardonically rated by some pilots as an asset in itself—enemy fighters and antiaircraft gunners, they said, could not credit it and missed them accordingly. Nine of these aircraft had reached Malta shortly before the fall of France.

London had always had doubts about the British ability to hold

Malta in the event of war, but after the French collapse and the isolation of the British Mediterranean fleet at its port in Egypt, these doubts became virtual certainties, particularly among the Air Force and Army chiefs. The prewar policies that had denied Malta its proper complement of antiaircraft defenses, its fighter squadrons, and its proposed submarine pens cut out of the rock (all subjects that had been discussed and then put aside, partly through ill-reasoned argument and partly through financial stringencies) now seemed to a number in authority to have been justified: The island was untenable. Churchill, however, felt differently.

It is interesting to note that in the councils of the Knights prior to the Great Siege of 1565 very similar arguments had been advanced against spending money on forts and fortifications to defend against attack by the Ottoman Empire. Then it was Grand Master La Valette who had said that there could be no withdrawal and that it was the fate of the Order "to defend the bare rock to the end"; in 1940 it was Winston Churchill who maintained that Malta must be held on all account, or the road to the East would be open to the Axis forces. In this view he was fully seconded by Admiral Cunningham, who had never had the slightest doubt about the small island's importance in any conflict that might take place in or around the Mediterranean basin. Fortunately for Malta, Hitler was considerably less percipient than his predecessor Napoleon. Both would-be world conquerors were ill-at-ease with the sea and ill-educated regarding the use of sea power, but Hitler was more so than his master. An early strike by the Germans with their immense preponderance of air power against the poorly equipped island might well have succeeded, and the face of history would indeed have been changed.

Malta was a dyarchy in theory, with legislative and executive powers divided between the British governor and the representatives of the Maltese people. This complicated system never worked very effectively, and while it had always been agreed that imperial strategic interest came first and foremost, on other matters there had been some friction. Throughout the whole period of the siege, however, the politics of the island were more or less in abeyance, and the governor was in effective control. One point rarely enough made in official accounts and personal records of these years is that, if the Maltese people had not willingly and fully participated in the defense of their island, the position would indeed have been completely untenable. This is a fact that was constantly ignored by historians and annalists of the first great siege, but it should never be forgotten in any account of the second and greater siege that was to follow.

Throughout the prewar years the Italians had made great efforts through cultural and educational links with the island, as well as more flagrant devices such as promoting the Fascist Youth party, to infiltrate the social structure and to subvert the Maltese from their old allegiance and into some form of union with Italy.[4] It was natural enough for geographic and mercantile reasons that Malta should feel a close affinity with Italy, added to which was the fact that Italian was the accepted cultural language among many of the upper classes. Until 1934 it had indeed been the language of the courts, with English or Maltese used as secondary languages. But only about fifteen percent of the population spoke Italian (and almost none of the working classes); so this anomaly was removed when it was decided that proceedings must be conducted in Maltese since "it is the national language of the Island, and the one which every Maltese speaks."[5] This official recognition of Maltese as a written language with the full authority of the law did much to strengthen the people's sense of national identity. It was, as Sir Harry Luke put it, "its elevation from the kitchen to the Courts."[6]

After the outbreak of war a comparatively small handful (about seventy) of Maltese whose dedication to Italy, if not to the Duce, made them necessarily suspect to the authorities were detained, most of them being transferred to Kenya in 1942. Although there was never any evidence that any of them was liable to emulate Norway's Quisling, an island about to be besieged could not afford the slightest risk.

One of the strange things about the siege that was about to develop was the way in which the island sank back almost into its medieval past. The small archipelago had never really become involved with the Renaissance, which had no part in the consciousness of the ruling Knights and, insofar as it had, was something to be distrusted. The later developments in Europe were perfectly reflected in the magnificence of the Italo-Spanish baroque that was the style of the palaces, churches, and auberges built by the Knights, and the very latest in fortress architecture had always been evident in the immense stone walls, scarps and counterscarps, bastions and demibastions that frowned over Grand Harbour or encircled the dock-yard cities on the southern side. This penchant for increasing the fortifications of the island was carried on even into the nineteenth century by the British in their Victoria Lines. These spread right across Malta at the geological line known as the Great Fault, and were designed to secure the harbors and populous areas against an improbable French landing.

Intellectually, as is shown by the contents of the library of the Knights, Malta had been somewhat (some would say deliberately) cut off from the mainstream of European thought. Here the Counter-Reformation had triumphed. The militant Catholicism displayed by the Knights of St. John, long after the Crusades had become but a distant memory to the new nations of Europe, had become absorbed into the very fabric of the island. The brief French episode and the new spirit of revolutionary France, far from being accepted, had been the principal cause for the Maltese revolt. It is significant that the priests had been foremost among their leaders, and vengeance for their vandalized churches had lit the torch for their liberation from French rule. The British Army and Navy officers, the governors, civil servants, and others who had taken the place of the Knights were conservative by nature and had been careful not to affront Catholic susceptibilities. Inevitably, there had been some incidents involving ardent Protestants attempting to wean Maltese away from Rome, but one of the least successful governors of the island was an Irish Anglo-Catholic, and the general policy had always been to leave the clergy to organize the lives and the education of the islanders. Despite all the social and other changes of the twentieth century this policy had remained very much unaltered, with the result that in Malta there was to be found a socioreligious pattern of life that seemed cut off from the modern world. Of Valletta, far more accurately than of Oxford, could Matthew Arnold have written: "Beautiful city! so venerable, so lovely, so unravaged by the fierce intellectual life of our century, so serene! . . . whispering from her towers the last enchantments of the Middle Age."

The early Italian bombing raids aroused a deep feeling of anger and affront. Apart from the death and wounding of relatives and friends, the devastation of churches and familiar landmarks was felt far more deeply by a small race, interconnected, intermarried, and insular in almost every respect of the word. Furthermore, the Maltese, quite unlike their Latin neighbors, although volatile enough in sport and politics, had a distinctly dour strain. It was to serve them in good stead as the regular pattern of air attack from the north continued by day and, worse, by night, when it was inevitable, in view of the technical abilities of the time, that the bombing was almost indiscriminate. To the surprise of the population, however, the long-anticipated gas attacks never occurred, nor did the invasion by sea for which the gunners of the Royal Malta artillery and the British Royal artillery had prepared in their gun positions around the coast. The island, which the British had always been happy to keep relatively uninfluenced by the modern world (rejected by most pre-war travelers or cruise liners as an army garrison, a fleet base, not scenically attractive, and somehow secretive), now became completely Fortress Malta.

4

Thunder Afar

Thunder echoes all around the islands on heavy summer nights, and sometimes at the beginning of the first heavy rainfalls in September. From June 1940 its man-made counterpart would only be absent for a day or two at a time over a period of years. At first, however, the normal processes of life on Malta continued almost unchanged. Bars, cafés, and the few restaurants remained open, and if business was not as usual because of air raids, it was superficially little changed. The reason for this was the nature of the island itself. Malta, as the Knights had found out centuries ago, was an ideal fortress because the limestone was so easily quarried, and within a comparatively short space of time the butter-yellow blocks developed a hard exterior from the briny wind that is always present, even on days when the hot sky seems airless.

In 1940 an old railway tunnel outside Valletta was reopened and turned into an immense dormitory that served many of the capital's inhabitants and those of its suburb Floriana in the years to come. Tunnels were also dug out of the solid rock, some within the dense fortifications left by the Knights. Individuals armed with pickaxes excavated other smaller shelters. Caves outside the cities in many parts of the rocky island were reoccupied for the first time in millennia, as the ghosts of Phoenicians were disturbed from their urn-burials by the life of displaced families. Throughout the island mass was now celebrated in catacombs and communal shelters, as a new persecution of Christians roared through the world. It was in many strange respects the dawn of Malta's Second Neolithic Age.[1]

Eager to test the Italian fleet and the striking power of the Duce's air force, Admiral Cunningham had earlier provoked them as much as possible by fleet raids along the North African coast. Apart from the loss of an old light cruiser *Calypso* to an Italian submarine (bold and efficient where the majority remained supine), these essays had done no more than show that the Italians seemed unprepared to defend the ports and installations of their North African colony by bringing their warships out to sea. The fleet was used, however, to cover their convoys transporting men and munitions to Libya, and in the second month of Italy's war one such convoy provided an occasion for a trial of strength between the two fleets.

The Italian fleet was out covering an important convoy southward bound for Benghazi, but it was for the protection of two convoys from Malta that fortuitously had the British fleet at sea on the same date. These convoys, one fast and one slow, were bound for Egypt. One carried naval stores now needed for the fleet in Alexandria, while the other was full of civilians and the wives and children of naval and other service personnel. Their departure from the island seemed to many of the defenders to mark the real opening of the siege. It had always been the practice in times past to remove as many noncombatants as possible from a place threatened by siege, before the gates closed and the real trial began. But in this case the children and old people and the other dependents of the Maltese could not be taken to safety. This would have required a vast assembly of merchant ships, even in the calm seas of peace. As it was, one of the only ships available in Malta for this operation was a captured Italian transport, the *Rodi*. This ship had brought to the island Italian prisoners of war, the first of the many thousands who, captured in later desert campaigns, would need transshipment to detention in East Africa and elsewhere. When these prisoners left the lean eastern flanks of the island, the Duce's voice was loud in Italy, the legions under the fasces of old Rome marched in parade before him, the Regia Aeronautica proudly rode the skies, and the noble great ships of their navy seemed to dominate the central Mediterranean.

Cunningham was steaming westward in his flagship, the *Warspite*, accompanied by two other older battleships, the aircraft carrier *Eagle,* five cruisers, as well as accompanying destroyers. They were not only covering these two convoys from surface attack but hoping to provoke the Italian fleet under its commander-in-chief, Admiral Inigo Campioni, to a trial of strength. Cunningham was soon to find out for himself the effect of modern air attack on a fleet—something he had been trying to test along the North African coast. Ashore in Malta the defenders might later become almost indifferent to Italian bombing (secure as most were by then in shelters of their native rock), but at sea Cunningham was soon to find out that the Italian Air Force had squadrons specially trained in high-level attack on shipping. Operating out of Rhodes (once the home of the Knights of St. John) and the other islands of the Dodecanese, the Italian bombers soon proved that they were in no way to be despised. At that time few sailors in the British fleet had had any real experience of bombing—of the high-screaming, ear-piercing whistle of the bombs' descent or the sight of those dark shapes swiftly falling, every one conveying the illusion that it was directed at the individual onlooker. Over and over again the ships would thud and pound to the blast of their own guns (comparatively few light antiaircraft guns in those days as compared with later), the staccato yammer of the pom-poms, the hard crack of four-inch, as the ships became hidden from one another by high-rising curtains of water from near-misses. (Dark they seemed against the brightness of sky and sea.) Exploding fragments hammered against steel hulls or swept through sides never designed to ward off high-velocity fragments.

Coming in on a level course at about twelve thousand feet—regardless, it seemed, of the bursting fire around them—their bomb bays opening, their patterned clusters falling, the Italian aircraft presented something completely new and chilling in naval warfare. Up until now sailors had fought against other sailors over the centuries, the ranges increasing as technology improved, but the raw facts of an engagement remaining much the same, even when shells became explosive and no longer the simple roaring rotundity of death-dealing ball. It was a comfort to remember, remarked Admiral Cunningham, "that there was always more water than ship"— but not very much, for a ship stood up huge, bare, and exposed above the absorbing flat acres of the sea. Years later he wrote: "It is not too much to say of those early months that the Italian high-level bombing was the best I have ever seen, far better than the German. . . . I shall always remember it with respect."

The astonishing thing about that first meeting of the new force from the air and the old force on the sea was that only one ship took a direct hit. There were near-misses by the dozen, but only the cruiser *Gloucester* received, direct on her bridge, a bomb's full, penetrating, and high-lifting blast. The captain was killed, as were six other officers and eleven ratings, while a number of others were wounded. Modern, lightly built ships dependent on the immense complexity of their electrical and communication systems would probably have succumbed. But the *Gloucester* had been designed for more old-fashioned actions involving bursting shells (speaking tubes and hand communications if all else failed), and she did not burn disastrously or fall from action. Within a short space of time she was brought under control, being steered from her after position. Although her speed was much reduced, the *Gloucester* resumed her place in the line.

Admiral Cunningham had by now confirmed the information that he had earlier in the day received from the submarine *Phoenix:* An Italian fleet including two battleships was at sea, two hundred miles east of Malta headed south. On the afternoon of July 8 a flying boat, also out of Malta, old and unsuited for modern warfare but containing trained eyes, sent a further report. There were two battleships, six cruisers, and seven destroyers. Clearly, they must be covering some important convoy, and the reason for the day's heavy bombing of the British fleet became more apparent: It was to deny them use of the central Mediterranean. Even more important, then, was it to strike toward the heart of the sea and attempt to cut off the Italian fleet from its base. Cunningham turned his ships toward Taranto.

The action, in which both battlefleets were covering important "soft" convoys of merchantmen—out of sight and unharmed in both cases—was in itself the justification for such fleets. But the conclusions that were to be drawn were correct on the Italian side, wrong on the British. The engagement was to reinforce the opinion of the Italian High Command that their fleet should be kept as a threat (as the classic "fleet in being" of naval strategy), while the British conclusion that air attack could be considered acceptable was to be proved false in later phases of the war, after the German

Luftwaffe had arrived in the Mediterranean. The ensuing Battle of Calabria, as it came to be called, was to bolster British morale (somewhat shaken by the first day's air attacks) and to confirm a wise decision on the part of the Italian High Command. But the fact remained that if the Italians had risked a stand-up fight they might have gained the Mediterranean forever. Of Cunningham's three battleships only the *Warspite* had recently been modernized; the *Malaya* and the *Royal Sovereign* were both slow, the latter notoriously so.

Across the summer sea of the central Mediterranean, broomed by the light but steady northwesterly common to those months, the two fleets drew together, the one anxious to provoke an action, the other to avoid it. Admiral Campioni, having covered his convoy to a position northwest of Benghazi, had turned north. He had been expressly directed by his High Command to keep well to the west so as not to risk an engagement until noon the following day, by which time his fleet would have come under air cover from Sicily and the Italian mainland.

It was a flying boat out of Malta that once again was the first to report the Italian fleet—about 145 miles west of Cunningham at 7:30 next morning. This was soon confirmed by reconnaissance aircraft flown off from the *Eagle.* Admiral Campioni should have been informed of the position of the British fleet, but he was badly let down by the Italian Air Force—an argument not only in favor of fleets having aircraft carriers with them, but of shore-based aircraft operating with ships being trained by, and coming under the control of, the commanding officers afloat. Indeed, it was not until nearly noon, when the fleets were some eighty miles apart, that the Italians located the British by means of an aircraft catapulted off Campioni's flagship, the *Giulio Cesere.* He was only about fifty miles from Cape Spartivento on the toe of Italy, close to the Messina Straits, and he had every reason to expect that his opponents would by now have come under heavy air attack from shore-based aircraft of the Regia Aeronautica. They did not. Nevertheless, he had many more destroyers than the British and twelve cruisers—six of them heavy cruisers—against Cunningham's five light cruisers (one of which, the *Gloucester,* being damaged, was held back in support of the *Eagle*). Campioni's two battleships were considerably faster and recently modernized, and could outrange the British battleships with the sole exception of the *Warspite.* The odds were more than favorable, particularly since every mile he steamed drew him more and more under the protection of his own air cover.

The Italian fleet officers were both dismayed and infuriated by the lack of cooperation from their air force, and the British were disappointed by the performance of their own torpedo-carrying Swordfish. Two attacks were launched from the *Eagle* during the day, the first shortly before noon and the second four hours later, but neither scored any hits. The British, too, were learning for the first time and at firsthand. But the very presence of these aircraft contributed to an increased nervousness and some loss of morale on the part of their opponents. The threat implicit in those torpedo-carrying biplanes was worth more than a battleship with fifteen-inch guns.

"The breeze was in the north-west, with a slight sea and a sky dappled with thin cloud. The visibility was fifteen to twenty miles when, between 2:52 and 3 P.M., the *Orion* and *Neptune* sighted enemy destroyers and cruisers."[2] These two cruisers, together with the *Liverpool* and *Sydney,* were fulfilling a classic function, spread on a line of bearing about ten miles ahead of Cunningham's flagship and designed to locate the opposing fleet. A few minutes after three in the afternoon Captain Rory O'Conor in the *Neptune* had the privilege of sending the signal "Enemy battle fleet in sight," the first time that this had been seen in the Mediterranean since the days of Nelson. Such high moments are few and far between in naval history, often, because of their special rarity, eclipsing all the long, hard-slogging times of convoy duties or the harsh moments of action itself, when the guns crash and the wounds are given and received.

Six minutes later four Italian heavy cruisers, also outriders of their fleet, opened fire with their eight-inch guns. Outranged and outgunned, the smaller British cruisers replied, but only the fact that the *Warspite* had drawn far ahead of the two other battleships, *Malaya* and *Royal Sovereign,* prevented Cunningham's cruisers, well-handled though they were, from receiving a mauling. At an extreme range for her fifteen-inch guns of twenty-six thousand yards, the *Warspite* opened fire on the Italian cruisers. For the first time in the history of warfare on the Mediterranean, the summer air was now rent by the long rumble of those great cordite explosions, followed by the noise, like a giant sheet being torn, of the shells' swift passage. Menaced from afar, the Italian cruisers prudently withdrew under cover of a smoke screen.

During the ensuing lull the *Warspite* was turned through 360 degrees to allow her slower partners to catch up. She was traveling at her maximum speed of 24.5 knots, and this necessary turn (to bring the full firepower of the British battleships into line ahead) provided an opportunity for two of the Italian heavy cruisers to attempt a cast to the east, with a view to getting at the *Eagle*. A few salvos of fifteen-inch shells dissuaded them. Then, at 3:53 P.M., the opposing battleships were in sight of one another, and the *Warspite* opened fire at twenty-six thousand yards. The two Italian battleships replied, both sides shooting well even at this great range and straddling their targets almost at once. Seven minutes after the action began, Cunningham saw "the great orange-coloured flash of a heavy explosion at the base of the enemy flagship's funnels." Smoke rose as fires broke out below decks in the *Giulio Cesare,* and the Italian fleet turned away under cover of smoke. Admiral Campioni's flagship had been hit at a range of thirteen miles.

With the smoke screen lying heavy and greasy over the sea, rolling slowly under the summer wind, a confused action took place with cruisers and destroyers on both sides looming or jinking out of the dark veils. Unwilling to risk what might well be a trap (submarines lying in wait for him in defense of their fleet), Cunningham took his own ships around to the north of the smoke. His opponents in any case had the legs of him and were away for the Messina Straits and the supposed safety of their air cover. The Regia Aeronautica did at last appear in large numbers and made a concerted attack, mainly on the *Warspite* and the *Eagle*. Once again, despite their comparative accuracy, the bombardiers were not accurate enough, and their ground control was obviously in some state of confusion. The *Warspite*'s own aircraft, which had been flown off during the action and had kept up a running commentary throughout the brief engagement, were happy to report that Admiral Campioni's fleet was now being bombed by his own air cover.[3]

Although damaged, Admiral Campioni's flagship was able to maintain her speed unimpaired. Although outraged by the criminal inefficiency of his air command, Campioni returned to harbor with the knowledge that his important convoy had been passed through safely to the army in Libya. Although engaged by the prestigious

Royal Navy, his fleet had not disgraced itself. It had also proved to the Italian High Command that nothing was to be gained by the fleet attempting to provoke a major action. They could pass their convoys to and from North Africa without any such risk—so long as the British fleet was based far away at Alexandria, and so long as the island of Malta did not possess sufficient offensive power by air or sea to threaten this lifeline.

Cunningham's fleet, heavily but again ineffectively bombed on their return voyage, had received a boost to morale by the enemy's evident unwillingness to face them, but they had been somewhat shaken by their new experience of air attack. The tendency, however, was to draw the wrong conclusion from the events of the past few days—that they could command the Mediterranean from their Egyptian base and that bombing, although very unpleasant, was acceptable. Even their admiral had not as yet appreciated the true situation, for he was to write: "It must have shown the Italians clearly that their Air Force and submarines cannot stop our Fleet penetrating into the Central Mediterranean and that only their main Fleet can seriously interfere with our operating there."

The arrival in due course of the Luftwaffe with its highly trained dive-bomber squadrons, and then—as and when they could be spared from the main Battle of the Atlantic—the incursion of German U-boats, with their skilled captains and their hardy crews, was to change things totally. But it was hardly surprising that the wrong conclusions were drawn in these early days, for they were based on the indifferent performance of the Italian air and submarine arm.

At the heart of the matter was the fact that Mussolini was an opportunist who had no real long-term plans for the war on which he had embarked. With the fall of France he had anticipated an early British withdrawal and some form of patched-up peace that would enable him to continue with the expansion of his North African empire. He was aware that Hitler had no wish to continue the war with Britain; indeed, the German dictator was to make many peace proposals through every avenue available to him throughout 1940 and well into 1941. Unknown to Mussolini, Hitler's real aims and ambitions were always directed toward the east and Russia. He considered the war, as it developed in the Mediterranean, no more than a sideshow. Certainly, it would be useful if Egypt and the Suez Canal could be brought under Axis control, but the maps that revolved constantly in his head consisted of the frontiers of Prussia and the lands that lay beyond. A small fly-speck to the south of Sicily, the island of Malta had probably hardly crossed his consciousness until that day when his ally had first bombed it.

This encounter between the two battlefleets was to be the only one of the war in which the main units engaged one another. When news of it reached Malta, it was seen as proof of the fact that the British still ruled the sea—even if they no longer did so from their principal base, the Grand Harbour of the island.

5

Parochial and Other Matters

This was the summer and the autumn in which the fate of the Western world was being decided in the Battle of Britain. Irrevocably, the whole pattern the war would follow over the succeeding years was being shaped by a handful of young men. Few indeed—like those in the Pass of Thermopylae—"their shoulders held the sky suspended."[1] It was hardly surprising that when the fate of Britain itself was in the balance, little enough could be spared for that other island far away under the sun, and now under a similar threat. What was perhaps surprising was that anything at all could be spared, yet in August an old aircraft carrier, the *Argus,* covered by a powerful striking force that had been assembled at Gibraltar (Force H), flew off twelve Hurricane fighters for the relief of Malta from a position off southern Sardinia—right in the heartland of the Middle Sea. That fighter aircraft could be spared at such a moment in Britain's history was evidence that Churchill had convinced certain reluctant quarters of the importance of holding Malta at whatever cost. It is a fact that not long before this event a department of the Admiralty in London had sent an indignant signal to Malta demanding to know why Fleet Air Arm property (the four Gloster Gladiator biplanes) had been handed over to the RAF—whose pilots were now flying the three of them that were left against overwhelming Italian fighter and bomber superiority![2]

At this moment in its history the mood of the island was largely expressed, and to some degree determined, by the governor-general, a man who deserves to go down in history with his name bracketed with that of La Valette, that supreme grand master of the Knights who had defied the overwhelming might of the Ottoman Empire at the height of its military power. Lieutenant General William Dobbie, later to be knighted for his services in Malta, was a Scot and, rare among Scots and rarer among soldiers, a Plymouth Brother. Nothing could have been further from the somewhat baroque Catholicism of the Maltese than the austere Protestantism of the Plymouth Brethren; nor more remote from the almost medieval power of the priesthood in the island than the Brethren belief that official ministry is a denial of the spiritual priesthood of all believers and of the guidance of the Holy Spirit. Yet, Dobbie, who conducted family prayers every evening and to whom his own household accorded such respect that his wife and daughter would rise to their feet when he entered a room, was a man whom the Maltese took to their hearts. Admiral Cunningham rightly assessed what it was about this soldier that so appealed to the Mediterranean islanders: "[He was] an Ironside of a man. His profound faith in the justice of our cause made a great impression upon the religious Maltese. The complete and calm faith shown in the broadcasts he made nearly every evening contributed immensely towards keeping up the morale of the people."[3] On the day that Italy declared war, Dobbie's first act as commander-in-chief had been to issue a special order of the day to the British and Maltese garrison:

"The decision of His Majesty's Government to fight until our enemies are defeated will be heard with the greatest satisfaction by all ranks of the Garrison of Malta.

"It may be that hard times lie ahead of us, but I know that however hard they may be, the courage and determination of all ranks will not falter, and that with God's help we will maintain the security of this fortress.

"I call on all officers and other ranks humbly to seek God's help, and then in reliance on Him to do their duty unflinchingly."

Read many years later, such words sound like a call from a past that seems far distant indeed.

The refugee problem (later to engulf the whole of Europe) was the most pressing one for the authorities on the island. After the first bombing raids the flood of families out of the capital and its suburb Floriana (and especially out of the Three Cities that held the heart of the dockyard communities) into houses, schools, and other institutions in other townships and small villages on the island led to inevitable complications with landlords and other authorities. The areas that were left behind teemed with dogs and cats, so much so that at various times these descendants of former domestic pets had to be ruthlessly culled. Drainage and sanitation problems, which were to remain a permanent hazard of the siege, showed themselves from the earliest stages. The abandoned central areas were on main drainage systems, but most of the outlying villages into which families now poured were dependent on cesspools. The emptying of these with inadequate equipment to meet the demand, and later the shortage of transport, meant that for many months the medical authorities were on tenterhooks about the possible outbreak of virulent diseases. But the islanders enjoyed one great benefit unknown to the crowded industrial cities of northern countries when these came under heavy air attack: The sea air, day and night, from north, south, east, or west, poured constantly over their heads, rinsing out even the underground shelters where so many thousands were to make their troglodytic homes.

After the first months it became obvious, even to those in Whitehall who had had earlier discarded Malta as indefensible, that the weight of the Italian air attack was something that the island, almost unprotected as it was, could clearly endure. With each day, too, the concept of Malta as a dagger leaning against the ribs of Italy was better understood. Churchill, Cunningham, and a number of others had long recognized this, and now with the flying in of further Hurricanes (making the Regia Aeronautica even more disinclined to offensive action over the island, at any rate by day) and some torpedo-carrying Swordfish for strikes against Italian shipping, together with the arrival of convoys with further stores and military supplies, the island's potentialities became clear. The submarines that were later to have so devastating an effect on the Italy-Libya shipping route had as yet played little part. Those based on the island when Mussolini had declared war were large boats that had formerly been stationed in the Far East and were particularly vulnerable to sighting in the pellucid waters of the Mediterranean. It was not until the arrival of the smaller U class from Britain via Gibraltar that their lethal potential began to be fully exploited. Kala-frana, the flying-boat base in Marsaxlokk Bay, received the welcome addition of Sunderland flying boats from Alexandria, which were vulnerable to modern fighter aircraft, but were efficient enough for reconnaissance and for the detection and destruction of enemy sub-marines. In September four Marylands were flown in to provide ad-ditional air reconnaissance, shortly to be followed by Wellington bombers—an efficient striking arm that was to pound enemy ports and harbors and shipping for the duration of the war, increasing in fury as the years went by and their numbers increased.

Marooned on what Churchill called "that unsinkable aircraft car-rier," a strange transformation affected the people. For one thing, difficult to understand though it may be for those who live in large countries with modern transportation systems, Maltese society had remained almost medieval—and this meant that people traveled but rarely. Until the war the inhabitants of the dockyard area, familiar with ships and the sea and the rough manners and mores of British and other foreign sailors, were very distinct in their outlook from country people who lived no more than three miles away. The early exodus from harbor towns and settlements meant a return to peas-ant roots for the semisophisticated port people, just as the men and women who lived entirely within a circumscribed village (church and social club, bar and store, plow and horse) now encountered their cousins from the early twentieth century (it was still the early twentieth century even in the waterfront world of Malta). One Brit-ish Army officer wrote: "When the Hampshires [his regiment] ar-rived in Malta early in 1941, after settling in and getting to know the people, we felt that we had somehow suddenly slipped back in time; that everything about us was some twenty-five years behind our known civilization, our thinking and our normal everyday struggle for existence. For one thing there was not the same struggle to achieve and we discovered the 'Not to worry, Joe' attitude which in the Maltese produced a happier, easier way of life."[4] Dr. Jeremy Boissevain in a monograph on Maltese social anthropology has commented: "The war itself was a major force in the same direction [social integration], for British troops and people from the urban areas were evacuated to the country to escape the bombing attacks, and so shared the life of their rural neighbours. All learned a good deal from one another. It is not surprising, therefore, that many

Maltese, especially in the villages, regard the last war as a social milestone, a dividing line between past dependence upon agriculture and present wage labour, between poverty and relative prosperity."[5] War is always a disastrous and malevolent force, but the changes effected by it are not always so.

Toward the end of 1940 the giant pattern in the desert sand to the south of Malta took a dramatic shift. In the early stages of the war the Italian Army, overwhelming in numbers but poorly equipped and low in morale—few wanted to be in any desert to start with, and all sensibly regretted leaving home—had advanced against the thin line of the British Army and had prodded forward into Egypt. The Suez Canal and the route to the oil of the Persian Gulf lay behind all the moves and countermoves of those years—objectives little understood by the sweating soldiers and sailors, who as always had to endure the death and havoc initiated by their remote masters.

Prior to the long-prepared advance of the British against the Italian forces in the western desert the most momentous event of the early sea war had already taken place. This was the British air attack on the Italian fleet in their base at Taranto, an attack carried out by torpedo-carrying Swordfish aircraft from H.M.S. *Illustrious.* H.M.S. *Eagle* was also to have taken part but had developed too many defects caused by near-misses from high-level bombing attacks during recent months. The *Illustrious,* a modern carrier with an armored flight deck, had been sent out to join Admiral Cunningham's fleet—a proof that his needs in the Mediterranean were understood and that the importance of the air arm in the landlocked sea had not gone unremarked in London, even though it had been somewhat downplayed by Cunningham himself. The brilliant example of the use of sea-air power at Taranto changed the balance of power in the Mediterranean, restoring to the British, even if only momentarily, the confidence that had been theirs before the fall of France.

From the moment that the *Illustrious* had arrived at Alexandria plans had been afoot to launch an airborne attack on the battlefleet in Taranto. Since it seemed impossible to force a fleet action upon the Italians, the only thing was for the air arm to effect the same damage (or worse) as might be achieved in a major engagement at sea. Taranto was of course very heavily defended, and only a night attack from some distance away (which might normally be considered as out of range for planes from an aircraft carrier) could achieve this. The *Illustrious* had brought out with her from Britain just such long-range fuel tanks for the aircraft as made this feasible. At a time when Maryland reconnaissance planes out of Malta showed that all the Italian major fleet units were present in the port, and using as cover for the presence of the British fleet at sea the passage of a convoy to Malta, the planes were launched from the vicinity of the Greek island of Cephalonia on the night of November 11.

The attack was overwhelmingly successful and deservedly ranks in the annals of the Royal Navy with Nelson's Battle of Trafalgar.[6] At one blow the strength of the Italian fleet was reduced by three battleships, the *Littorio* and the *Duilio* both being out of action for months, the *Cavour* beached and out of the war for good. Only the *Vittorio Veneto* and the *Cesare* escaped. The aircraft carrier showed itself to be the most potent weapon of war at sea, and the battleship joined the long ranks of ships that had once dominated the oceans and whose day was over. The subsequent withdrawal of the Italian fleet to Naples out of reach of air attacks and the exultant improvement in morale in the British fleet obscured at the time the salient fact of the victory at Taranto—the dominance of the air over the sea. So long as the Italian Air Force remained inefficient and ill-directed, the British could feel that they had secured control of the central Mediterranean as well as the eastern end of the sea.

After Taranto, two convoys, one from Alexandria and one from Gibraltar, were passed through to Malta, both covered by battleships and aircraft carriers (the *Ark Royal,* so often "sunk" in German broadcasts, being with the western convoy). Despite a threat by the Italian fleet from Naples—wisely withdrawn when the composition of the western convoy became known to Admiral Campioni—both arrived unscathed in the island. Additional troops, stores, motor transport, guns, and ammunition all served to confirm a confidence that had been growing ever since Cunningham's first action against the Italian fleet and had been immensely reinforced by Taranto. "Life," wrote a British artillery officer, "was not very different from normal. Still no mails arrived and so there were no home papers, but food and drink were to be had in plenty provided you could get them—transport was very scarce. Dances were held once a week at the Club; women wore their evening dresses and many officers changed into their 'blues' at night."[7] The amateur dra-

matic society flourished, and regular concert parties toured the outlying posts, where groups of soldiers waited at their guns for assault
from the sea.

Small though it is—ridiculously so on a map of the Mediterranean—Malta is a strange island in its ability to evoke an immense
depth out of less than one hundred square miles. The whole group is
smaller than the Isle of Wight, yet it gives the sense of extraordinary
complexity and density—something reinforced by the onionskin
pattern of its old townships and villages. Away from the dense population areas of the east coast, the biblical landscape unfolds. Few
trees break its sun-varnished canvas, a scattering here and there of
olives, the lonely and ancient carob, small fields contained against
the wind and the winter rains by drystone walls, remote farm buildings often seeming to slump back out of the rock from which they
were built, and at night a profound and dense darkness. There were
hardly any good roads on the island, the best being the military road
on the east coast and one between Valletta and the ancient inland
capital of Mdina. The other roads were dust and dirt tracks, fading
away in veinlets that wandered off between rocks and prickly pear
and scattered tumbles of stone, where walls had been abandoned
and never repaired. Along most of the coastal areas, particularly in
the west, where the high cliffs stoop into the sea, the paths became
little more than goat tracks. In this countryside, at carefully selected
points, the soldiers had built gun emplacements and machine-gun
posts, where the dimmed blue flicker of a kerosene lamp or the high
buzz of a Primus cooker were all that revealed their presence against
the dark and ancient rocks. Bare, steep-sided limestone ridges, uninhabited since the islands rose from the sea, yielding little even for
goats, now sometimes echoed to the tang of soldiers' metaled boots
or equipment. Those who spent weeks or months on patrol in these
lonely places did not escape the immense weight of time that seems
to engulf the Maltese islands more deeply than any others in this
sea. On moonlit nights the Neolithic temples threw their profound
shadows, and the remains of Roman buildings in comfortable valleys seemed almost modern. For the soldiers the daytime arrival of a
concert party, carried about in a horse-drawn cart, was an event of
far greater significance than ever had been the weekly visit to the
cinema in their distant home towns.

Malta lies well south of the latitude of Tunis. Its climate is North
African, and in summer temperatures of 90 degrees in the shade are

not unusual as the island bakes like a dry bleak bone. The land lies asleep, waking only with the first rains of late September or early October. Then the island steams and roars under the monsoon weather, as the water pours down cart tracks and roads and pathways in sudden rivers of dust and mud. Seen from the air, the island spreads around it at those times a khaki stain in the clear blue sea. Even after the rains have stopped, winter is not without its discomforts. Although the temperature rarely falls below 50 °F., the wind off the snow-capped mountains of Sicily and great Etna to the north blows down piercing cold, and the island becomes damp and drafty like an old stone corridor. During this season the people in their shelters and the radio operators, coders, and cipher officers, deep down under fortresses like St. Angelo and Lascaris, badly needed the kerosene brought in by the convoys. If summer meant the minimum of clothes—shorts and steel helmets at gun positions—winter meant the same level of clothing for the British as if they had been back in their native country.

It was against a winter background in 1941 that the news reached them all of the British advances in the western desert. The Italians under Marshal Graziani were expelled from their foothold in Egypt by General Wavell's Army of the Nile, which took some 30,000 prisoners almost immediately. Meanwhile, Mussolini's misguided attack on Greece, with its inevitable demands upon the Italian Air Force, meant an even further easing of the pressure on Malta. Unfortunately, the attention of Adolf Hitler had now inevitably been drawn to the Mediterranean by the misfortunes and incompetence of his ally. Hitler's immense successes on the continent, eclipsing by far those of any previous European warlord, had hitherto prevented him from paying much attention to the sea to the south and its potential importance as a theater of war. In Malta, the year drew to a close with the happy feeling that the Royal Navy had proved itself master of the sea yet again, the British and allied forces were routing the Italian military in the desert, and the threat from the air had diminished and dwindled. Many Maltese even began to return to their houses and abandon their shelter life. Food seemed relatively plentiful, bars that had been closed opened their old-fashioned swinging doors again, schools in the threatened areas began to reopen, and soldiers, sailors, and civilians alike began to hope that the threat by air from the north had been endured and outlasted.

As if to crown this feeling of optimism, the watchers on the defenses and the people of Valletta received a surprising Christmas gift from the sea. Early in the afternoon of December 20 Admiral Cunningham's flagship *Warspite* and a destroyer escort hove into sight off the eastern coast. She and the battleship *Valiant* had just been helping Britain's Greek allies by bombarding the Albanian city of Vlona, the main port for the Italian Army in that area, while other fleet units swept for enemy convoys off the Tunisian coast. Cunningham wrote: "We then went onto Malta, and as things had been very quiet for some time I decided to take the *Warspite* into Grand Harbour for a night or two while the destroyers refueled. . . . It was our first visit since May, and news of our arrival had been spread abroad. As we moved in with our band playing and guard paraded, the Barracas and other points of vantage were black with wildly-cheering Maltese. Our reception was touchingly overwhelming.

"I went round seeing all our friends in the intervals of more official visits. Admiralty House looked very stripped and deserted, and in the hall I was met by my bandmaster and our two Maltese maids, both the latter weeping with emotion and asking if I could not persuade my wife to return.

"I went all over the dockyard next morning with the Vice-Admiral [Sir Wilbraham Ford] and was mobbed by crowds of excited workmen singing 'God Save the King' and 'Rule Britannia.' I had difficulty in preventing myself from being carried around, and had to make more than a dozen impromptu speeches telling all and sundry how greatly the fleet still depended upon them, and congratulating them on the fine way they were working under incessant attack and great difficulties. It was a very moving experience, and once again I realised what a great acquisition we had in Sir Wilbraham Ford. I had several meetings with the Governor, Lieutenant-General (later Sir) William Dobbie, another fine man and a tower of strength. My staff discussed the supply situation. We stayed in Malta about forty hours completely undisturbed by any air attack. It was a most useful visit."[8]

When the *Warspite* steamed out of Grand Harbour again, the destroyers weaving and jinking around her on the winter-blue sea, those who watched her go hoped that she was the harbinger of happy days, when the great gray ships would once more dominate the harbors and the clouds of lesser vessels infest the creeks and

inlets. Hitler, however, had decided that the actions of his Axis partner—first over Malta (which he had expected to be invaded long
ago), then in the western desert, and now in Greece—could no
longer be dismissed as incompetent buffoonery. They represented a
real threat to the New Order in Europe. The continent was conquered, and for the first time he could spare for the Mediterranean
theater of war the kind of planes that were unsuited for the Battle of
Britain but ideal for the reduction of civilian areas where there was
little or no air defense. During December *Fliegerkorps X* began
moving from Norway, down through Europe, to airfields in southern Italy and Sicily.

6

The Germans Intervene

Fliegerkorps X, commanded by General Geissler, was a crack unit that had been seasoned during the Norwegian campaign and in later attacks on England. The cream of the Luftwaffe, it had been specially trained in antishipping tactics and was composed of dive-bombers—the Stuka 87 "pure" dive-bomber and the twin-engined Junkers 88 shallow dive-bombers. They spearheaded the arrival of some 350 other Heinkel and Junkers bombers together with an escort of Messerschmitt fighters, the latter more than a match for the few Hurricanes on Malta. The German High Command, seeing the weaknesses of the Regia Aeronautica and the successes that the British had achieved by the use of the *Illustrious* as well as the other two aircraft carriers, had drawn up a list of priorities—to which the Italians had happily agreed. *Fliegerkorps X* was to act in collaboration with the Italians in attacking enemy maritime units at sea, to put the bases at Malta and Alexandria out of commission, and to mine the Suez Canal as well as the approaches to all ports and harbors in enemy hands. At the top of the list was simply "Sink the *Illustrious.*"

The Christmas of 1940 in Malta, despite the blackout and the permanent state of readiness, had something almost peacetime in its quality. True, the illuminated cribs could not appear in the doorways of churches, nor the Christmas-scene figures in the windows of private houses, and the traditional Christmas Midnight Mass was not held, but throughout the island the liturgy was celebrated on Christmas Eve afternoon. Soldiers, sailors, and airmen organized their own celebrations and parties, but the Maltese whose homes had been destroyed and who had moved into shelters or out into the evacuee centers were not forgotten. Air raid wardens and members of the special constabulary gave Christmas parties for the children. Joseph Micalleff records how at Cottonera, right in the heart of the dockyard area, after mass and communion, "during the day men enjoyed themselves singing and playing string instruments."[1]

Most of the cinemas had reopened some time before Christmas, encouraged by the lull in the bombing (there had been two hundred air raids by the end of the year), and motion picture shows were often shown three times daily to meet the demands of the throngs of British and Maltese servicemen. Newsreels of the distant war in the Atlantic and elsewhere seemed to remind the besieged that they were not alone in their struggle. The Royal Opera House in Valletta opened a Christmas series of entertainments, starting with a comic opera in Maltese. Air-raid shelters were decorated with festoons and flags, military bands enlivened the holiday, and football matches were held, as civilian and military teams played one another in the Empire Stadium. (The Maltese, many years before Europe and the rest of the world, had developed a passionate enthusiasm for this British sport). The Italians, true to their old traditions, kept the Christmas peace, and the Regia Aeronautica was grounded over the week. But at Catania and Comiso airfields in Sicily the Luftwaffe was settling in.

It was a hard, cold winter over all of Europe, and everywhere the conquered learned to adjust themselves to their new status. The cold to the north of the island—snow on the Madonie and Nebrodi ranges of Sicily as well as Etna and its foothills—effected one of those little miracles that happen in Malta only once or twice in a generation. On the morning of December 17 flurries of snow fell over the old walled capital Mdina and its suburb Rabat. Snow is so rare in Malta that people called their children out from their homes and held up babies to see the brief swirls of evanescent "mystery stuff."[2] Meanwhile at Luqa Airbase and at other military bases throughout the island thousands of Maltese children were entertained with parties and presents.

The jinx-winged, wheel-spatted Stuka 87s began practicing concerted attacks off the Sicilian coast on a mock-up target representing the flight deck of an aircraft carrier. Operation Excess, the passage of two important convoys through the Mediterranean, one from Gibraltar and the other from Alexandria, had been planned to take place early in December. This date was scrapped, however, because of disruption caused in the Atlantic by the German cruiser *Hipper* and rescheduled for early January 1941. Four large merchantmen under Admiral Somerville's Force H out of Gilbraltar were to be passed through to the central Mediterranean, three of them destined for Piraeus, to aid Britain's Greek allies, and one for Malta, with four thousand tons of ammunition and—almost as important— three thousand tons of seed potatoes. At the same time from the east Admiral Cunningham aimed to pass an oiler to Suda Bay in the island of Crete and two merchant vessels with general supplies, oil fuel, and gasoline to Malta. Empty merchantmen waiting in Malta would then be escorted back to Alexandria. The threat still posed by the Italian battleships in the area was almost eliminated on the night of January 8, when Wellington bombers operating out of Malta raided Naples, now the headquarters of the Italian fleet. The bombers badly damaged the battleship *Giulio Cesare,* with the result that both she and the *Vittorio Veneto* were hastily withdrawn to Genoa in the north. The island was proving how much it could affect the issues of the war.

With little threat of intervention by Italian surface forces, it now looked as if the complicated operation of moving these two convoys through the Mediterranean would proceed without a hitch. Two of the Duce's destroyers covering a convoy were unfortunate enough to run into the British cruiser *Bonaventure* and the destroyer *Hereward;* one Italian ship was sunk, the other was damaged. The only British casualty so far was the destroyer *Gallant,* which fell afoul of a mine-field off the Italian fortress-island of Pantellaria and had her bow blown off. Taken in tow by the stern, she was escorted by cruisers to Malta, where along with other casualties of the war she was to be beached for years to come.

In the morning of January 9 the convoy and escort from Gibraltar were attacked by ten Savoia bombers in the usual high-level fashion—ineffective even if alarming. The battleship *Malaya* and the cruiser *Gloucester* were straddled but survived intact, while Fulmar fighters from the *Ark Royal* clawed two of the bombers out of the sky.

Meanwhile, Cunningham's ships advancing from the east were preparing to cover Somerville's convoy once Force H turned back to Gibraltar. Cunningham's main force now consisted of his flagship *Warspite*, the battleship *Valiant*, the carrier *Illustrious*, and an escort of five destroyers. They were reported by shadowing enemy aircraft, one of which was brought down by fighters from the *Illustrious*. Although the position of the British fleet had been known to the Axis air forces for some time, a number of bombers looking for the fleet from Alexandria had failed to find them on the previous day. By January 10 it was clear that they were pinpointed, and the Fulmar fighters had to be constantly aloft on the watch for further planes. It was a clear, almost windless day with that wintry clarity often found in the Mediterranean. The fleet was on alert, expecting high-level attacks or torpedo-carrying aircraft—all of which they had become accustomed to during recent months.

At 12:20 P.M. a pair of Savoia torpedo bombers coming in low over the sea drew everyone's attention to their attack, clearly designed for *Illustrious*. The patroling fighters, seeing the gunfire from the fleet, at once began to descend. The Savoias loosed their torpedoes, which missed the aircraft carrier but passed narrowly astern of the *Valiant* and made off for Sicily low over the water. It was 12:28, an attack had been repelled, the Fulmars that had been on patrol were in pursuit of the Italians, and the sky was empty. Another flight of Fulmars was due to take off at 12:35.

At 12:30 a jagged thickening on the screen of the early radar aboard *Illustrious* indicated a large group of aircraft to the north. No one aboard the ship had ever seen anything quite like it before. Usually a few "indentations," as it were, would disclose the arrival of a reconnaissance plane or—as recently—the approach of a few bombers. This was something different—a large group of aircraft coming down from Sicily. Captain Boyd of the *Illustrious* had just made the customary signal to his commander-in-chief, asking for permission to turn into the wind so that his next flight of Fulmars could take off at 12:35. Suddenly, a darkening mass of aircraft came into sight. These were the Junkers 87s and Stukas, forty in all, and behind them a further wave of Junkers 88s. *Fliegerkorps X* had arrived over the Mediterranean.

The attack that followed was, as Ian Cameron wrote, "one of the great flying achievements of the war (comparable with the crippling of the Italian fleet at Taranto; Guy Gibson's breaking of the Mohne dam; the Mosquito bombing of Amsterdam gaol; and the Air Arm's Barracuda attack on the Tirpitz)."[3] Disregarding the intense barrage put up by the fleet, they approached at twelve thousand feet and then broke up into two formations, one of thirty planes concentrating entirely on *Illustrious* while the other ten broke away to attack the two battleships.

For the first time in war the vulnerability of the sea to the new air power was made evident. Everything was suddenly changed. There had been other such moments in the long violent history of man—when a flight of arrows directed against armored knights or the thunder of early siege guns against stone walls have transformed forever the whole technique of war. This was one of those moments, and even the threatened spectators could only marvel: "We could not but admire the skill and precision of it all. The attacks were pressed home to point-blank range, and as they pulled out of their dives some of them were seen to fly along the flight deck of the *Illustrious* below the level of her funnel."[4] Admiral Cunningham was so engrossed that he hardly seemed to notice when a thousand-pound bomb hurtled over his own bridge and, missing the foredeck, struck the fluke of the battleship's starboard bower anchor.

Some of the attackers dived in from the full twelve thousand feet at which they had approached, others dived to about half their approach height, checked with a neat twist, and then turned into their bombing dive. The angles at which they finally dived varied slightly pilot by pilot, but some were as steep as eighty degrees before, using their air brakes, they flattened out after releasing their bombs. The screaming siren-sound of a Stuka's dive, its guns flashing, and the knowledge of the hurling death it carried, were sensations that those on the ships would never forget, even amid all the other terrors of war.

Six and a half minutes after the attack had begun, it was all over, with the Stukas zigzagging away at sea level in the direction of Sicily. The earlier flight of Fulmars that had been lured away in pursuit of the Italian torpedo bombers had never been able to regain height before the German attack started, and the relief flight had only just got airborne. Caught completely unawares, and below instead of above the attackers, they fought desperately to catch the bombers in their downward plunge. Five of the dive-bombers were shot down, and the last ten to attack had their bombing runs severely disrupted by the wheeling, spitting fighters.

As the raid ended, one thing became immediately clear to the *Illustrious* pilots: They would not be returning to their mothership. Indeed, had it not been for the desperate efforts of her own aircraft, it is doubtful if the *Illustrious* would have survived at all. As it was, she had sustained such severe damage that she would be out of the war for many months. Her only destination now could be Malta.

The British had known of the Luftwaffe's presence in Sicily from reconnaissance flights made from the island. What some of those involved, both civilians and military, noted as a "singular feeling of unease" had no doubt been communicated to them by the silence of their senior officers—who knew but were not telling. The success in Europe of the cataclysmic bombing of cities was fully appreciated by all those who had to consider Malta's place in this Mediterranean war, which was now fast becoming the only battleground where the opponents could get at each other. If the full weight of the German might was to fall upon the small island, could the people endure it? It is very doubtful if at that moment the moral question was ever raised in the minds of Britain's war leaders—*should* they be asked to endure it? The only question was would they, or could they? The answer was soon given by the welcoming reception for the H.M.S. *Illustrious* as she arrived in Grand Harbour. It was true that the people of Malta had asked to become a British colony, but that had been in a different century, and although the Maltese men had constantly exposed themselves to French fire during the siege of Valletta, they had always been secure in the knowledge that their women and children were safe at home in their villages.

The relief flight of Fulmars had taken off as the attack started, and some planes actually flew through the fountains of water raised by near-misses of thousand-pound bombs. If they had not managed to get airborne, there is no doubt that *Illustrious* would have been hit even more than she was, possibly even sunk. Only her armored flight deck saved her from this fate and, although hit by six thousand-pounders, she staggered on. Her steering gear had been put out of action; bombs had damaged the elevators that took the aircraft to and from the deck below; some fifty percent of her 4.5-inch antiaircraft guns were knocked out; giant fires fueled by aviation gasoline roared through the hold; fuel tanks and ammunition were exploding. In addition, human casualties were heavy. The one all-important thing was that, despite the vast damage, the ship's main engines were still working and she was able to steam at nearly twenty knots.

With her steering gear gone, however, the only way of making for Malta was by jamming the rudder amidships and varying the revolutions on the main engines to maintain a more or less steady course.

For hour after hour the fight to save her went on, stokers fainting in the boiler rooms from the intense heat, and the captain permanently in anguish that the magazines might explode (he did not flood them for fear of further attacks and the necessity of using what was left of his firepower). His decision was proved right, for the enemy planes came back.

First there was an attack by Savoia bombers, but as usual they did not descend to face the gunfire of the fleet and, again as usual, their high-level attacks were unsuccessful. Then, shortly after 4 P.M., the Stukas returned, only fifteen of them this time, with an escort of Messerschmitt fighters. The Fulmars, which had earlier flown on to Malta to refuel and rearm, were waiting for them this time, high up and prepared. Although the Fulmars were slow-climbing aircraft, hardly a match for the Messerschmitts, they still managed to break up the attack, several Stukas being shot down and others damaged. This dogfight over the fleet raised the morale of the British, who had been badly shaken by the first evidence (hardly yet absorbed) that efficient land-based dive-bombers were almost unstoppable. If the attack on Taranto had signaled the end of the battleship as the most powerful vessel afloat, the attack on the *Illustrious* heralded the vulnerability of the aircraft carrier—certainly in a landlocked sea like the Mediterranean.

Listing heavily, with thousands of tons of water sluicing about inside the ship, with some fires still out of control, and with many dead and dying aboard, the *Illustrious* was about fifteen miles off Malta at sunset. In the last Stuka attack only one bomber had got through, but its thousand-pounder almost sounded the ship's death knell, falling near the after lift, penetrating the armor plate, and bursting within. The moon was up and the great ship, still steering under engines alone, was heading for the swept channel off Grand Harbour when a radio signal from Malta advised that torpedo bombers were approaching. Thus alerted, the carrier and her destroyer escorts were able to send up an antiaircraft barrage that beat off the enemy—one torpedo strike would almost certainly have sent the *Illustrious* to the bottom.

Throughout the day the progress of events had been plotted in operations rooms deep below the rock of Malta, and as the Fulmar pilots arrived at the Fleet Air Arm base of Hal Far for fuel and ammunition, they had told their stories. But even in the remotest villages the sound of the action and the thunder of the guns over the sea had alerted the islanders to the fact that some naval battle was taking place nearby. The flights of Fulmars coming and going during the day had hardly escaped the eyes of country farmers accustomed over the years to gazing skyward in spring and autumn for the annual migration of birds between Africa and Europe—before reaching for their shotguns.

The cargo ships, for which the whole action had been fought, had already reached Grand Harbour safely. The unloading of vital equipment, ammunition, and stores had begun. At ten o'clock that night, with powerful side-paddle tugs assisting her, the *Illustrious* came darkly down the harbor like an exhausted gladiator and secured to Parlatorio Wharf in French Creek. Smoke still rose from her, she stank of burning and cordite, of aviation fuel and oil and blood and tired sweat. So the very face of war was seen in the heart of the island.

7

Full Fury

Upon the old and indomitable fortress of the Knights of St. John there was to fall the weight of an attack far heavier than even the Grand Turk at the peak of the Ottoman Empire's power could have conceived. But first there was a lull. It was as if even the conquerors of Europe had been momentarily disturbed by the losses that their crack squadrons had sustained from the gunfire of the British fleet. Their principal target, as they knew from reconnaissance on January 11, remained obstinately afloat at the far end of Grand Harbour, and reports from the Italians of the density of antiaircraft fire over the area (doubtless somewhat magnified to excuse the ineffectuality of their own bombing of the island) prompted some cautious preparation in the attack that must certainly follow. In the meantime they had other successes to report.

The two British cruisers that had escorted the damaged destroyer *Gallant* into Malta were withdrawing to rejoin the fleet when they were attacked by dive-bombers coming in out of the sun—a classic tactic, which proved effective since neither ship was fitted with radar. The *Gloucester* was struck on the bridge by a bomb that went down into the bowels of the ship but failed to explode, and the cruiser *Southampton* was hit twice, so badly that she had to be abandoned and sunk by torpedo. Thus, the arrival of the Luftwaffe in the Mediterranean had abruptly changed the whole balance of power.

It was fortunate that early in the New Year a very experienced artillery officer, Brigadier General Sadler, had arrived in Malta to take charge of the antiaircraft defenses. He had previously served in Dover in a similar command during the Battle of Britain, when the guns of Dover were credited with ninety planes destroyed. Malta had hitherto been unfamiliar with dive-bombing tactics, but now that they might be expected, Sadler had immediately set in train the preparation of a box barrage to cover the whole area of Grand Harbour. The details of such a barrage, designed to cover French Creek where the *Illustrious* lay, were rushed to completion. There was just time for the coordinates of fire to be worked out, more guns brought from other positions to saturate the area at fixed angles, and heights of shell burst determined so that, as one gunner put it, "no gaps should be left through which the Stukas could bomb with comparative immunity."[1]

There was no question of repairing *Illustrious* in Malta even if there had been no threat from the air. All that could be done, if there was enough respite from attack, was to patch her up temporarily to make her fit for sea. It was clear that she would have to run the gauntlet yet again (if she got to sea at all) and make for Alexandria. From the moment of her arrival, the work on the ship had gone on relentlessly. After the dead, the dying, and the wounded had been taken ashore (the latter transported to the large hospital at Mtarfa on its high ridge near the old city of Mdina), the work on the ship had begun. Throughout that first night, with dockyard hoses playing on still-smoldering fires and surgeons and medical orderlies attending the wounded, shipbuilders and engineers were aboard to survey the damage. The final assessment by the ship's engineer commander was: "Her engines are not too bad, we'll get her away all right."[2]

Night and day, during that almost unbelievable lull in the battle, the ship echoed to the sound of workmen. "At first light on the morning of the 11th the Maltese dockyard workers took over. Their specific orders were not to deal with the smashed deck and twisted alleyways, and anything else above the waterline, but to attend only to the bare essentials that would make it possible for the ship to go out to sea and quickly. Divers went down to examine the bottom, the fitters invaded the engine room, and the welders began to take out the wooden pegs in her punctured hull and to weld the holes. . . . That morning the news had flashed all over the island and onlookers began to appear over the bastions and in boats outside the creek to see the fantastic ship that had withstood so much, so that Malta could have her convoy."[3]

The writer, who was a boy at the time, goes on to tell how five days later, on Thursday, January 16, his father, who was working aboard the *Illustrious,* asked him to collect a cap for him and bring it down to the dockyard. The boy was thus one of those who, without being in any way involved in the action, witnessed the arrival of the force sent to ensure that the *Illustrious* never again haunted the sea-lanes of the Mediterranean. Others who were engaged at the guns, including one British artillery officer, have also left us their record of the attack, still remembered by old men in the island as they sit in peace at home or in the dark caverns of local bars.

> Old men forget: yet all shall be forgot,
> But he'll remember with advantages
> What feats he did that day.

At a quarter past noon on January 16 a special announcement was made throughout the island over the cable radio system: In the event of an air raid, all civilians must immediately take cover and go into shelters because a new form of air defense tactics was about to be employed. The reason for the announcement was that in the recent past, after the alarm at the first air raids had given way to something of a contempt for the high-flying raiders, many of the Maltese living and working around Grand Harbour had got in the habit of gathering on the high vantage points of Valletta or in the Three Cities on their own rooftops to watch the defending fighters rise up and the ensuing dogfights, as if it were all some spectacular opera. This time, with *Fliegerkorps X* coming over, the box barrage would be of such density that any watchers were as likely to be killed by falling shrapnel as by the enemy.

At 1:55 P.M. the radar plot darkened. It was the largest that had ever been recorded in Malta till then. All who were watching the sky recorded the same impression of a multitude of dark dots approaching, "wave after wave of them." The air raid warning sirens wailed over the island as the red flags went up. Everywhere, forewarned by the radio, the people scurried for shelter. All around the harbor, all along the mile after mile of the strange configurations of its indented creeks, the mouths of guns lifted, light antiaircraft, heavy antiaircraft, pom-poms, machine guns, and 4.5-inchers. Even some of the heavy guns in the forts, hitherto unused because they were valueless against high-level bombers, swiveled and turned to provide massive death-dealing blasts in the air at the height where dive-bombers might be expected to level off.

That day there were only four Hurricanes, three Fulmars, and two of the old original Gladiators in serviceable condition to rise against the enemy. They were ordered to patrol outside the harbor area and to pick off stragglers or damaged planes as they emerged from the bursting forest that was shortly to grow over the sheltered water. (Not all of them, as will be seen, obeyed.)

Brilliantly directed, bravely sustained, the attack was something in the nature of another Charge of the Light Brigade—but more effective. Messerschmitt fighters and Italian Fiat and Macchi fighters hung like a swarm of gnats above the darker approaching cloud of bombers. The attack came in two main waves—first the shallow-dive twin-engined Junkers 88 and then, in the larger wave, the Stukas—over seventy bombers in all. The barrage that rose up to meet them was universally described as "hell let loose," beating on the eardrums in such waves of sound that some of those who heard it felt as if they were going mad. Apart from all the shore defenses and antiaircraft guns guarding the area, every ship in the harbor including the *Illustrious* herself opened fire, the thunder clamoring round and round the stony heights above the harbor, while the ramparts and fortresses of the Knights reverberated like a great drum. Joseph Attard remembers "the shaking of the shelter as bombs were hitting the Dockyard part which was beneath the bastion where the shelter stood, only fifty yards away. I felt the strong wave of blast in the shelter and pressed myself to the wall in the first cavity I found. Women and men alike, screaming prayers, were toppled on each other. . . . Children began to cry while the shattering noises outside continued, with more diving, whistling bombs, explosions, blocks of concrete that were lifted from the dockyard below and smashed against the face of the shelter, and of course the never-ending gunfire. It looked as if the world had come to an end and no one would live."[4]

The *Illustrious* was at times completely hidden from view by the fountains of bomb splashes and exploding near-misses, and yet, despite the great bravery (which all accounts acclaim) with which the pilots pressed home their attack, they only managed to score one direct hit on the carrier—on the quarterdeck, causing relatively minor damage. An eyewitness described the ship at that moment: "HMS *Illustrious* herself struck me as being rather like a great cat at bay. She had her back arched up against the walls of the cliffs rising sheer from the docks and her guns were spitting back defiance at any and every target that came within range."[5] The island rocked to the shock of the battle, and the Three Cities rumbled and roared with the weight of exploding bombs and the crash of heavy masonry as stone ramparts and walls came thundering down.

An officer of the Royal Artillery watched one fighter disregard the orders to stay outside the area of the box barrage: "I was on a light-aircraft gun position in the harbour area for one of these attacks, and I can still see clearly a German bomber diving through that terrific curtain of steel, followed by a Fulmar, release his bomb almost at the last moment and then turn and fly out only a few feet above the water and turn right-handed towards the entrance of the harbour. He was so low that he had to rise to clear the breakwater, which is only some fifteen feet high. As the Stuka rose to clear the mole the Fulmar pilot shot him down into the sea on the far side. He later landed at Halfar remarking that he didn't think much of Malta's bloody barrage! However, he never flew that particular plane again, so badly was it damaged."[6]

Lying on the opposite side of the creek from the *Illustrious* was a merchantman from the convoy, the *Essex,* which was hit by a heavy bomb in the engine room with a loss of thirty-eight dead and wounded. Fortunately for everyone in the area, the bulkheads of the engine room contained the explosion—for the holds of the ship were loaded with four thousand tons of ammunition and torpedoes. Had these gone up, the whole creek and everything in it would have been destroyed.

One Stuka hit in the barrage released its bombs over Valletta before crashing into the sea beyond Fort St. Elmo. The bombs brought down a large building in the city's Old Mint Street. Everywhere the men of the Passive Defence Services were rushing to the rescue of victims trapped inside shattered houses, beneath shelters, and in cellars. After the second wave of the attack had passed and the gunfire ceased, a sudden silence was remarked—a silence that seemed to be compounded by the crash of buildings still falling. Over the

whole harbor area there hung a thick pall of smoke and yellow limestone dust, turning and eddying in the blue air.

Many were killed or wounded that day. Buildings were demolished not only in Valletta but most widely throughout the Three
Cities surrounding the dockyard; the peninsula of Senglea fared the
worst, with over three hundred houses badly damaged or destroyed.
The ambulance men and mobile squads of rescue and demolition
workers moved cautiously through streets blocked by fallen masonry. The yellow limestone blocks that formed the houses,
churches, ramparts, and indeed almost every building in Malta had
proved how effective they were against incendiary bombs and how
well they could withstand the blast from high explosives, but direct
hits were another matter; shifting the blocks as quickly as possible to
get at survivors buried beneath them was a herculean task. (The lack
of relief squads to carry on this work when the first workers were
exhausted was something that had to be corrected before further
raids.)

After this first day's attack the inhabitants of the Three Cities immediately took up the great exodus that had practically been reversed during recent months. It was quite clear, now the Luftwaffe
had arrived, that houses must be abandoned and that families must
either move to outlying districts or find deep shelters within walking
distance of the dockyard, Malta's main source of employment.
There was not much work out in the countryside, where already
there was a surplus of idle men whose shops or small businesses had
been forced to close down.

During the raid of January 16 ten of the attackers were shot
down, five by fighters and five by the antiaircraft defenses. Others
were badly damaged, and the command in Sicily decided to give
their squadrons a rest over the next day. The work on the *Illustrious*
continued, as fitters and welders and construction officers worked
ceaselessly to get her to sea before the bombers came back. This next
raid took place on the eighteenth, but the German plan had
changed—the aim now was to eliminate the airfields from which the
fighter opposition came. Luqa and Hal Far were heavily attacked by
eighty raiders, the former being so badly cratered that for a time it
became unserviceable.

The German commanders reckoned that if fighter opposition
could be eliminated, a further attack on the *Illustrious* would be suc-

cessful. But the word had inevitably gone round the pilots, even those of General Geissler's crack formation, that the harbor of Malta was a kind of hell such as they had not encountered before during the course of the war. The fact was that the Stuka, still to sink many ships and damage the morale of many a sailor during the next few years, was obsolescent: Terrifying in its dive, and accurate enough against the gunfire of a single ship, it was too slow in flight against modern fighters or the concentrated barrage of a fleet. The Stuka depended very largely upon the nerve and skill of its pilots, and as crack veterans were lost or wounded and less experienced hands took control, the impact of the Stuka declined. In due course the arrival of Spitfires in the Mediterranean would signal its demise, although the dour courage of the Germans kept it flying successfully for some years to come.

Despite the weight of the attack on the airfields *Fliegerkorps X* suffered badly, seven falling to the British fighters and four to the guns. The last raid launched against the aircraft carrier itself came on Sunday, January 19. A color-sergeant of the Royal Marines manning one of the guns on top of Fort St. Angelo (La Valette's headquarters in the Great Siege of 1565) described how "Bombs were dropped in and around all the creeks, causing terrific clouds of dust, flying masonry and iron. Although I did not see it myself, it was stated that a motor-car complete went sailing over the top of us. The dust and spray often blinded our view, but the dive-bombers always came on. As they broke through the dust they seemed like hawks looking for their prey." He added: "You lose all sense of fear and self-preservation while it lasts. You get the same feeling as being at a football final."[7] A curious touch!

Six Hurricanes, one Fulmar, and one of the old Gladiators were up that day and accounted for eleven of the raiders, the guns bringing down another eight. This was reckoned to be about one quarter of the attacking force—sufficient deterrent in itself, especially since later Italian reports revealed a number of funerals taking place in Sicily for Luftwaffe airmen. An Italian Red Cross seaplane was spotted assiduously searching the Malta-Sicily channel, presumably for aircraft that had failed to reach home. The *Illustrious* received no direct hits but suffered underwater damage through the mining effect of near-misses that exploded on the bottom of the creek. Teams of technicians and welders and divers set to work on her once again.

There were no further air raids, for the rate of loss borne by the Luftwaffe could no longer be sustained. Preparations were indeed being made for a further attack, but early on the night of January 23 the great ship slipped away and headed east for Alexandria, gradually working up speed until she was making over twenty knots. Ian Cameron wrote: ". . . no warship of any Navy ever lived through such punishment—eight direct hits (at least five of them with 1000-pounders) with seven fractional misses."[8] It was a tribute to the ship's builders, crew, and the dockyard staff of Malta that she ever sailed again. So fast did she move during that night that the cruiser squadron sent to escort her back missed her, underestimating her speed, and were themselves heavily bombed. She reached Alexandria safely and after further temporary repairs went on to Norfolk, Virginia, for a complete refit. Her place in the Mediterranean was taken two months later by another carrier with an armored flight deck, the *Formidable*.

The *Illustrious* blitz, as it came to be known among the besieged, was recognized by everyone as the beginning of a new phase in the history through which all were living. Two days after the first attack on the aircraft carrier the government ordered the evacuation of the Three Cities. All available transport was ordered to the area, and soon army trucks, private cars, buses, and horse-drawn carts were raising clouds of dust along the roads. Festooned with people (reminiscent of the sticky paper that hung from summer ceilings to catch flies) and piled high with furniture and family treasures, the stream of transport made for outlying townships and villages. It was clear that so long as the harbor remained in use—which meant so long as Malta was not conquered—the whole area must be evacuated except for people who, in the safety of deep-tunneled shelters, could remain close to their source of work. Housing the refugees was one problem, but almost as difficult was feeding and clothing them. In January the rocky island is cold, damp, and windy, and depots distributing clothing and blankets were immediately opened to try to meet the people's needs, while communal feeding centers and the first mobile canteens began to distribute food and hot drinks at minimal prices.

The Maltese, as befitted a Mediterranean island race, were both hardy and frugal. These virtues were to be tested almost to destruction in the months to come. As in all communities under similar pressures, however, not only does the good become evident but the bad thrives. The black market in every kind of commodity continued to grow, and the abandoned cities around Grand Harbour could hardly escape the looter. Archbishop Caruana might condemn this as "a very grave sin," but even in most Catholic Malta there were many sinners, and in dockyard areas rats thrive. The simpler rodents were kept down by the dogs and cats that, abandoned yet again, haunted the tumbled buildings and the empty streets.

8

Island, Desert, and Sea

That same January 1941 the British Army attacked in North Africa. The Italians were rolled back and the borders of Egypt were left far behind as General Wavell's troops advanced. Moving rapidly into Cyrenaica up the desert road that was to become so sadly familiar to the soldiers during the years to come, the army took Bardia (yielding some forty-five thousand prisoners) and then the useful deep-water port of Tobruk—a name familiar in world headlines when it later became a solitary garrison in enemy-held territory. By February 6 the Italian forces had been driven right out of Cyrenaica, thus securing the safety of Egypt and producing—for the time being, at any rate—a useful buffer state between the Suez Canal Zone and Italian-held Tripolitania. There was no doubt that Wavell's army could have pushed right on to Tripoli itself, perhaps ending the desert war before ever the Germans got involved in it. But Churchill already had his eye on Greece and was pressing the Greek government to accept British tanks and weaponry and troops to aid them in their successful stand against the Italian invasion of their country. So, at a moment when the Axis forces might have been thrown out of North Africa for good, Wavell was compelled to send some of his troops to the aid of Greece.

Hitler was alarmed by the collapse of his ally in the desert and ordered the transfer of nearly half of *Fliegerkorps X* to Tripoli to

stiffen the Italian resistance. This in its turn meant that the scale of
the air attack on Malta began to decline. Luckily for the island this
happened just when a series of day and night raids had begun to tell
on the defenders. In addition to attacks on the airfields a new technique was the dropping of parachute mines over the land: Their
blast effect was enormous, shattering houses and nerves equally. At
the same time the systematic mining of the approaches to Malta, as
well as the creeks and harbors, by magnetic mines was beginning to
increase the hazards of navigation near the island, contributing to
Malta's sense of isolation from the outside world. Dive-bombers
escorted by fighters continued to attack by day, while the nights
were rendered sleepless by the incursion of high-flying raiders, some
bombing and others mining.

The attacks continued throughout January, February, and
March. The principal aim of these raids was to wear down the resistance of the defense and at the same time to occupy the energy and
the attention of everyone in Malta. For Hitler had already decided
that his ally must be reinforced in North Africa, and the crumbling
Italian resistance stiffened by an injection of German troops. The
advance guard of the Afrika Korps began to reach Tripoli in January, no more than a light motorized division at first, but soon
followed by a complete armored division, the 15th Panzer. On February 12 General Erwin Rommel arrived in Tripoli to take command of the *Deutsches Afrika Korps.* With support from units of
Fliegerkorps X and from long-range aircraft based in Sicily, the general had at his disposal a really efficient fighting force. Though still
unskilled in the ways of desert warfare, the Germans would inflict
grave losses on the extended line of British troops, soon to be depleted through the demands imposed by their leaders' commitment
to Greece.

The weakness of Malta as an offensive base was shown by the fact
that the Afrika Korps reached its destination with scarcely any
losses. Shortage of aircraft and, for some time, a shortage of suitable
submarines on the British side meant that the Italian Navy was able
to transport men and matériel comparatively unscathed. However,
the arrival in the island in February of the first of a new class of submarines, the U class, was the beginning of a change in Malta's position. As more of these deservedly famous "boats" reached Malta,
the attacks on Italian shipping would grow and grow, until the is-

land dealt out more damage to the Axis war effort than ever it received itself. Yet even in this early spring of 1941 Wellington bombers were attacking the airfields of Sicily, while the few Swordfish available, acting in concert with the Sunderlands for air reconnaissance, were displaying the first evidence of Malta's potential against the Axis lifeline between Italy and Africa. Fortunately for the islanders the damage was still so slight that it did not provoke an immediate response—invasion.

It is doubtful if an invasion could have succeeded even at this moment. The Italians had long possessed a plan for the conquest of Malta, but anyone may plan something—some dreamy fantasy—it is the carrying of it into execution that counts. And the Italian High Command had suspected all along that this plan, "Operazione C3: Malta,"[1] was little more than a pipe dream. It called for some forty thousand trained troops, including paratroops, landing craft, an air cover of five hundred planes, and—for the time that it took to establish troops successfully ashore—naval superiority in the area. Exercises had indeed been held with the relatively few motorized barges that existed and a limited number of troops, but these were more in the nature of a propaganda act for visiting dignitaries and officials to witness yet another facet of Mussolini's grand army and navy in operation. It was all so much opéra bouffe, and while the Germans had indeed expected something in the nature of an invasion to take place within days or hours of Italy's entering the war, no one in the Italian High Command ever imagined that such a thing was possible. For one thing the difficulty of landing troops on the stony island of Malta was heightened by the fact that there were very few beaches of any size where troops could be put ashore from flat-bottomed barges.

"Malta lies in the sea like the deck of a sinking aircraft carrier, with the side to the south-west high out of the water, sloping towards the north and east, with the deck awash at several points. To the west, with the exception of the mouths of some water-courses and of the main valleys which traverse the Island at three points, the cliffs are sheer and high and the beaches narrow."[2] The only suitable places for landing, on the northeast coast in the areas of Mellieha and St. Paul's Bay, were so well-covered and so well-defended that it would have been suicide for any craft to try and approach by day or night. Paratroopers would hardly have had more success against Malta. As Hitler was perspicacious enough to point out at a later date, the miniature fields, each bounded by irregular drystone walls, were obstacle enough in themselves and death to gliders.

Malta was hard. The bony island frame, which the Knights of St. John had despaired of after arriving from their home in fertile and gracious Rhodes, made it a natural fortress. The only other place where a landing might have been attempted (and here the Italian plan was for a diversionary thrust) was in the big open bay of Marsaxlokk in the south. This "south harbour," with its sloping ledges of rock surrounded by immediately rising ground, would have been another death trap. The defenders' task was made the easier by the intractable nature of the island, and the Italian (and later German) staff officers who contemplated relief maps and models shook their heads in despair. To neutralize Malta by such a weight of bombing, coupled with mining of the approaches, so that no aircraft could rise from its airfields and no shipping could get through to relieve the island, was seen as the only answer to the problem. This neutralization of Malta was tried in 1942.

Despite their new commitments in North Africa the Luftwaffe kept some pressure on the island. Determined to establish air superiority and to wear out the pilots and the aircraft of the small core of defending Hurricanes, sweeps of Messerschmitt 109 fighters were sent over Malta in daylight. Quite apart from their numbers, the Messerschmitts were more than a match for the Mark 1 Hurricanes, and by the close of February these daylight raids were almost routine. The watchers on the ground, who in the early days of the island's aerial warfare had been happy to see how a handful of fighters would spring up like the knights in their old tales of chivalry, putting to flight large numbers of the enemy, now grew sadly used to seeing the parachutes of their defenders opening over the barren hills and the patchwork green of the small fields. Sometimes Luqa Airfield would be rendered completely unserviceable by a Stuka raid. The accompanying fighters seemed to fly with easy insolence lower and lower overhead, spraying anything that moved on road or dusty track. The Wellington bombers, which had managed to make Naples unsafe for heavy units of the Italian fleet and which had closed Sicilian ports and raided that island's airfields, were caught on the ground, some of them burned out and others badly damaged.

While far more ominous signs were visible in other parts of the Mediterranean theater of war—the Afrika Korps making ready for desert warfare and the Germans poised to invade Greece—the linchpin of the sea was itself being eroded. "A Blitz raid of several formations," was reported, "totalling no less than one hundred aircraft. . . . Sixty bombers attacked Hal Far." The seaplane base at Kalafrana was also bombed and machine-gunned. To repulse this last attack every serviceable Hurricane was put in the air, leaving no reserves either of aircraft or of men. A few days prior to this the main airbase at Luqa had also been heavily attacked, the old village from which the base takes its name receiving the residue of bombs dropped by pilots unwilling to face the lightning storm of flak over the airfield itself.

The *Times of Malta*, a remarkable newspaper that never ceased publication on any day throughout the war, sent a reporter to the scene: "There is hardly a street without a demolished house or one seriously damaged or shaken. . . . The villagers told me that tons of bombs have fallen in or about the village. There were signs of destruction everywhere. Seventy-seven houses have been completely demolished, 25 others seriously damaged and uninhabitable, and it is reckoned that only about 25 percent of the homes there have so far escaped completely unscathed. So many bombs—some of the biggest ever dropped—have fallen all round that village . . . that almost all houses and farms on the outskirts facing the fields bear marks of the shrapnel, which hit holes into the walls. . . . These people, most of them miners, stone-cutters and farmers, are among the most courageous and confident one can be privileged to meet. They have dug shelters, carried away to other villages the most valuable portions of their furniture and household goods, and they continue to live and work there, notwithstanding the severe punishment the village has had to submit to at the hands of the enemy."[3] So well had the Maltese stonecutters dug shelters for their wives and families and fellow villagers that in all the thunder of this raid, the collapse of houses and the bursting of walls and splintering of great stones, there was only one casualty.

In the early raids the attackers had concentrated on the harbor and any shipping in it as well as on the all-important dockyard. Then it had been the turn of the airfields, but now, during the clear spring nights, the indiscriminate bombing of residential areas, familiar in London and other British cities, became common in the miniature world of Malta. The residents of the dockyard area had suffered worst in the *Illustrious* blitz, but now the well-to-do seaside suburb of Sliema, which bore a marked resemblance to similar Victorian outcrops along the shores of Britain, learned the anguish of total war. Twenty-two were killed and thirty-six injured in one raid alone in March—small figures compared to those in Britain and Europe, but heavy enough in view of the size of the island and its population. A survivor recalled the aftermath of this raid: "The bright moonlight bathed the scene of utter devastation, the acrid reek of explosive filled the cool night air. The uncanny silence was broken only by muffled groans and long drawn sighs. Husky and terse remarks from men who were looking for signs of humanity, accentuated the grim poignancy of the disaster."[4]

Throughout the months following the arrival of the Luftwaffe in Sicily only a handful of individual merchant ships (their crews sailing with old-fashioned blockade-runner's panache) had managed to reach the island with stores and weaponry. The first convoy of the year, consisting of four merchantmen, escorted by the battlefleet and the new aircraft carrier *Formidable* from Alexandria, reached Grand Harbour unobserved early on March 23. But reconnaissance from Sicily immediately spotted the new arrivals, and two of the freighters were sunk at their moorings before they could be unloaded. This disclosed a dangerous weakness in port arrangements for cargo handling, not to be properly dealt with until further losses had made such an overhaul tragically imperative.

Prior to the arrival of this convoy Admiral Cunningham, who never wearied of reminding London of the importance of Malta, had received something of a rebuff from the First Sea Lord, Admiral Sir Dudley Pound. The latter pointed out that the Battle of the Atlantic transcended all other commitments, though it was still hoped to pass some more Hurricanes through to Malta by carrier from Gibraltar as soon as circumstances permitted. In his reply Cunningham once again stressed the alarming condition of the island: "The most drastic and early measures are needed to restore the situation at Malta, which alarms me seriously. Enemy air forces operate over the island as they please."

It was toward the close of March that the British Mediterranean fleet managed to reassert itself. But the fleet action, which came to be known as the Battle of Cape Matapan, served to highlight the supremacy of the air arm at sea. Insofar as it had any major bearing on the course of the Mediterranean war and Malta's part in it, Matapan reconfirmed the superiority of the British over the Italian fleet, strengthening the latter's High Command in their reluctance to engage in any major actions. When it came to further assessments as to the feasibility of invading Malta (with the necessity of having naval superiority, even if only temporary, in the area), Matapan played its part in deterring any such considerations.

While the Germans had congratulated the Italians on their successful convoying of the Afrika Korps to Libya with scarcely any loss, they were now extremely disturbed by the ease with which British convoys were making their way to Greece laden with supplies and troops, on the very eve of the German invasion. Pressure was accordingly brought to bear upon the Italians from the highest level to use their fleet to disrupt this supply line. Hitler had his eyes obsessively fixed upon his major ambition, the invasion of Soviet Russia, and did not want to get heavily embroiled in Balkan enterprises. He had already come to his partner's aid in the desert war, and now he was prepared to save Mussolini's face once again by sending troops to Greece. He wished to cover his southern flank before his major enterprise. Despite the objections that Admirals Riccardi and Iachino had already raised to any fleet ventures into the eastern Mediterranean, pleading accurately enough the superiority of British naval and land-based air reconnaissance in that area, they were at last compelled to take some action. They were promised the full cooperation of the Luftwaffe together with the Regia Aeronautica from bases in the Dodecanese. After his previous experience off Cape Spartivento of the inefficiency of his own air force, Admiral Iachino may well have hesitated, but the promise of the Luftwaffe's support, combined with the fact that these orders came from the very top, gave him no option.

Flying his flag in the *Vittorio Veneto,* Iachino passed through the Messina Straits early on March 27, in company with four escorting destroyers and preceded by the heavy cruisers *Trieste, Trento,* and *Bolzano* together with their destroyer screen. East of Sicily they were met by three heavy cruisers from Taranto, *Zara, Pola,* and *Fiume,* and two light cruisers from Brindisi, all with their attendant destroyer screens. The object of this fleet was to position itself in the area south of Crete near Gavdos and intercept merchant traffic northward bound for Greece from Alexandria. Admiral Iachino's fears about the cooperation that he might expect from the air were sadly confirmed. Neither Italian planes nor, even more disappointing, the Luftwaffe made their anticipated appearance to protect him from being observed by British reconnaissance. Sure enough, a Sunderland flying boat out of Malta sighted one of the cruiser divisions steering southeast in the direction of Crete. This report alerted Admiral Cunningham, who had already become suspicious that an increase in enemy air reconnaissance over Alexandria meant some major move by the Italian fleet. Putting to sea overnight (Alexandria was full of prying eyes) in *Warspite*, along with the battleships *Barham* and *Valiant*, the aircraft carrier *Formidable*, and escorting destroyers, he steered for the same position south of Crete toward which the Italian fleet was heading.

In the battle that followed the collision of these two fleets, the battleships never came within fighting range of one another. This was fortunate for the Italian admiral since he was heavily outnumbered. In any case, the possession of the aircraft carrier by the British made the whole difference to the engagement. Without the benefit of air reconnaissance Admiral Iachino was at the gravest disadvantage, being ignorant of what enemy forces were opposing him and of their position. His own ships were soon under attack from Royal Air Force bombers and then from the *Formidable's* planes. The cruiser *Pola* was hit and immobilized in a torpedo attack by Swordfish, then left behind as the Italian squadron turned about. She later provided the unintentional bait whereby Admiral Iachino, having misjudged the position of the British battlefleet and believing them to be far from the scene, sent back two heavy cruisers with escorting destroyers, either to take survivors off the *Pola* and sink her or to tow her back to safety. On the night of March 28 this rescue mission fell right into the path of Cunningham's battlefleet in pursuit of the withdrawing *Vittorio Veneto*, which had also been damaged in a torpedo attack. The two cruisers and two of the destroyers were blown to pieces, and the *Pola* was sunk at leisure. The British picked up what survivors they could, but after saving some nine hundred men, they were compelled to leave the scene by the arrival of the Luftwaffe the morning of the twenty-ninth. A message giving the exact position of the survivors was sent to the Italian Admiralty, which dispatched a hospital ship. Other survivors were also picked up by a Greek destroyer flotilla that arrived on the scene.[5]

The Italians were without radar and untrained in night fighting, two fatal deficiences that led to their being overwhelmed. They were fortunate in one respect only, that the torpedo strike on Admiral Iachino's flagship was insufficient to slow her down, and she was able to join the other vessels in withdrawing at high speed to their home bases. The disaster could have been far worse. The failure of their own air force and of the Germans' in the action served to confirm the Italian Admiralty in its further unwillingness to venture the fleet at sea. Thus, Matapan, a fleet action in which the battleships never sighted one another and in which the air arm dominated, was conclusive in the history of war.

Italian naval morale was naturally even further depressed by this action, while that of the British, who had been shaken by the constant bombing they had to endure every time they went to sea, was correspondingly improved. They would need all the morale that they could call upon in the weeks that lay ahead.

9

Voices

In ancient sieges a dramatic keynote of the whole story was often the moment when a well-wisher among the besieging army, or a spy who has managed to infiltrate it, shot an arrow over the walls bearing, say, the word "tomorrow," thus ensuring that the besieged would be all prepared when the great attack was launched. (Something of this sort happened at a crucial moment in the Great Siege of 1565.) In the complexity of a modern siege such messages still arrived—and, indeed, still by air, but crossing not only the walls of the besieged fortress but often many miles of ocean. Malta throughout the siege was not only the recipient of innumerable messages by day and night, it was also a central distribution point for information throughout the Mediterranean, as well as back to Britain.

The island had long had a primary function not only as a fleet base but as a main headquarters for the reception of intelligence gleaned from Axis Europe and distributed to Allied forces. The threat that Malta posed to the lifeline of convoys between Italy and North Africa made its reduction all-important to the German and Italian leaders, but this was not its only importance to the British. It was Malta as an intelligence center, listening in to occupied Europe from Greece and the Balkans throughout the whole of the southern part of the continent, that made it so deadly. Army, navy, and air force all had their W/T (wireless telegraphy) and R/T (radiotelephony) stations scanning the airwaves twenty-four hours of the day and night. From the capital Valletta itself, to Fort St. Angelo, to airfields and remote parts of the countryside, the island bristled with radio masts. Malta was a giant ear in the Mediterranean.

So far we have told the story of the siege in the traditional manner, as presented in the many accounts of those days. Soldier, sailor, and airman, of both high and low rank, have given their accounts of the siege, the air battles, and the relief convoys as these were seen in terms of action and events. Yet, there was another side, a fourth dimension, as it were, to the story of the siege, just as there was to that of the whole war. Very few of those involved ever knew of this other dimension, and even the few who did know were constrained by their obligations of official secrecy never to reveal it. Thus, Admiral Cunningham in his autobiography published in 1951 maintains that it was a combination of "unusual Italian wireless activity," coupled with the sighting of an Italian cruiser squadron by an aircraft flown off by the *Formidable,* that put him in position for the Battle of Cape Matapan. Both these facts are true, but what Cunningham omitted was the fact that, prior to taking his ships to sea from Alexandria, he had already received information from London that the Italian fleet was about to move against the convoys to Greece off the island of Crete.

The astonishing story of how the theoretically unbreakable German ciphering machine called Enigma was cracked at Bletchley Park in England could not be told before 1974.[1] The incredibly valuable intelligence service named Ultra had sprung out of this achievement. This "decisive factor in the allied victory," as General Eisenhower called it, played an incalculable part in the Mediterranean, as it did everywhere else in the course of the European war. One of the main centers for the reception of Ultra information was the island of Malta. Throughout the war, while many of the top-secret messages of the enemy were being read, the information contained in them was being assessed, classified, checked, and put together by the brilliant team at Bletchley Park. The sum total of this was then transmitted to Special Liaison Units (SLU) for the attention of commanders-in-chief and a selected handful of senior officers. One of the largest SLUs anywhere was in Malta. Also installed in Malta was the new RAF Type X machine cipher, which had been carefully developed after the breaking of the German

Enigma machine, thus putting it far in advance of that used by the Germans. Type X machines were only installed in main headquarters that served two or more of the services; Malta served all three. Dozens of men and women passed the whole war in Malta with earphones clamped to their heads, listening in at the intercept stations and striving to catch signals being transmitted by the forces ranged against them.

The Y services (as they were known) of the army, navy, and air force worked long hours—six-hour watches were common—inconspicuously and, indeed, completely unknown to the men at the guns, the pilots, or the men in the ships whose lives often depended on the intelligence gathered by Ultra. The working conditions of those employed by the Y services on Malta would hardly have been tolerated by any civilian in whatever form of employment, for many of them worked deep underground in limestone tunnels carved out beneath the immense Lascaris Bastion in the walls of Valletta. The naval operations room had been moved to this deep, bombproof heart after Fort St. Angelo had received too great attention from the enemy, standing up as it did conspicuous across the waters of Grand Harbour. Despite the fact that this old headquarters of the Knights of Malta received over sixty direct hits during the siege, the great walls, bastions, and cavaliers stood firm, proof indeed that in the centuries for which the fortress had been designed it would have been impregnable. Other men and women were ciphering and coding, deciphering and decoding, in what had originally been the tunnels excavated to make quarters for the galley slaves in the days of the Knights. This area, like that below Lascaris Bastion, had been considerably enlarged by further tunneling to accommodate these new citizens, whose work, however remote from that of the slaves, was as arduous in its different way, and the circumstances almost equally disagreeable.

The benefits of air-conditioning were unknown in Malta during World War II, and the air that filtered through these tunnels (into which boxlike offices had been built) was inevitably hot, humid, and dusty.[2] Limestone is quite easy to cut, but equally, until it develops a hard skin after exposure to the briny sea air, it crumbles easily. Roof-falls were not uncommon in the new tunnels, and the freshly cut stone sweated with damp. In Malta, when the hot and damp sirocco blows—mostly in spring and autumn—the outside walls of buildings often stream with moisture as if after rain. In the tunnels of Lascaris and St. Angelo clothing would grow mold within a day or so, and a film of moisture often lay over everything. The porosity of the limestone, which had allowed the great lakes to form beneath the island (from which Malta drew much of its water), was sadly in evidence in the tunnels during the rainy season. Pools of water formed in the passages, and sea-boots were often the rig-of-the-day. It is hardly surprising that chest and lung ailments were found among the operators who spent long working hours down there.

These circumstances were special to Malta, but another factor that is hardly mentioned in accounts of the eavesdropping intelligence services during the war was the stress of the work itself. The island was under siege, but so were the nerves of the radio operators, merely from the nature of their work. This was noted even in the comparative peace of Bletchley Park. Listening intently for long hours with all attention fixed is a great strain, and *tinnitus,* a constant buzzing in the ears, became a common affliction among operators. But these, and other installations like them, were the brains that helped to direct the war, and Malta, unlike other communications centers such as Cairo, was in the heart of the war itself.

When the action was fiercest during the long months of the siege, particularly in 1942 when the island was almost cut off, the only communication with the outside world was over the airwaves. The wireless telegraphy for which the operators listened out was mostly on medium or high frequencies, and on these emanated traffic from the Italians and the Germans in a number of codes and ciphers, including the all-important Enigma, and even *en clair.* Radiotelephony was mostly employed by fighter pilots in their single-engined machines talking with fellow pilots or responding to their ground controller. These communications were conducted on very high frequencies, which meant that the range of communication was short— but then it was only sixty miles from Malta to Sicily. Whether by day or by night the approach of the attackers could be recorded, the raid reaching its crescendo when the air was also filled with the voices of the defenders. R/T was also used by the Italian high-speed motorboats and, when they later reached the Mediterranean, the German E-boats. The torpedo boats most often came into action against convoys striving to reach Malta from the west during the height of the siege. Their main operating ground was in the Narrows

between Sicily and Tunisia, where the Italian fortress-island Pantelleria and the lesser islands of Lampedusa and Linosa barred the
channel. The intercept stations closest to Malta were at Gibraltar
and Alexandria, and there were others—from Baghdad to Aden—
listening for traffic from all over the Middle East, from North
Africa, and as far afield as the Balkans. Sailings from Italian and
Greek ports were monitored, and Italian naval ciphers read as well
as German Luftwaffe traffic on Enigma, the whole being put together at Bletchley Park, whence the intelligence picture was transmitted to the commanders-in-chief.

It was known in Malta, for instance, that *Fliegerkorps X* was
moving down through Europe to Sicily. (This fact does not appear
in earlier accounts of the siege because the existence of Enigma and
Ultra was not known to most of the authors; the few senior officers
who knew about it could not reveal their source.) If this was so, it
may be asked, why did the subsequent deadly attacks on H.M.S. *Illustrious* and the blitz on Grand Harbour take place? The answer is
that it is one thing to have advance secret intelligence, but quite another to be able to act upon it. Action demands resources, and at this
stage in the war these were spread so thin as to be almost minimal in
places. Malta had to receive its convoy, and the *Illustrious* was the
necessary aircraft carrier to be in the escort. The deadly efficiency of
Fliegerkorps X in dive-bombing attacks might have been anticipated
but could hardly have been obviated. On the other hand, the Luftwaffe was quite surprised by the reception it got over Grand Harbour when it arrived to finish off (as it thought) the aircraft carrier.
The air defenses of the island against the Italians had given nobody
an inkling of what had been prepared for the Nazis. (The losses sustained by the Luftwaffe during those attacks from the newly installed box-barrage proved unacceptable, and the escape of the
Illustrious, even given some element of luck, was made possible.)

Throughout the course of the war Ultra information was acted
upon *where resources permitted* and often enabled commanders in
the field—particularly in the western desert—to "box canny" and to
make the greatest use of what they had at a time when the Axis
forces possessed considerable numerical superiority. On the other
hand, it was always understood by those in high command that
Ultra could be used only in such ways that the Germans would
never suspect that the most secret information being conveyed on

their Enigma machines was being read. This often entailed cover plans to make it appear as if the action that was subsequently taken had been the result of ordinary reconnaissance that had chanced upon the passage of a convoy or the movement of an armored unit through the desert. If it might be suspected that some particular move could only have been the result of Enigma ciphers being read, then no action could be taken. This was an obligation of the utmost stringency that was laid upon all commanders-in-chief. So valuable was Ultra information that losses had to be accepted if it looked as if this great secret might be compromised.[3]

Apart from receiving Ultra information from Bletchley Park and routinely eavesdropping on the air, one of the functions of the Y service in Malta as elsewhere was direction-finding (D/F), or taking bearings upon enemy transmissions so that, for instance, the movements of ships could be plotted. Wireless silence at sea was of course the general rule, but submarines still had to report at times, and there are always indiscretions. The operations room used every scrap of information out of which, like many bits from a jigsaw puzzle, a picture could be formed. Quite apart from this, such things as an increased volume in activity from some known port or area could provide a hint of troop movements or indicate a convoy preparing to leave or a major fleet gathering for an operation. Of Malta during those years it could well be said, echoing *The Tempest,* that "the isle is full of noises" and "a thousand twangling instruments."

10

Spring Forty-one

The Battle of Matapan had been fought because the Italian Navy, relinquishing its sensible policy of avoiding action and remaining a fleet in being, had been compelled to strike at the British convoys making their way with troops and matériel between Egypt and Greece. Just as these intentions had been revealed by Ultra, so the very convoys that lured the Italians into the eastern Mediterranean had been prompted by Ultra information. Early in 1941 the buildup of German forces in southern Romania had become known, and further signals had shown that Hitler's aim was for his forces to move through Bulgaria and attack Greece.

The British decision to go to the aid of Greece, which was quite contrary to the wishes of General Wavell and was to lead to the German successes in North Africa, was a political one. A similar political decision, when the British forces had to be withdrawn from Greece, to try and hold the great island in Crete in the face of overwhelming German air power, was to lead to such heavy losses in the Mediterranean fleet that the whole British position in the sea was changed and the achievements of Spartivento, Taranto, and Matapan were largely nullified. Just as Ultra information had led to the British reinforcement of Greece, so it had forewarned of the later German intention to attack Crete. Winston Churchill became particularly impressed at this time with the efficiency and accuracy of

Ultra, but the use of this information remained a political judgment. To attempt to stop the German advance in Greece with British forces that depended on a supply line running back to Egypt (and subsequently all the way round the Cape of Good Hope) was illogical. Similarly, so was the attempt to hold Crete against overwhelming German air power.

During that bad spring of 1941, which was to lead to an even worse summer—the nadir, so it seemed, of Britain's fortunes during World War II—it was evidence of the understanding of the true importance of Malta in the war that, despite the situation in Britain, twelve Hurricane Mark IIAs, reckoned to be more than a match for the Messerschmitt 109s, were put aboard the carrier *Argus* for transfer at Gibraltar to the *Ark Royal*. Even the old Hurricanes that had seen such service in Malta had shown what a toll they could take of the invaders. The addition of some of the new Hurricanes to the island's defenses was as appreciated as it was important at the time. Later, a further twenty-three Hurricanes were transferred from Britain by the same means, being flown off the *Ark Royal* from a point south of the island of Sardinia.[1]

Despite the reduction in daylight air attacks due to the movement of part of *Fliegerkorps X* to North Africa, the grip of the siege upon the island began to tighten. In February 1941 a law had been passed giving the authorities the right to call up all able-bodied men between the ages of sixteen and fifty-six for military service. Government employees, dockyard workers, farmers, quarrymen, and stonecutters were exempted, but by the end of the year nearly four thousand men in the nineteen-to-twenty-nine age group had been drafted. The introduction of conscription was in itself a reminder of distant days. The last time that this had happened was in 1792, when the islanders were besieging the French locked in Valletta. Now it was they themselves who were besieged.

Other evidences of war were to be found in the worsening shortage of food: Sugar, coffee, tea, margarine, matches, lard, and rice were all rationed, as was household soap.[2] Goats' milk was available but cows had not then been introduced to the island, and one of the staples was condensed milk, also rationed. Tea and coffee, particularly tea—with condensed milk, heavily sweetened, and drunk out of glasses—had long been a source of relaxation to the islanders, and its increasing unavailability was to be one of the sorest trials as the siege developed. Olive oil and bread—the excellent wood-oven-fired Maltese bread—had long formed the basis of the island diet, and these were as yet untouched. Pasta was nothing like as popular as in Sicily and Italy, for bread had always been the staff of life for the Maltese. Many of the great beehive-shaped granaries excavated out of the rock—as at Floriana—had been built in the days of the Knights.

Early in April of 1941 the islanders rejoiced to see four of the most powerful new fleet destroyers station themselves in Malta—the *Mohawk* and *Nubian* of the Tribal class and the *Jervis* and *Janus* of the J class. The choice of such a time to reinforce the island with a powerful striking force was clear enough. The presence in North Africa of the Afrika Korps and of its general, Erwin Rommel, meant increased demands on the supply line between Italy and Tripoli. Rommel's arrival had been known since February, and the fact that throughout the desert campaigns his headquarters sent a situation report every evening at almost the same time on a known frequency and from a known location was a great bonus to intelligence. German radio communications between their headquarters in Europe and their forces in North Africa often revealed supply requirements, and these, read by Ultra, led to anticipation of the convoys being run to meet them. The German buildup could not be interfered with while Malta was barren of fighting ships, short of aircraft, and without an efficient submarine force, but all these defects now began to be remedied. A flotilla of the small U class submarines had been assembled. These submarines were to prove immensely effective in future months, and their activities were in evidence from the very beginning.

Earlier that year Field Marshal Kesselring, airman turned soldier, had been sent to Rome to coordinate the actions of air and land forces. It had become clear that, although ostensible deference must be paid to the Italian High Command, in the end the Germans would have to look after more than their own. For the moment the existence of a German army assisting the Italians in North Africa was sufficient reason for so high-ranking an officer to be appointed to coordinate Luftwaffe and Afrika Korps. He informed Rommel that he and an Italian general would be visiting him in mid-July. Hero though he was later to become, almost as much admired by his enemies as by his own troops, Rommel did not command great confidence among his senior officers. Although a stalwart supporter of the Nazi party, he had the reputation of acting independently and without consultation with the OKW (Supreme Command of the Armed Forces). On his own at the far end of a communications link with Germany, the desert might suit Rommel well, but his superiors mistrusted his impetuosity. Army Chief of Staff Franz Halder was one of those who suspected that Rommel might take the bit between his teeth unless suitably restrained, and so toward the end of April he sent his deputy, General Friedrick Paulus, to check on Rommel's intentions and to discuss the whole desert campaign with him. After two weeks in North Africa Paulus sent a lengthy report to Berlin detailing the strategy that he and Rommel had together agreed to pursue in the desert. Curiously enough, seeing that it dealt almost exclusively with army matters, this important message was sent in the cipher used by the Luftwaffe—and this was one that had been most satisfactorily broken at Bletchley Park, while German Army ciphers proved more difficult. Thus, the British commanders now had a complete picture of the overall German strategy. While this could not prevent the British and Imperial forces having to retreat in the face of superior arms, it meant that the retreat was conducted without the disaster that might otherwise have occurred.

The reading of German Luftwaffe Enigma traffic and Italian naval ciphers was an intelligence operation coordinated back in England and then transmitted directly to the Commander-in-Chief, Mediterranean. Sailings from Italian ports were known about from Italian ciphers, and details of air escorts for convoys came from Enigma—something that accounts for some of the surprisingly accurate attacks made by surface craft and submarines in those early days. Later in the war contacts made with Italian convoys could often be ascribed to radar as well as to highly developed air reconnaissance. Certainly, radar would confirm the presence of the enemy when the attacking ships or aircraft were within its range, but it must be noted that the four destroyers that had just reached Malta to form an attacking force were not yet fitted with radar. Nevertheless, on April 15, an enemy convoy of five ships escorted by three destroyers was located off the Tunisian coast by the 14th Flotilla (*Mohawk, Nubian, Jervis,* and *Janus*). In the ensuing action all five transports, laden with troops and supplies for the Afrika Korps, were sunk as well as two of the destroyers, the third being put out of action and drifting onto the Kerkenah Bank (later to be salvaged). In the last stage of this action the Italian destroyer *Tarigo,* with her captain mortally wounded and with his ship hit time and again, yet managed to lay herself between the attackers and their prey and launch three torpedoes, sinking the *Mohawk.* As later events in the war would show, the Italians could show a spirit second to none, particularly in escort work and small-boat actions. The stories of cowardice carried in the British press, like all things else always in wartime, were designed for home consumption by civilians.

April showed the island most clearly in its dual role—attacked and attacker. Malta was somewhat like an old counterpuncher in the boxing ring who, though battered and bloody, still comes forward with blows that make his apparently superior opponent hesitate and then reel back. Swordfish and Wellingtons operating from the island served in a coordinated attack with Cunningham's battlefleet on the main Libyan port and capital of Tripoli on April 20, at the same time a convoy was passed through to Malta and empty merchant ships taken out. That night RAF bombers and the Fleet Air Arm attacked the port first, so that when the battleships *Warspite, Barham,* and *Valiant* and the heavy cruiser *Gloucester* arrived on the scene with their destroyer escort, complete surprise was achieved. The defenders of Tripoli were disoriented by the air attack and totally unready for this sudden whistling thunder from the sea. From the beginning of the year up to the end of April Malta-based submarines sank ten ships—just an earnest of what they would do later.

Throughout the Mediterranean T. S. Eliot's "cruellest month," April, justified the poet's epithet in the activities of man, but from the beginning of the month all the islands of the sea were, as always, peacefully crowned with wildflowers. Nowhere was this more true than in the Maltese archipelago, where, apart from the hundreds of indigenous species, there had been numerous deliberate and accidental imports during the years of the British occupation. As the islanders felt the warmth of that most delicate and delightful season of the year creep over their fields and streets, invading even the cavernous mouths of their underground shelters, they were encouraged not only by Easter—a festival always celebrated in southern lands more than Christmas—but also by the relative absence of daylight bombing. They did not know that this was a result of the withdrawal of planes for the campaign in Greece and the offensive in the western desert, but it was part of an Easter bonus all the same. The night raids continued, however; on the twenty-ninth the dockyard area of Cospicua was hit as well as the outlying townships of Zabbar, Zurrieq, and Zebbug. On the following night Cospicua was again bombed, and the village of Kalkara on Grand Harbour, as well as Valletta and Sliema. Casualties fortunately were few, and those mostly in the farming township of Zebbug, which was unprepared for such attacks (Zebbug means "olives" in Maltese), but many houses were damaged or demolished, thus adding to the never-ending problem of refugees.

A member of the Hampshire Regiment, which had come to reinforce the island in February 1941, straight from service in the desert, recorded some years later his remembered images of Malta at that season of the year: "To us Poor Bloody Infantry from the desert, with its undulating expanses of sand from horizon to horizon, Malta appeared as it must have looked to those early Arabs and Moors, especially in the spring of the year with grass in the low-lying Marsa area and bright yellow chrysanthemums all the way from Porte des Bombes to Pieta Creek.

"The solid limestone houses of the villagers with pumpkins ripening in the sun on the flat roofs, colourful washing there, too, gave promise of companionship after the bleak months in North Africa where even the nomads ceased to roam. There were crops in the tiny fields surrounded by the never-ending lines of stone walls, and fig trees and olives as well as orange and lemon orchards."[3]

Under the spring sun the island was as always at its most gracious—a far call from the dusty aridity of summer, when it shows its North African face and is almost as barren as the desert that the soldier remembered. Now it was European *Primavera,* with its hundreds of varieties of wildflowers and flowering plants (over nine hundred species have been recorded by botanists), ranging from miniature wild orchids to the diminutive ancestors of the garden iris. On the high garigue, among the bare rocks, stony ground, and sandy patches, were scattered low bushes of thyme, rosemary, sage, and many other herbs as well as grape hyacinth, garlic, star of Bethlehem, and narcissus, to name but a few flowers whose brief spring would soon be extinguished, leaving their dusty seed-heads in the parched land of summer. Everywhere, alongside the white roads and growing thick in the lanes that were too narrow for even the smallest army trucks, waved the yellow Cape sorrel. Legend has it that this was introduced by an Englishwoman from South Africa in the early nineteenth century, since when it had spread all over the island and become known in Maltese as *Haxixa Inglesa,* the English weed. The fields were still green, and the island was enameled with its flowers.

Meanwhile the German armies were advancing in Greece and the British forces (too little and too late), confronted by overwhelming air power, were falling back, finally to be evacuated. On April 27, 1941, German troops entered Athens.

11

War and Weather

The fast mechanized columns of the Afrika Korps were sweeping everything before them in the desert to the south. In the east the German 12th Army was overrunning Greece. Agonizingly conscious of German tank and air superiority on both flanks of their besieged island, the people in Malta looked out over a sea where the enemy's grip was tightening around them. The prospects of the summer ahead looked bleak indeed. One of the only sources of hope, though unperceived as yet in the island, was that the port of Tobruk in Cyrenaica was being held even as the enemy was moving up to the borders of Egypt. Tobruk in due course was to become, like Malta itself, a thorn in the side of the triumphant Axis powers, another besieged garrison, but unlike Malta able to strike back over land.

The withdrawal of part of *Fliegerkorps X* to assist in the desert war and then of the remainder to Greece, where *Fliegerkorps VIII* was already engaged in strafing the retreating British, meant that Malta was now only under attack by night from the Regia Aeronautica. This, as has been seen, was unpleasant enough, but the respite from the efficient daylight bombing by the Germans seemed to the Maltese people an added bonus to the late-spring weather. Although news of the retreats in the desert and in Greece came to them over the cable radio, it was natural enough that the long-term effect these defeats would have on Malta's part in the war was not at first perceived. The relief from the Luftwaffe attacks seemed enough in itself on those fine days when, curiously, official announcements and news broadcasts could still be heard issuing from houses that had been deserted or too badly damaged to be occupied. Coming out of dusty Bakelite radios that had been left switched on, the crackled voices sounded strange on the still, blue air amid white rubble or glassless window frames.

News of the final withdrawal from Greece and the occupation of Crete came by word of mouth—rumor on an island where almost every family knows one another runs faster than any brushfire—and was fully understood. Its implications were clear enough: Not only was the British Army having to be evacuated from Greece, but the Mediterranean fleet was taking such punishment from the air that its victories at sea would be rendered meaningless. By April 24 over fifty thousand troops had reached their evacuation beaches in Greece, some near Athens and others at selected points in the Morea. That the losses among warships engaged in escorting the troopships in this evacuation were not greater was a result of the fact that the Luftwaffe had not been able to move its bases forward fast enough to catch up with the disciplined retreat (described by Rear Admiral Baillie Grohman as "magnificent—especially considering that they had been fighting a rearguard action for some weeks, from Salonika almost to Cape Matapan"). Evacuation could only be carried out during the hours of darkness for fear of the Luftwaffe; on any occasion when this was disregarded the result was disastrous. One troopship late in leaving Nauplia was sunk as soon as daylight discovered her. Two destroyers sent to pick up the survivors, having collected some seven hundred men from the scene of the sinking, were themselves sunk by dive-bombers as they headed for Suda Bay in Crete. Only forty-one sailors and eight soldiers survived out of the hundreds involved. The writing that had been on the wall since the attack on the *Illustrious* by *Fliegerkorps X* was now plain for all to see: Ships could not operate safely or efficiently in the face of massive air superiority. Crete was to prove the final scene where this fundamental fact of modern warfare was to be made explicit.

Another fundamental rule in warfare later to be pronounced by General Montgomery, "Never march on Moscow," was about to be broken by the German dictator during that year. Incomprehensible though it seems with hindsight, Hitler in his fanatic absorption with the eastern territories, the conquest of Russia, and the destruction of the "subhumans" who lived in the giant land, was to close his eyes to the potentials of the desert campaign. In this area, the only one where the British and the Germans could get to grips, there lay at that moment the key to the whole struggle. A concentration of German forces behind the spearhead of Rommel's Afrika Korps could have swept the British back and out of Egypt and the entire Middle East. The Suez Canal would have come under Axis control, along with the oil of the Persian Gulf. The British would have been deprived of this essential of modern warfare as well as ignominiously expelled from the African continent. The rankling wound of the war in the west with Britain would have been removed at a stroke. At his leisure, and without any further worries about sources of oil for his military machine, the Führer could have turned his attention to the invasion of Russia.

Hitler never saw the desert war as anything other than an unfortunate sideshow into which he had been dragged in order to bail out his incompetent partner. In Greece and the Balkans, too, he had had to intervene to save Mussolini's face and so as not to leave his right flank unguarded or in a state of confusion when he made his major move east. The arrival of the British in Greece, honor bound to come to the aid of an ally even though at grave disadvantage to their main interests, caused Hitler to take the Greek campaign seriously. He recalled what the British had tried to do via the Dardanelles in the First World War, and a threat to his flank and to the Romanian oil fields could not be tolerated when he was about to march on Russia. Hitler prided himself on a mastery of grand strategy and military geopolitics, but by failing to see what success in the desert could have meant to him and how it could have ensured a successful invasion of Russia by two giant prongs striking into the heart of that country (one from Europe and the west, the other from the south), he deprived himself of ultimate victory. Hitler's eyes were European eyes; he could see the east only in terms of Russia.

Even at the moment when the evacuation of the troops from Greece had not yet been completed, a major operation was taking place in the Mediterranean in which Malta figured conspicuously. This was an elaborate operation code-named Tiger, in which the great risk was taken of passing right through to Egypt a convoy from the western end at the same time as two convoys came from the east to Malta. The convoy for Egypt was made up of transports full of tank reinforcements for the Army of the Nile. Churchill, unlike his adversary, was fully aware of what the loss of Egypt and the Suez Canal would mean and was determined when the German panzers had shown their hand in the desert to reinforce General Wavell as far as possible. The risk was considerable, for convoys passing from Gibraltar all the way through to Egypt had not been considered acceptable since the arrival of the Luftwaffe in the central Mediterranean. However, in the hope that German air power would be fully stretched with the Greek and desert operations, the gamble was taken.

The convoy from the western end was escorted by Force H from Gibraltar, the only loss occurring when one of the transports struck a mine and sank in the narrows of the Skerki Channel. This area, which was later to be the setting for many desperate actions involving convoys to Malta, was shallow and mine-infested, an ideal attack ground for torpedo boats, submarines, and torpedo aircraft. On this occasion, however, the convoy made a successful passage except for the loss of the one transport. Force H then withdrew to Gibraltar as Cunningham's Mediterranean fleet took over as escort to Egypt.

On its way to the rendezvous Cunningham's fleet had also successfully covered the two highly important convoys to Malta. This was one of the most creditable moments of the Mediterranean sea campaign to date for the fleet from Alexandria—battleships, cruisers, and destroyers alike—at a time when it had been working at full stretch since the campaign had started in Greece. Although in need of a respite—which it was not to get—the fleet escorted these two convoys into the beleaguered island in time to ensure Malta's survival through the long summer that lay ahead. One of the convoys consisted of two slow tankers carrying twenty-four thousand tons of fuel, and the other a fast one of four supply ships with troops, food, ammunition, and the thousand and one other requisites needed by the garrison and the people.

The successful passage of these two convoys through to Malta must largely be ascribed to the state of the weather at the time. Without the poor visibility there can be little doubt that, although the Mediterranean fleet had the carrier *Formidable* with them for fighter cover, the convoys would certainly have been spotted and heavily attacked. Indeed, a great many enemy aircraft were reported on the fleet's radar, clearly searching for them and their precious cargo ships, but, as Admiral Cunningham reported, the weather was "thick with low cloud down almost to our mast-heads." The admiral comments in his autobiography that "for the time of the year the weather was most unusual," a curious remark coming from one who had served in the Mediterranean in the First World War and often during the interwar years and who might well have called himself, in the words of Nelson, "an old Mediterranean man." It was in fact very typical sirocco weather, which is more common in the month of May than any other. Starting in the desert as a dry, dusty, southerly wind, varying in direction from southeast to southwest and known as the *Khamsin,* it picks up moisture as it crosses the sea. The hot desert air cools from contact with the sea's surface, the relative humidity rises sharply, and the resultant sirocco wind is warm and hazy and full of moisture-laden clouds. Known as the *xlokk* in Maltese it causes the buildings and gutters on the island to stream with water, the enervating air exacerbating tempers and causing even the mildest to swear as they sweat.[1] But since the war and the bombing the besieged islanders had learned to bless this normally cursed wind for the respite that it gave from air attack. It was during just such a period that these two all-important convoys were approaching the island. Traditionally known as Calypso's Isle from the secret "hidden" island of the goddess in Homer's *Odyssey,* Malta low-lying on the face of the sea was now completely obscured by cloud.[2]

Admiral Cunningham learned while at sea that the island was encircled by more than the sirocco cloud—it was completely mined in. During their night raids the Regia Aeronautica had been sowing mines in all the approaches, and the vice-admiral of Malta[3] reported to his commander-in-chief that the destroyer flotilla stationed in the island could not sail to escort in the convoys because it could not get out of harbor. The channel normally used could not be swept because all the minesweepers capable of dealing with magnetic mines had been lost or put out of action.

Fortunately, Cunningham had among the escorts for the convoys one corvette that was equipped for magnetic minesweeping, but one ship alone would clearly not be capable of dealing with the situation around Malta. A method was quickly devised by the fleet torpedo officer,[4] and a signal was sent to Malta instructing the authorities to blast a channel out through the approaches to the island with depth charges. There were plenty of depth charges available, and to the thunder of underwater explosions a channel was gradually cleared outward from Grand Harbour, the pattern of exploding charges having the effect of countermining or otherwise disturbing the firing mechanism of the magnetic mines in the approach channel. Even so, when the *Gloxinia,* Cunningham's lone corvette equipped for magnetic sweeping, preceded the convoys into the harbor, at least a dozen mines that had survived the previous rough treatment went up in thunders of spray.

Finally, under the steamy cotton-wool clouds of the south wind, the convoys sailed into Grand Harbour and were unloaded, unseen by any aerial reconnaissance. The special supply ship H.M.S. *Breconshire,* whose name was to become synonymous with the siege of Malta during the months to come, also entered Marsaxlokk, the southern harbor, with fuel and ammunition. As the most critical period of the war for the Mediterranean fleet developed to the east around the island of Crete, Malta stood replenished, refueled, and rearmed. The limestone fortress was all set to confirm the German opinion that "a gross error had been committed [by the Italians] in not starting the war with the conquest of Malta."

12

On Another Island

Following the success of the German Army in Greece, it was almost inevitable that the next scene of action would be the great fish-shaped island of Crete, lying across the foot of the Aegean Sea and dominating all the eastern Mediterranean to the south. The capture of Crete would mean that from its airfields the Luftwaffe would have Alexandria and Suez and the Canal within reach and could make the passage of Allied merchant and naval ships in support of the ground forces along the North African coast so hazardous as almost to cut this lifeline. As yet the German Navy, with its U-boats and light craft, had hardly been committed to the Mediterranean, the area by tacit agreement being considered the province of the Italians and their fleet.

The dominant pressure on the Mediterranean theater of war was then to be exerted by the Luftwaffe. Here again, as in the Battle of Britain, Reichsmarshal Goering was not only supremely confident but determined to obtain the laurels of victory for his own service. Units of *Fliegerkorps X,* as has been seen, were detached from Sicily to join *Fliegerkorps VIII* in Greece. The latter could deploy over seven hundred aircraft for the operations in Greece and the subsequent attack on Crete, several hundred of them being dive-bombers. These would have been sufficient in themselves to devastate the airfields available to the RAF, which had fought a rearguard action in

DODECANESE ISLANDS

RHODES

SCARPANTO (Italian)

Enemy airfield.
21–22 May, night
bombardment.
26 May, bombed
by Fleet Air Arm.

29 May, Decoy damaged

29 May, Orion &
Dido damaged

28 May, Ajax
damaged

21 May
Juno sunk

KASOS

Kasos Str.

29 May
Hereward
sunk

Kasos

29 May
Hereward sunk

29 May
Imperial
sunk

28–29 May
Night evacuation

Dido
Orion
Ajax
Hasty
Kimberley
Hereward
Janus

21–22 May
Convoy
engaged
by Rear-
Admiral
Glennie's
force

Heraklion Ⓐ

CRETE

Suda Bay

Retimo

Canea

Maleme Ⓐ

Sphakia

25 May
Kashmir &
Kelly sunk

28–31 May
Night evacuations

22 May
Convoy
engaged
by Rear-
Admiral
King's
force

Kandahar
Kingston
Nubian
Calcutta
Perth
Naiad
Carlisle

23 May
Warspite damaged

22 May
Greyhound sunk

ANTIKITHERA

Antikithera Channel

22 May
Valiant
damaged

22 May
Gloucester
sunk

Kithera Channel

KITHERA

22 May
Fiji sunk

30 May
Perth damaged

MEDITERRANEAN
SEA

0   20   40   60   80   100 Miles

Ⓐ Airfield

30 May   Kelvin damaged near Alexandria
31 May   Napier & Nizam damaged 30 miles south
1 June   Calcutta sunk 100 miles from Alexandria

35°

27°

26°

25°

24°

23°

34°

35°

25°

34°

M.V.

the air all the way down Greece and was now reduced to a few Hurricanes and some old Gladiators.

It might have seemed reasonable for the bulk of the German troops to be transported for the invasion of Crete under the escort of the Italian Navy, covered by German fighter aircraft. After all, the British during their withdrawal from Greece had transported sixteen thousand men to hold the island of Crete, the bulk of the troops being taken to Egypt to reinforce the desert army. Large-scale landings protected by overwhelming air superiority would have succeeded in getting through the defenses of the Royal Navy, which would have been required to work in narrow waters without fighter cover and under dive-bomber attack, and in conquering Crete in a conventional manner. But the Germans decided to take Crete by airborne assault, not only because they were mistrustful of the Italians' ability to provide adequate protection at sea for troop convoys but also because Goering wished the whole operation to come under the aegis of the Luftwaffe. General Kurt Student, who commanded *Fliegerkorps XI,* consisting of the parachute and airborne troops, was the author of the scheme. He was naturally eager to try out his elite troops and was confident that they would achieve a far swifter victory than would conventional units. Such a large-scale airborne assault had not been previously tried during the war, and it was hoped that the element of surprise would aid in swiftly overwhelming the British defenses.

Even if the British could not prevent the attack, they had known about the projected airborne invasion of the island since the end of April. Ultra had given warning from the moment that gliders and transport aircraft had begun to assemble in Bulgaria. The vast buildup of Luftwaffe bombers, dive-bombers, and fighters, the sheer weight of all the preparations, revealed the urgent desire of the German High Command to complete the occupation of Crete as quickly as possible. Hitler had given his approval to the scheme, for he was anxious to see the whole campaign in Greece and the Aegean concluded before turning to the invasion of Russia.

That this too was known about due to Ultra is now common knowledge—even the fact that Stalin was warned in advance by Churchill of the German plans. In the case of Crete, not only was Churchill informed some time prior to the invasion, but General Freyberg in command of the Allied forces on the island was fur-

nished with the German plans in elaborate detail. General Kurt
Student was a German of the almost obsessively meticulous order
and was determined to ensure that every unit involved in the forth-
coming operation was kept fully briefed. The result was a stream of
signals read by Ultra, giving full information several weeks in advance—from the date that the invasion would take place to landing
grounds and the strength of airborne formations.

This being so, the inevitable question must be asked: Why was
Crete lost? Ultra information could only forewarn a commander
about some intended enemy move, but there was little that he could
do about it unless he had the necessary weapons at his disposal. In
the case of Crete it was impossible to bring the strength of the RAF
up to anything approaching practical standards. The Hurricane
squadrons that had fought their way down through Greece were reduced to under a dozen aircraft, and the few Gladiators of the Fleet
Air Arm were too old to cope with the waves of Messerschmitt fighters that escorted the bombers and transport planes. In the first stage
of the action, when the Luftwaffe began softening up the island
prior to the main assault, these few survivors of the many weeks of
fighting were reduced to four Hurricanes and three Gladiators.
Hard-pressed in North Africa, with few enough planes even to defend Malta, the British had no reserves left for transfer to Crete before the blow fell on May 20. Only the day before, the seven
remaining aircraft were rightly judged incapable of withstanding
the wave poised over the island and were sent back to Egypt. Thus
there was no fighter defense at all. What surprised General Student
and subsequent commentators on the campaign was that it almost
seemed as if the airborne assault had been anticipated. It was true
that General Freyberg might well have learned from sources in
Greece of the buildup of gliders and transport planes and of the
presence of paratroops on the mainland—and certainly in that case
he would have prepared his defenses around the most likely airfields: This seemed good enough cover for the Ultra source.[1]

The attack began with heavy bombing around Canea and Maleme airfields, followed by waves of gliders coming in to land. German plans called for these landings to drive away the handful of
troops that were all that might have been expected to be left to
guard the airfields. In fact, General Student's airborne troops ran
into an opposition such as had never been anticipated. Losses were

heavy on both sides, and Maleme airfield, which had been expected to fall within the day, remained a battlefield at nightfall. Similarly, at Canea the invaders were firmly held, and the ground remained disputed.

With his crack paratroopers in trouble at both these landing places, General Student may have hoped for better things on the airfields of Heraklion and Retimo, but here too the Germans met with unexpectedly fierce resistance. The key to the battle for Crete was the landing ground at Maleme, where it was hoped to bring in Junkers 52 transport planes carrying the 5th Mountain Division as reinforcements. The airborne assault on Crete might indeed have been completely defeated if General Freyberg had thrown into Maleme two New Zealand infantry battalions held in reserve at Canea. Aware, however, that the bulk of German reinforcements must come by sea, General Freyberg held back the New Zealanders to deal with the expected landing. Had he but known that during the night of May 21 Royal Navy ships sweeping north of the island had encountered these seaborne reinforcements and that all of them had either been sunk or turned back, Maleme might have been held. As it was, the German transport planes landed, Maleme was taken, and the way was clear for massive reinforcements by air. Crete was lost.

The fact remains that Heraklion and Retimo airfields were held until the general evacuation of Crete by the Allied forces had been ordered; the former not being abandoned until May 28 and the latter not until the thirtieth. This was proof, if such was needed, that the landings by General Student's airborne forces, which had been expected to clear all the airfields within a few hours, had failed. At every point where these crack troops had been thrown in they had been held and had suffered such heavy casualties that the German command was in a state of despair. What seemed so inexplicable to the Germans at the time as well as to subsequent writers on the Battle of Crete—the failure of the paratroopers to secure the airfields within a matter of hours—is clearly explained by the prior knowledge obtained from Ultra. Once Maleme had been captured, however, and the way cleared for massive reinforcements, the loss of the island was inevitable, since the Allies had no air cover and their ground troops were ceaselessly harassed by the overwhelming numbers of Luftwaffe fighters and dive-bombers.[2]

The political decision to hold Crete, taken with the full knowledge that the Luftwaffe would overwhelm the skies and that there could be no response from the RAF or the Fleet Air Arm, was an act that was to have grave consequences for the Mediterranean fleet. The list of warships sunk, severely damaged, or so badly damaged that they had to be sunk to prevent them from falling into enemy hands, covers every type of vessel afloat from destroyers to cruisers to battleships. Operating in confined waters with two objectives—to prevent reinforcements reaching the island by sea and to withdraw Allied troops when the order came—meant that ships without air cover had to be constantly active in waters where, from the Greek mainland, from Aegean islands, and in due course from Crete itself, the Luftwaffe and the Regia Aeronautica could enjoy a field day such as only political folly could ever have offered them.

The ships were operating under such conditions of almost continuous attack that it was not uncommon for them to have to retire from the scene of action because all their antiaircraft ammunition had been used up. At one point Admiral Cunningham responded to a message from the Admiralty that he found "singularly unhelpful": "The experience of three days in which two cruisers and four destroyers have been sunk, and one battleship, two cruisers and four destroyers severely damaged shows what losses are likely to be. Sea control in the Eastern Mediterranean could not be retained after another such experience." He went on to say that "the effect of the recent operations was cumulative, and that the officers, men and machinery were nearing exhaustion."[3]

Yet, no major German reinforcements had been able to reach Crete by sea, as transports and escorts that attempted it were either sunk by the fleet units patrolling north of the island or were forced to turn back under cover of darkness. Radar also played a part in one of these major actions, when a convoy attempting to reach Crete at night was badly shot up, despite the gallantry of its Italian escort endeavoring to protect its charges against attackers who could "see" in the dark. The last British reinforcements were sent into Crete the night of May 26–27; the next day the order finally came through from London to evacuate the island. Yet even as late as May 26, Winston Churchill cabled General Wavell: "Victory in Crete essential at this turning point of the war. Keep hurling in all you can."

As an example of the total impracticability of the prime minister's command was the story of the landing ship H.M.S. *Glenroy,* which was sent up from Alexandria at the last moment to try to land more troops on the island even though British, Australian, and New Zealand forces were everywhere in retreat: "The *Glenroy* escorted by the *Coventry* [antiaircraft cruiser], *Stuart* and *Jaguer* [destroyers] was also on her way to try landing troops at Tymbaki [on the south coast of Crete]. They were bombed during the morning of May 26th. and at 6:20 P.M. were heavily attacked by dive-bombers and then by low-flying torpedo bombers. The *Glenroy* avoided the torpedoes, but was slightly damaged and had some casualties from near misses and machine-gun fire. Three of her landing craft were holed, and a large dump of cased petrol on the upper-deck was set ablaze. To cope with the fire the *Glenroy* had to turn south to bring the wind aft, and one of the landing-craft at the devits had to be jettisoned. With eight hundred troops on board and a large cargo of petrol the situation was most unpleasant; but when the flames were mastered the convoy again resumed its course for Crete."[4]

Finally, owing to the time lost, the *Glenroy* was turned back because her late arrival would have meant landing the troops in daylight—an impossibility with the Luftwaffe everywhere dominant. The bloodbath that was the sea around Crete would not be cleared until the last of the Allied forces able to reach any of the embarkation points had been taken off.

As the evacuation proceeded, the harbor at Alexandria presented a panorama of increasingly disastrous proportions: ships of all classes with gaping holes in their decks or sides, cruisers with gun turrets blasted apart and gun barrels pointing askew at the sky, a destroyer with so much of her stern blown off that it was amazing her propeller shafts and screws had remained to drive her back to port, and other vessels that looked as if only the breakers' yard awaited them. By June 1 all those who had gotten off the island had arrived in Egypt—over sixteen thousand men, leaving five thousand or more still in Crete to surrender (some took to the mountains). Admiral Cunningham's covering dispatch summed up what had been achieved and at what cost: "Apart from the cumulative effect of prolonged seagoing over extended periods it has to be remembered that in this last instance ships' companies had none of the inspiration of battle with the enemy to bear them up. . . . They had started the evacuation already over-tired and they had to carry it through under conditions of savage air attacks such as had only recently caused grievous losses to the fleet."

The fatigue caused by the constant bombing attacks and long periods at sea under trying conditions was such that both men and ships were at breaking point. The surviving destroyers, those maids of all work, were worn to pieces, even when they had not been badly damaged. It was not unusual for a man to be rescued from one sinking ship only to board another destined to be sunk and survive to join a third that, if not sunk, was hit. During the two full months before, during, and after the Battle of Crete, one of the cruisers had spent fewer than ten nights in harbor—and then only to refuel and rearm. The days at sea were not days on patrol but of constant Action Stations. But, as Admiral Cunningham wrote, "it was impossible to abandon the troops in Crete. Our naval tradition would never survive such an action." But the cost was greater than anything that might even have been expected. Two battleships, the *Warspite* and the *Barham,* and the aircraft carrier *Formidable* were so badly damaged as to be beyond local repair and to be out of action for some months; three cruisers and six destroyers were sunk; two cruisers and two destroyers were damaged beyond local repair; and three cruisers and six destroyers were damaged sufficiently to be out of action for some weeks.

Despite all these losses, the Royal Navy had fulfilled its prime function, for throughout the whole of the battle no warship or transport of the Axis powers had succeeded in reaching the island. Apart from this and the evacuation of so many fighting men, it was difficult to discern anything else on the credit side. What could not have been foreseen was that the Cretans in company with some of the Allied survivors in the mountains, later to be reinforced by agents landed at night from submarines, were to make the island a permanent running sore in the side of their occupiers. The Cretans had a long tradition of guerrilla warfare, dating back to the centuries of their occupation by the Turks. From the ancient, almost inaccessible caves in the high, remote mountains they defied the German occupiers just as their ancestors had defied the Ottoman Empire. But the most important outcome of the battle was the fact that in the course of the airborne attack *Fliegerkorps XI,* the only paratroop and airborne division in the German Army, had been practically annihilated. No further airborne operations were ever carried out by

Goering's Luftwaffe; later, when further proposals were made for a similar attack on Malta, the events of Crete were well remembered.

The whole of Malta was a giant fortress, whereas Crete was a large island with many landing places available and held by an insufficient number of men. Hitler's own comments about the nature of Malta's terrain and the thousands of stone walls that created a death trap for gliders and paratroopers, making any form of airborne assault almost impossible, combined with the memory of Crete, were to preclude any invasion. Of course, none of this was apparent to the people of Malta at the time. The news of the paratroopers' attack on Crete naturally caused great concern among the islanders, suggesting that a similar attack might soon be launched against them. Many on the island—servicemen and civilians alike—anticipated a return of the Luftwaffe to Sicily now that Crete had fallen. What they could not know was that *Fliegerkorps VIII* was to be withdrawn to the north for Hitler's Russian campaign starting on June 22, and that *Fliegerkorps X* had abandoned the airfields in Sicily and was now responsible for the whole of the Mediterranean theater. Since the war in the desert was the main Axis preoccupation at this time, those units of *Fliegerkorps X* that were not stationed in North Africa were concentrated in Greece and Crete, giving them operational access to Egypt and the Suez Canal. The Mediterranean fleet would find that the eastern waters of the sea were now heavily threatened and that convoys to beleaguered Tobruk were increasingly at hazard (so, too, would be future convoys to Malta). For the moment, Malta was threatened by no more than the Regia Aeronautica, the scale of whose attacks had long since become of relatively little importance—at any rate from a military point of view. Thus, the summer of 1941, which many in Malta had anticipated would be even more fearsome than the previous winter, proved to be a time of relative tranquillity during which island-based forces began to hit hard at the lifeline between Italy and North Africa. Once German attention was concentrated on the Russian front, the importance of Malta was somewhat lost to sight. With Operation Barbarossa engrossing Hitler's attention, the small island to the south of Sicily was temporarily overlooked.

13

The Besieged Strike Back

Living on tight rations is difficult to get used to, but after a time the body becomes adjusted; even then, however, the steady monotony of the diet begins to wear down the morale. During the autumn of 1940 and the winter and spring that followed, garrison and civilians alike were kept vibrant by the air attacks and by the constant vise-like pressure that seemed to firm the spirit without breaking it. In the summer of 1941, without the attentions of the Luftwaffe, with fewer night raids, and with the daytime raids made by the Regia Aeronautica—high up, ready to turn back at the sight of either bursting flak against the summer sky or the silver glint of rising fighters' wings—induced something like a melancholy resignation among the islanders.

The war now seemed interminable. The reports from the desert—except for those describing the stubborn resistance of the defenders of Tobruk—were indeed melancholy, and the fall of Crete had engendered a deep fear. The obvious countermeasures could not escape notice: The airfields were being mined, and the few other possible landing places were being obstructed. But the inhabitants could now at least escape out of the railway tunnel, the bomb shelters, the caves, and the modern catacombs—from all the damp walls that had housed them—knowing that only a week or two would see all of these refuges as dry as bone again. But the dryness itself would soon become oppressive, for the summer sun is the enemy in southern lands. Spring and autumn are the happy times, the winter is dull and damp and windy, but the summer—the season of *la grande chaleur*—is the time when the ennui that seems to rise like a steam from the hard blue sea engulfs peasant and priest alike. Both had survived the first twelve months of this second great siege equally well—the peasant because centuries of unremitting toil on that difficult, stone-hedged land had bred men and women accustomed to hard lives and simple joys, and the priest because the disciplines of the faith had trained him under the same austere sky. The townspeople—shopkeepers, civil servants, small businessmen, and others—were less well equipped. The dockyard workers, skilled and unskilled, were as tough as their country cousins, but many of their small houses lay in ruins, and their slightly more sophisticated forms of entertainment had come to a standstill.

The cheap entertainment for all classes in Malta during the summer months had always been the sea: The Maltese were as native to the water as fish. Fishing itself with rod and line as well as swimming in the lukewarm water were pastimes that never cost a penny. Fresh water was never too great a problem during the siege (whatever else had been forgotten, the water supply for a growing population and a large fleet had been borne in mind), but its supply had often become disrupted through mains being burst under bombing. Very few working people as yet had baths with running water, and even where they existed and where the mains were intact, it was likely that home supply pipes had been broken. All beaches that were anything like beaches were out of bounds because they were potential landing areas; in fact, most of the coastline, except in very rocky or otherwise unapproachable parts, was similarly forbidden. Hazards were everywhere, and it was difficult to find a place in which to enjoy the simple pleasure of bathing. The soldiers and the gunners in their remote concrete pillboxes, scattered all around that mostly inhospitable coast, might spend much of their free time living in the water, but the dockyard workers and townsfolk, unless they were lucky, were condemned to sweat and swelter as the lion-sun grew steadily higher at noon. *Le Cafard,* that old familiar of the French Foreign Legion, was not unknown in Malta. The island lies farther south than the latitude of Tunis, and its cockroach mumblings were insistent in the summer.

Thanks to recent convoys, the shadow of real hunger had not yet visited the island, and reserve stocks of essential commodities had been built up. The system of kerosene distribution, which had been maladministered and had become a source of black marketeering, was radically altered, and policemen now accompanied the kerosene carts through townships and villages to ensure a fair supply. There were still large stocks of butter (little in demand among a Mediterranean people), but other unrationed goods were beyond the reach of all but those with private money or large incomes. Although stonecutters and miners earned a good wage, the average for Maltese servicemen and government employees was about five shillings a day. Bread, the staple diet of the Maltese family, had not yet been rationed, but bread suppliers tended to sell over the odds, and it was not unusual for workingmen's wives to spend several hours a day walking from one place to another to find bread for their families at a reasonable price.

Far from Malta, at the eastern end of the sea, further attempts were made by the Axis powers to seal off the British from the vital oil supplies and thus bring the Mediterranean struggle to a close. These hinged on an attempt by the pro-German administration in Iraq to drive out the British forces that were stationed there by agreement. The operation depended upon the Vichy French colonial administration in Syria (which had been far from neutral in its conduct) supporting an Iraqi rebellion and allowing German aircraft to make use of Syrian airfields. Seeing that the German aim was ultimately to occupy northern Syria and thus threaten Egypt through Palestine, the British were forced to launch an expedition into Syria shortly after the disaster of Crete and the withdrawal in the desert.

Had these eastern maneuvers by the Axis been successful, Malta's part in the history of the war would have soon been over. But the British succeeded in compelling the pro-German Vichy French general in Syria to capitulate in July. During the naval operations off the Syrian coast in support of the army, shore-based French aircraft damaged several destroyers—a further blow to the Mediterranean fleet at a time when it could ill afford it. The fact that Syria from now on was controlled by British troops relieved the pressure at the eastern end of the sea, but the weakness in the fleet resulting from all these campaigns meant that the task of supplying Malta from Alexandria would be increasingly difficult.

In the meantime, as if it were some earlier siege (as had in fact happened in 1565), those within the walls began to sally out by secret ways to attack the enemy's supply lines. Again, they could only do this when the latter were distracted by more important events—and, of course, the cover of darkness was essential. (When those besieged in a fortress begin to break out and attack their investors in broad daylight, it is a clear sign that their morale is so high and the surrounding forces so weak that the siege appears to be drawing to a close.) In June the Axis forces were concerned by a counterattack launched by General Wavell in the western desert, the main aim of which was to relieve the garrison of Tobruk. Thus, the distraction existed, and the very fact that this was the moment when the supply line to the Axis forces in North Africa was most important provided added incentive for the besieged to strike out.

The sortie by night was still the tactic adopted by the bombers operating from Malta. During the worst period of the spring, before the Luftwaffe had been withdrawn for the Greece and Crete operations, the last of these Wellington bomber squadrons had been withdrawn to Egypt. By May they were back, however, and by June there were sometimes two squadrons of bombers available, as well as at least one squadron of Blenheims and two of Fleet Air Arm Swordfish. The strength of the island as an airbase, reduced to almost nothing over the winter, began to increase. The old Swordfish, lumbering but accurate with their torpedoes, achieved major successes on the sea routes between Italy and North Africa. The Wellingtons' bombing of the North African ports, while not so successful in sinking ships, caused considerable disruption in the loading and unloading of the transports upon which the Axis desert armies relied. In the villages and scattered farmsteads of Malta the country people heard the thudding of the engines overhead at night and knew—as their ancestors had once known from the hoofbeats of the cavalry raiding the Turkish encampments—that their defenders were active. The importance of this to the morale of a beleaguered people is scarcely measurable; 122 bomber sorties were made out of Malta from June 30 to July 13—a record for the island since the beginning of the war.

The submarines used the dark tunnel of the sea to make their forays against the enemy's supply lines. In the early days of the large P and R class these patrols had been heavy with suspense and danger, for in the pellucid Mediterranean waters big submarines were often spotted by overflying aircraft. The smaller and far more maneuverable U class, six of which were for a time based on the island, soon achieved success on the convoy routes in the restricted confines between Sicily and North Africa. The submarines' headquarters was on Manoel Island, which lay north of Valletta in Marsamuscetto Creek. The island itself was connected by a causeway to the main island and distinguished by a large eighteenth-century fort designed to protect the capital from this quarter in the days of the Knights. Originally garrisoned by five hundred men, it now housed the submarine command—workmen, artificers, spare crews, and sailors resting from patrol. Where eighteenth-century cannon had once glowered seaward, antiaircraft batteries now pointed skyward. "Fort Manoel is the classic example of a Baroque fortress—bold yet precise, elegant yet a hard functional machine"[1]—it was a cornerstone of Malta's function during these years. Both the fort and its surrounds were heavily attacked during a later stage in the siege, and so dangerous did the whole area become that submarines in from patrol often had to lie submerged on the bottom to escape the rain of bombs.

Apart from attacking Axis shipping, the submarines had other functions during these years, some of which were to become vital to the later landings in Sicily and southern Italy. As a by-product of their patrols submarines sometimes surfaced after dark and, particularly in Calabria, where the railway lines ran close to the coast, shelled bridges and railway lines or landed raiding parties to disrupt these and other communications. Months later, when the planning for the Allied attack on Sicily got under way, submarines from Malta would embark parties with folding canoes to make detailed studies of potential landing areas, to take inshore soundings, to investigate beaches, and to check on the strength of enemy defenses. The information that could not be gained through aerial reconnaissance or through the radio waves reaching Malta would have to be won by individuals who operated in the darkness of night and then slipped back to the shelter of their submarines before the eastern sky lightened and the bright day set in. If so much of the espionage success achieved during the war has rightly been attributed in recent years to the code- and cipher-breaking of Bletchley Park, it must not be forgotten that the old primitive method of reports brought back by spies from behind enemy lines remained as important as in earlier centuries. Many of these brave men disappeared without trace.[2]

Acting in conjunction with torpedo-equipped Swordfish, the submarines began to wreak havoc on the convoy route to Tripoli. The area off the Kerkenna Bank, which was marked by a number of navigation buoys, was one of the great hunting grounds, and it was here that commanders whose names and whose submarines were to become part of wartime legend found their raison d'être. In March 1940 three of the Malta submarines—*Unique, Utmost,* and *Upright*—all scored successes in this navigationally hazardous and much-mined area. "When a heavy concentration [of shipping] on the Tripoli route was reported on the 8th March, every available boat was sent to sea. The *Utmost* (Lieutenant-Commander R. D. Caylet), recently returned from patrol, was off again after only twenty-four hours in harbour, and on the 9th torpedoed and sank the Italian transport *Capo Vita.* The next day Lieutenant A. F. Collett in the *Unique,* whose patrol had been extended for the same reason, sank the *Fenicia.* The *Utmost* was off the Tunisian coast again on the 19th and, falling in with a convoy of five German ships with supplies for the Afrika Korps on the 28th, torpedoed two of them, the *Heraklia* and the *Ruhr.* The former sank but the *Ruhr* was towed to port. The same convoy was further depleted on leaving Tripoli on its return journey when the *Galilea,* straggling astern of it, was torpedoed and severely damaged by the *Upright.*"[3]

Only a month earlier the *Upright,* commanded by Lieutenant E. D. Norman, had sunk the Italian cruiser *Armando Diaz* off the Kerkenna Bank. This cruiser and another of the same class had been quite unnecessarily hazarded by the Italian command as escort to a large convoy of German transports—unnecessarily because the British had no surface forces at this time in the central Mediterranean. (This was well enough known from air reconnaissance over Malta.) A cruiser was no threat to submarines, but was at the same time an ideal target. Lieutenant Commander Malcolm D. Wanklyn, V.C., D.S.O., in the *Upholder* was himself a scourge of the convoy routes. Between April 1941 and March 1942 the *Upholder* sank ten merchant ships (three of which were troop-carrying liners of over eighteen thousand tons), one destroyer, and two U-boats, damaging a further cruiser and three merchant ships. He and the *Upholder* were finally lost off Tripoli in April 1942.

With Malta sending out submariners like these, it was hardly surprising that the Italians, unable to contain losses so great, would demand large-scale action against Malta and that Rommel, bitterly aware of the men, munitions, fuel, tanks, guns, and transports that were failing to reach him, would begin to call for an antidote to the poison of "that scorpion in the sea." It has always to be remembered that in these early days the Italian convoys were without anything approaching the British Asdic (Sonar) or RDF (Radar). Blind on the surface at night and with only hydrophones for listening to the darkness below, they struggled bravely to maintain the supply line to North Africa, while being increasingly harassed by the aircraft and submarines operating out of the island that their Regia Aeronautica had earlier claimed to have been "rendered completely inoperative."

Large minelaying submarines from Alexandria also played an important part in the summer of 1941 by bringing to Malta such limited quantities of essential stores as they could carry in their mine-bays. After unloading, they then took aboard their outfit of mines from the underground stores and proceeded north to lay them in important areas, such as around Palermo and other much-used ports. One of these submarines discharged these two main functions of her patrol and went on to use her torpedoes on an Italian submarine and a merchantman; when the latter refused to sink, the sub surfaced and sank her by gunfire.

The "magic carpet," as this supply system by submarines became known to the islanders, could only be of limited and temporary service (Malta had not received a real convoy since May). The *Rorqual* and the *Cashalot* were two of these visitors from Alexandria. Arriving off the island on a dark night, they would signal their identity and, lifting their whalebacks, come down the swept channel to Grand Harbour. The watchers on the shore—and there were many who now slept out in the warm summer on quaysides and paths and paving slabs—would see the water streaming phosphorescent from the submarines' casings, a light fume drifting over the surface, and hear the muffled thump of their diesel engines. As the craft passed they would catch the oily, hot-metal smell lifting from the conning tower. Sometimes on those nights the air-raid sirens would wail to announce what had become almost routine hit-and-run raids. Sometimes the all-clear would go without any raid having taken place, the radar pilot having signaled an approaching formation that had suddenly faded and disappeared. Extra-close attention was paid at first to see whether this was merely a diversion, and if the plot would suddenly thicken from another quarter. But after this had happened once or twice, it was realized that some of the Italian pilots, familiar from the past or by report with the Medusalike terror that the island inspired, preferred to drop their bombs in the safety of the sea and then return to their comfortable quarters in Sicily.

14

The Hot Summer

On June 22, 1941, German forces invaded Soviet Russia. Hitler reckoned that Britain could make no move, that his right flank in the Balkans and Greece was secured, and that the Mediterranean theater was dominated by the Luftwaffe and the Afrika Korps. He had chosen this moment to risk the strategic nightmare that the Germans had tried to avoid throughout their military history—a war on two fronts. Stalin, forewarned of the invasion by Churchill but strangely unbelieving that his partner in power politics of a megalo-Machiavellian kind could have so duped him—or that the hostile British under Churchill, of all people, would have informed him correctly—could do little as the mechanized gray waves rolled forward. The British could only hope that the two *hostes humani generis* would exhaust one another, meanwhile making such excursions as they could on the one front where they were active, while their enemy's main attention was engaged elsewhere. In view of the failure of General Wavell's counterattack in the western desert the revictualing and reinforcing of Malta was more important than ever.

Sweltering under the summer sun, the naval fuel carrier H.M.S. *Breconshire* and six large merchant ships waited empty beneath the protection of the island's barrage. They had long ago discharged their contents but had been forced to remain immobilized for fear of air attack. Concern was also growing about the need in Malta for mines and torpedoes for the submarines, torpedoes for aircraft, ammunition for guns, fuel for aircraft, for ships, and for shore installations, as well as food for the garrison and the people. In June 1941 planning had started for a large convoy to replenish the island and at the same time to take away these empty ships that were urgently needed elsewhere. Operation Substance was designed to forward a convoy from Gibraltar under the escort of Force H as far as the Skerki Channel, the fleet from Alexandria at the same time creating a diversion with the intention of deceiving the enemy into thinking that this convoy was designed to pass right through the Mediterranean to the east.

On the night of July 21 the convoy entered the Straits of Gibraltar (it was always necessary to pass convoys through at night because of the many agents in the area). As so often happens where the cold ocean meets the warm sea, there was thick fog in the straits, and the troopship *Leinster* ran aground. Unfortunately, she was carrying among much else RAF personnel to maintain the aircraft in Malta, but even so, her loss was of less concern than would have been the loss of any of the other heavily laden merchantmen. As the convoy moved on to the east with fighter cover provided by the *Ark Royal,* Force H with the addition of the battleship *Nelson* moved north of it to provide protection as far as the Skerki Channel. Meanwhile Cunningham's fleet made a sortie from Alexandria, having sent two submarines to the west of Crete to make wireless maneuvering signals that would suggest to listeners that the fleet was operating in that area. This stratagem had the desired effect, drawing out the Luftwaffe and Regia Aeronautica over the area, as the battlefleet turned back overnight to Alexandria. Although the Italians had at this time three divisions of cruisers and four battleships, in the western Mediterranean, no surface move was made against the convoy as it advanced toward Malta. The Regia Aeronautica, however, had some success in an attack by torpedo aircraft and high-level bombers on the convoy as it neared Sicily. One cruiser was crippled and forced to turn back to Gibraltar, and one destroyer was sunk. The Italians were skilled in such a combination of high-level bombing and low-level torpedo attacks. In the last dangerous night, as the convoy sailed through the narrow Skerki Channel, motor torpedo boats registered a hit on the *Sydney Star,* which managed to survive and finally reached Malta alone and apart from the rest of the convoy. The ship went through further bombing and torpedo attacks in the kind of saga that was to become only too familiar on what was already euphemistically known as "the Malta run."[1]

Despite the losses, Operation Substance was a great success, with six large merchantmen laden with essential supplies reaching the island and the security of Grand Harbour. Now that the Luftwaffe was no longer in Sicily, it was reckoned that the island's barrage and its fighters could keep the Regia Aeronautica away while the valuable stores were unloaded. At the same time the *Breconshire* and the six empty merchantmen were escorted back through the Sicilian channel on their way to Gibraltar. At either of the two main points of the operation—the passage of the convoy to Malta through the Sicilian channel or the return of the empty ships—the judicious use of a cruiser squadron by the Italians could have led to a disaster, but they remained inactive in harbor. Previous encounters with British surface ships and the recent loss of the *Armando Diaz* to the submarine *Upright* had not helped their morale.

The Italian Air Force was a bit more active. Once their reconnaissance planes had established the presence of the ships in harbor, the Italians dispatched a high-level raid. As had become increasingly familiar, however, the raiders dispersed before the barrage. The many Maltese who had thronged the roads and walls around Grand Harbour to look with affection and some comfort on the merchantmen berthed below, stayed to cheer as the barrage lifted and the Hurricanes came in among the disorganized attackers. How often during those years, at times when they were not entirely deserted because of the weight of an attack, did the old ramparts and curtain walls erected in the days of the Knights echo with the cheers of the people as the fighter pilots rode the sky above! These were only to be exceeded by the roars of cheers, applause, and tears that were to greet the arrival of torn and bloody ships from savaged convoys in the months that lay ahead.

On the night of July 25 an incredibly brave but, in the final analysis, foolhardy attempt was made by the Italians to destroy the ships of this convoy whose presence unloading in Grand Harbour so mocked their Regia Aeronautica. The history behind this venture goes some way back in time. The Italians had always been adept at actions involving individual gallantry and cavalryman dash. In the

First World War they had sunk the Austrian battleship *Viribus Unitis* as it lay in harbor by attaching mines to it from a small submarine (the father of Count Ciano, Mussolini's foreign minister and son-in-law, had been among the crew on this occasion). The Italians had continued to work on such specialized attack craft as midget submarines, high-speed motor torpedo boats, and what amounted to manned torpedoes.

The *Decima Flottiglia Mas* (10th Light Flotilla) was responsible throughout the Second World War for everything connected with these types of operations, including explosive motorboats (EMBs) piloted by one man in an ejector seat (so that he could blow himself clear before the moment of impact), two-man chariots known as *maiale* ("pigs"), and skin-diving frogmen. A pig was a slow-speed torpedo on which sat a two-man crew wearing breathing apparatus, maneuvering themselves until they were below the target. The detachable warhead was then removed and clamped to the keel, a time-fuse was set, and the pig then withdrawn to safety. (Later in 1941 three of these were to change the whole balance of power at sea when they entered Alexandria harbor and crippled the battleship *Valiant* and the fleet flagship *Queen Elizabeth* and blew the stern off a large tanker.) The 10th Flotilla had already conducted successful operations in Gibraltar harbor, while during the Crete campaign six EMBs had penetrated the defenses at Suda Bay, sunk the cruiser *York,* and damaged a tanker. The naval authorities in Malta had long been alert to the possibility of some attack being made by one or other of these specialist craft, and the gunners had been trained to expect them.

The Italians had indeed been planning an attack on Malta for a long time, but their awareness that the island and its harbor were defended to an extent found nowhere else in the Mediterranean, and that the garrison was under siege and therefore on the qui vive far more than at Gibraltar or at Suda Bay (which was an open anchorage with temporary defenses), had been enough to cause some hesitation. A parent craft and escorting motor torpedo boats had to come down from Sicily, launch their small attacking craft, wait for survivors—if any—and get away again before daylight. It was a daunting task from the start, and if the Italians had had a full appreciation of Malta's radar system, they would never have attempted it. Indeed, on several occasions coastal batteries had opened up at night on unseen targets at sea, firing under radar control, it being assumed by the gunners at the time that these were probably minelaying motorboats. But, since it is known that members of the 10th Flotilla had come over on one or two occasions to examine the lie of the land and to test out defenses, it may have been they who provoked this "blind" firing.[2] If so, it is even more incomprehensible that the Italian commanders could have envisaged that an assault such as the one they prepared could have any chance of success. Mariano Gabriele, the official historian of *Operazione C3: Malta,* refers to it as "the unfortunate action."

Starting from the harbor of Augusta in Sicily on the night of July 25, the attack force consisted of a parent ship, the naval auxiliary *Diana,* carrying eight of the small EMBs that were intended to attack the convoy in Grand Harbour once the defenses had been breached, and two torpedo motorboats, each towing a two-man pig. One of the latter was to enter Marsamuscetto and find a target among submarines at Fort Manoel. The other was to blast a way through the outer defenses of Grand Harbour, thus creating a breach that would enable the EMBs to tear in and make their headlong attack on the merchantmen. Even if the defenses had been so simple that the piercing of one would have given access to the inner harbor where the ships lay, it was almost unthinkable that any boat, however small and however fast, would have got down the length of Grand Harbour without being blown to pieces. The Italians planned to cover the approach of the EMBs and the two-man submarines by an air raid, their theory being that the noise of the bombs and the thunder of the barrage would cover the whole attack sequence from the sea.

The first thing to go wrong for the Italians was that the parent ship *Diana* was picked up early on radar. The second problem was that their air raid was too short and over too early: The "cover" for the attack by sea was lifted long before it was needed. The harbor defenses were always alert, but especially so when there was a convoy in. The radar report of a vessel to the north of the island brought everyone to a high degree of readiness.

The *Diana* stopped about twenty miles from the island and put her EMBs overboard, they and the motorboats carrying on toward Grand Harbour. The plan was for Major Teseo Tesei, who had been actively engaged in experiments with manned torpedoes since the

1930s and who was one of the principal promoters of the operation, together with his crewman, Chief Diver Pedretti, to make for the viaduct that ran out to the breakwater from the shore by Fort St. Elmo. Having reached it, they would attach their warhead to the defenses and blow them up, thus giving the raiders access to Grand Harbour. The EMBs, taking the explosion as the cue, would then charge through the gap.

The exact pattern of events will never be known, since neither Tesei nor Pedretti was ever seen again, but the first explosion at the foot of St. Elmo (which should have been masked by the air raid) brought all the alert gunners into action. They were mostly Maltese of the Royal Malta Artillery, and their guns were mostly six-pounder pom-poms, Bofors, and small arms. They opened fire as all the searchlights trained on the entrance to Grand Harbour were snapped on. One of the EMB pilots seems to have reached the entrance under the viaduct, for it was either his boat exploding against the defenses or Tesei's warhead before him that brought down the whole span in a tangled heap of metal. This "entrance" to Grand Harbour, such as it was, was now irretrievably blocked. Meanwhile, caught in the full glare of all the searchlights, the EMBs racing toward the harbor were blown to pieces. The Maltese gunners had waited many months for attack from the sea, and when it came they let their feelings of frustrated vengeance come to the boil in the waters outside. Within two minutes most of the attackers were dead and every boat was sunk. All the bravery in the world could not avail against such a savage curtain of metal.

The people of Valletta were on their roofs and in the streets. The families sleeping outside and on the vantage points of the Upper and Lower Barracca were witnesses to that astonishing display: fire and light, parabolas of tracer, and a sea exploding in flames. With the dawn the Hurricanes were overhead battling the escort of Macchi fighters that had been promised the attacking team for first light. There was in any case nothing for them to escort back to Sicily. The *Diana* had long ago turned away after bringing her charges to the dropping point, the EMBs were destroyed, and the motorboats that had covered them and the two-man torpedoes to the harbor periphery were caught by the Hurricanes before they could make good their escape. In the dogfight above the scene, three of the Macchis were shot down and one of the Hurricanes. The pilot of the latter bailed out and got into his dinghy. As the sea lightened, he sighted a stationary torpedo boat and paddled over to it, only to find that all the crew had been killed. He took possession and hoisted a white flag. Later in the morning a Fleet Air Arm Swordfish equipped with floats landed alongside and took him off; the Italian torpedo boat was towed back intact. Miss Ella Warren, M.B.E., who at that time was among the many British women engaged in plotting duties with the Navy, later wrote: "Among things salved from the boat was a little mascot white furry dog, with a red bow; what girl gave it to what boy? We named him 'Bruno-Bianco' and he swung on a cord above my typewriter and his little black eyes gave nothing away."[3]

The crew of the two-man torpedo intended for Manoel Island and the submarines experienced some difficulties with their craft and were forced to abandon it. They were later captured swimming ashore in St. George's Bay, which is a good two miles to the north of Marsamuscetto, suggesting that they had been confused by the bays and inlets of the coastline and had never been on the right track for their target area. Never was Italy's Medaglia d'Oro, albeit posthumously, more fittingly awarded than to Major Teseo Tesei and Chief Diver Pedretti. They and their companions had tackled the most formidable fortress-harbor in the world and had died beneath the guns of Fort St. Elmo, where once the flower of the army of the Grande Turke had similarly perished.[4]

15

Aspects of War

Four days before the seaborne attack on Grand Harbour the island had once again shown its striking power. Malta-based Blenheim bombers, alerted to the passage of a convoy of one German and three Italian transports, closely followed by a tanker, on their way to North Africa, struck in a mast-high attack. An ammunition ship blew up, and the tanker, set on fire, finally drifted immobilized to become a total loss on Kerkenna Bank. The Blenheims specialized in low-level attacks, and although there were no more than two squadrons at a time based on the island, they achieved a success against shipping that was hardly equaled even by the submarines. Acting in close cooperation with the torpedo-carrying Swordfish of the Fleet Air Arm, they combined to spread havoc on the Libyan supply route, sometimes the Blenheims finishing off a ship that the Swordfish had torpedoed, and sometimes the torpedo-carrier finishing off a ship that had been bombed but not sunk.

By October 1941 over sixty percent of the Axis supplies designed for North Africa were failing to reach their destination. Rommel, who had seemed poised over Egypt even though the port of Tobruk still remained untaken, constantly complained in his routine nightly communiqué of almost every kind of shortage. Lack of fuel came first on the list, then demands for equipment, and then criticism of the Italians for stretching his land supply line by unloading at Tripoli instead of Benghazi five hundred miles farther east. Undoubtedly Rommel was a believer in the old principle of always asking headquarters for more than you expect, in the hope of getting something close to what you want, but the shipping figures bear out his complaints. By November 1941 over seventy percent of supplies was failing to reach North Africa. The bravery of the Italian merchant marine and their escorts who daily faced these attacks by air and by sea was remarkable. As for Rommel's complaints about the failure to use the port of Benghazi sufficiently, the coastal sea route from Tripoli to Benghazi was constantly patrolled by Allied submarines out of Alexandria, while the port itself was raided almost every night by RAF bombers from Egypt. His problem always remained that narrow lifeline between Italy and North Africa against which Malta pressed like a knife.

At the height of the siege of Malta the lives of the people on the island were dominated almost entirely by the raids, the deaths and injuries, the shattering sound of so many guns numbing the mind, the roar of aircraft, the rumble of collapsing buildings, and—worst of all—the scream of falling bombs that seemed to menace each and every listener with personal dismemberment and death. At such times all ordinary considerations of life, making money, making love, making a meal, making something connected with one's trade or craft, were subordinate to the simple demands of survival. But in the summer and autumn of 1941 the shelter life was largely abandoned. Many photographs witness the gypsy-encampment atmosphere that grew up around the mouths of the tunnels and the cavernlike entrances of public and private shelters. Mothers and children, barefoot as often as not, sometimes gathered around an improvised cooking stove (kerosene was in short supply, but fortunately the staple diet of bread and oil with a little tomato paste was all that most wanted in the hot weather). There were all Maltese soldiers in uniform, priests as much a part of the people as they always were in Malta, and the revered old, sitting on wooden chairs or boxes.

As everywhere else at that time the war itself was the enemy, and in the blank face of the monstrous evil and disruption of life the survivors on this raft of a crowded island drew together in a warmth of friendship. Apart from the many British servicemen (hardly foreigners, since generations of close companionship and intermarriage had made them part of the island scene), there were members of the old British empire, New Zealanders, Australians, and Canadians, some in ships, some in aircraft passing through to the Middle East, and some in the RAF stationed on Malta. There were many parties, for although spirits were scarce, beer at that time still held out, and local wine (mostly of doubtful parentage and brewed under conditions ranging from ingenious to absurd) was drunk more for effect than for palatable pleasure. Known to some as "jungle juice" and to others, familiar with the results if taken in excess, as "screech," this potent liquid enlivened many licit and illicit gatherings. Men who served during the siege remembered not only the hardships and horrors and the inevitable tedium of war but such things as "the mournful echo from an uncovered well" and "the sweet-scented stephanotis around the kitchen door and the colourful oranges and lemons catching the sunlight."[1]

Much of the atmosphere of those days is best perhaps expressed in the words of a Chinese sage: "A man getting drunk at a farewell party should strike a musical tone, in order to strengthen his spirit . . . and a drunk military man should order gallons and put out more flags in order to increase his military splendor."[2]

A traveling concert party had been marooned on the island when the siege began and continued throughout the months and years to carry on as if on an extended tour. The Malta Amateur Dramatic Association, a staunch survivor from the interwar years, still thrived on light comedy and drawing-room drama, though its ranks were now largely filled by men and women who spent most of their time either on the guns or underground in plotting or ciphering operations. Individual units put up their own teams of entertainers, and the RAF, true to its reputation of being more raffish than the other services, had a band called the Raffians. Small bars still opened throughout the island from Gzira and Sliema to such as remained in Strait Street, Valletta—the street where once by tradition the Knights had fought their duels, but which had long ago been taken over as the sailors' bar and brothel and cheap café quarter. Known to generations of servicemen as the gut, it had achieved a worldwide reputation among seagoers, but now, bombed in places and deserted in others, it was already but a shadow of its former self.

More and more as the weeks and months passed the people of the island and their many uniformed guests went back to almost medieval village patterns of life. With roads both bad and bombed, with travel discouraged and gasoline heavily rationed and very scarce, with civilians unwilling to be far from their homes and servicemen unable to be far from their place of duty, there was a return to life within small circumscribed areas. The country people had always lived like this, and now the refugees from dockyard areas and towns learned to share similar restricted patterns of living. Like miniature Japanese gardens the villages expanded to reveal an infinite variety as the eye became used to a microscopic view. There was a bar or two and a store, however little in it—the one a meeting place for the men, the other for the women—usually a square, however small; a particular streetcorner, under (almost certainly) the statue of some saint, known to be shady even when the sun stood high; and some natural feature, knoll, ridge, or declivity, where toward sundown a breeze or breath of faint, moist air could be felt drawing off the sea. Life was small but all the more fresh and memorable for it.

"It was evening coming on to dark. To the west, the sky was a vivid orange streaked with purple.... A few stars had begun to shine. The sound of generators on three British destroyers in the harbour seemed a natural part of the evening. The city was behind us, past the old, enormous hospital of the Knights and the narrower streets of downtown. We could hear very little of it. Just Esther and I at the great door of her house with the brass-dolphin knockers, the ornate shoe-scrapes on both sides of the upper step."

"The room I was living in was small but comfortable. Through the window, I could see part of a headland towering high above the sea. The rest of the cliff was invisible. Sometimes at night, when all was silent and no air-raid was on, I would lie still on my bed and listen to the distant sound of the sea far below breaking against the bottom of the cliffs."[3]

Writing in the nineteenth century in his *History of the Knights of Malta,* General Whitworth Porter had concluded his account of the Great Siege with what might have seemed imperialistic rodomontade, but which proved prophetic: "English hearts and English swords now protect those ramparts which formerly glistened with the ensigns of the Order of St. John; and should occasion ever demand the sacrifice, the world will find that British blood can be poured forth like water in defence of that rock which the common consent of Europe has entrusted to her hands. On such a day the memory of this great siege will have its due effect, and those ramparts already bedewed with so much noble blood, will again witness deeds of heroism, such as shall rival, if they cannot excel the great struggle of 1565."[4]

British blood was indeed "poured forth like water" not only on the land, as the general had envisaged, but in the air, on the sea, and under it, "in defence of that rock." The great distinction between the stories of this second great siege and of the earlier one is that the accounts of 1940–1943 give full credit to the Maltese people themselves. In the histories of the siege of 1565 it was inevitable, in the light of those times, that it was the Knights, the "noble blood," who occupied almost every corner of the canvas. Nameless peasantry, their wives and children, merited little except commendations for their general bravery and stoic endurance. The Abbé Vertot, Count Zabarella, General Porter, and many others tended to ignore the people of the island, forgetting that with a cowardly or even indifferent population the siege could neither have been won nor endured at all. Down through the years the Maltese have held a mass of thanksgiving on September 8 to commemorate the raising of the siege of 1565, while the boatmen of the principal villages and townships around Grand Harbour maintain the traditional *dghaisa* races in those oared boats that equal the gondolas of Venice in their elegant lines while surpassing them in the extravagance of their color and decoration.

But these, and the fireworks displays that followed, were not in evidence during the years of war, and it is doubtful if many of those in the British services knew much, if anything, of the siege that had preceded by nearly four centuries the one in which they were engaged—nor anything at all of the later siege of the French in Valletta by the Maltese themselves. Yet the roots of the islanders' resilience were as old as the leathery-leaved carob tree, and if, as some claim, their ancestry can be traced back to the Carthaginians, then it is worth remembering that the siege of Carthage was one of the most fiercely contested in the whole of ancient history.

Islanders tend to be fiercely patriotic, every island being superior to its neighbor, but usually islands are adjacent to large nations to which their language, religion, and patriotism are subordinate. Malta was different. Set alone in the sea, the Maltese had given their allegiance to the British at a time when their survival was threatened. But they had retained their own language, customs, basic laws, and nationalism. Britain, though a protecting presence, was far away. Had Malta become a colony or dependency of Italy the islanders' Catholic faith surely would have blended with that of the Italians, there would have been more intermarriage, and the Maltese language and customs might well have been submerged. As it was, the islanders had a great affection for remote Britain but had now developed a curiously deep hatred of their neighbors, the Italians. People with whom for centuries their fishermen and merchantmen had shared the same sea had violently attacked them. Many were intermarried, many bore Sicilian (if not Italian) names, and of course they shared the same Catholic faith. The Maltese upper classes and many among the middle class spoke Italian in preference to Maltese ("a kitchen language"), if they did not speak English. Their feeling of revulsion when the first bombs fell was very deep indeed. It was deepest in the hearts of the dockyard people and the country farmers and their wives. They often shared more in common with the red-faced British soldiers than they did with their employers and the upper strata of their own people.[5]

Admiral Cunningham related in his memoirs that "During the early Italian bombing a petty officer steward, one Talliana, had been left behind at Admiralty House. One morning he brought news to my wife that an Italian bomber had been shot down, adding fiercely that if the Maltese laid hands on the crew they would be lynched there and then. My wife remonstrated, pointing out that the Italians might retaliate against our airmen, and that in any case lynching was against International Law. Talliana regarded her with a pitying sort of expression. 'International Law not in Malta, Signora,' he said, shaking his head."

With almost identical words had the Maltese refused to take any more prisoners after the fall of Fort St. Elmo in 1565 (when the Turks had mutilated the dead bodies of the defenders). "St. Elmo's pay," they had shouted as they cut their throats. The expression is used to this day in Malta for any action in which no quarter is given.

16

The Fall of the Year

September, before the rains come, is the harshest time. The lion-sun of summer burns just as fiercely and the whole island is baked out, not a green thing to be seen save the prickly pear (those "figs of India" that feed both man and beast) and, ageless as the bony land from which they climb, the carob trees opaque with dust. Even the sea looks hot; it is certainly warm, cleansing but not refreshing to the swimmer. At such times, as throughout much of summer, the observer turning his eyes from the still, dark-blue water toward the sky will encounter a curious phenomenon. The great dome above, while free of cloud, is not the picture-postcard blue that might be expected but white—sometimes curiously dazzling, like the whitewashed walls in Greek islands, and at other times milky and soft. Whereas in the Aegean the summer sky, broomed by the northerlies, is crisp and sharply blue, and over much of Italy it is the misty azure of a hundred Renaissance paintings, this Maltese sky—perhaps reflecting back the harsh, rocky landscape—is in distinct contrast to the sea from which one's gaze has been lifted. Against the white skies of September 1941 few aircraft rose in defense of the island. With Sicily abandoned by the Luftwaffe and with *Fliegerkorps X* engaged in the eastern Mediterranean and over the desert, the Italians concentrated almost entirely on night bombing. Even this was on a lesser scale than before, though carefully designed to cause the maximum irritation to the besieged while encouraging them to waste the ammunition brought in by convoys at so great a cost. The technique was to send over from Sicily an almost continuous stream of single bombers, coming in high and straight and usually on a course to unload over Grand Harbour.

To combat this night bombing the defenders had earlier set up a Malta night fighter unit composed of some flights of Hurricanes. There were problems involving such a unit, since conditions were quite unlike those to be found in England or anywhere else. As the artillery commander on Malta put it at the time: "Not only were the airfields within the gun-defended area, but it was usual for aircraft to arrive either from Egypt or Gibraltar nightly, for bomber flights to take place almost nightly, or for the Fleet Air Arm to carry out strikes or reconnaissance. Night fighters were usually up, and the enemy was almost invariably present." All this activity in the night sky over an island only seventeen miles long by nine miles at its greatest width presented a kind of almost continuous three-dimensional chess game. "The problem of dealing with all these factors (of which the most difficult were the arrival of strangers from Gibraltar inadequately briefed as to our plans, and the return of damaged bombers from Sicily, who were not always able or willing to comply with the rules) necessitated very clear cut instructions to the guns and searchlights, as well as to the air defences. . . . Simplicity was essential, since personnel changed very rapidly, and any extended period of inactivity almost always meant beginning the work all over again, educating the pilots and the fighter controllers in the details of control."[1] The islanders who slept fitfully in their shelters during these nuisance raids (they did relatively little damage) could hardly have imagined the technicalities of the radar and communications war that was being conducted over their heads.

The night fighter unit was a fascinating example of the interlocking of searchlights, gun operations unit, and the Hurricanes themselves. In Britain, with factory sources of supply quite close to hand, it might by now be possible to be profligate with ammunition for the purpose of maintaining civilian morale, but in Malta the primary consideration was always the tenuous sea or air links to the sources of replacements for everything. In the scheme evolved for the destruction of bombers at night one of the main requirements was the conservation of antiaircraft ammunition. The radar of the artillery and the searchlights were used in combination to direct the fighters onto the targets. The island was divided into two sections, Valletta being on the dividing line, each of which was patrolled by a Hurricane kept informed by radio of the course, speed, and height of any approaching raiders. (No orders were given to them as they would have been in daylight interception.) When the raid was some fifteen miles off the island, the Hurricanes, each within its patrol zone, would position themselves on either side and on converging courses toward the target. The result was that as soon as an enemy aircraft was caught in the searchlights there was a Hurricane to port and one to starboard on closing courses.

The resulting analysis showed that, on an average, out of every seven raiders that crossed Malta's coastline, five were picked up by the searchlights; three out of every five were attacked; and two of these three were shot down. The figures were good but not quite good enough: Too many raiders were getting through to Grand Harbour. The sinking of the destroyer *Maori* by a direct hit was but one of a number of incidents that led to an improvement in the night fighter arrangements. In order to make the most efficient use of anti-aircraft fire together with the night fighters, the sky was now layered, as well as being divided in two sectors, with the Hurricanes operating above a fixed height and the guns below them. While this somewhat increased the expenditure of ammunition, it led to much greater efficiency, and this system with but minor modifications continued to be used throughout the siege. It was good also for the morale of all those islanders who, unable to be spectators (and thus occasionally to see a bomber caught in the searchlights being shot down), were only listeners to a raid. They could now hear from their shelters the sound of the guns—fearsome in the early days, but now become reassuring. It gave them all that satisfactory feeling of hitting back.

During the late summer and early autumn of 1941 the aircraft strength of the island was gradually built up. More Hurricanes arrived, brought by aircraft carriers from Gibraltar to flying-off range, until the island could muster about seventy of these invaluable all-purpose fighters. Not only had they now taken over night fighter duties but, equipped with bomb racks, they also had been turned into fighter-bombers. (When the important September convoy was entering Grand Harbour, they operated in this capacity against Comiso Airfield in Sicily, serving to ground the Italian fighters at this crucial moment.) The island now had for attack, in addition to its Fleet Air Arm Swordfish, a number of Marylands, two squadrons of Blenheims, seventeen Wellington bombers, and a few radar-equipped Wellingtons; the latter proved invaluable in guiding the torpedo-carrying Swordfish onto their targets at night. The Swordfish were also used as minelayers and sank or damaged about a quarter of a million tons of shipping between May and November 1941. The Blenheims striking by day at masthead height (and incurring inevitable losses) accounted for about fifty thousand tons over the same period. Even the German High Command, with their eyes firmly fixed on the progress of the great advances on the Russian front, could not entirely ignore Rommel's almost nightly cries of anguish at the failure of supplies to reach him.

With the winter approaching and with the Mediterranean fleet from Alexandria fully engaged with coastal operations in support of the desert army and the supply of the all-important garrison at Tobruk, it was clearly a good moment to run a convoy through to Malta from the west. This was a large one, consisting of nine merchant ships carrying eighty-five thousand tons of supplies and twenty-six hundred troops, and had as escort three battleships, one aircraft carrier, five cruisers, and eighteen destroyers. (The escort normally provided by Force H from Gibraltar was one battleship, one aircraft carrier, and two cruisers as well as destroyers.) The reason for the considerable increase was the hope that, expecting the usual force, the Italian fleet might venture out to give battle. Elaborate deception methods were employed to disguise the size of the convoy and the fleet, the convoy being passed through the Straits of Gibraltar in two groups on the night of September 24. The heavy ships kept well to the northward shortly afterward, while the body of the convoy kept along the Algerian coast, where they were certain to be sighted and reported. The deception that there was no more than one battleship in the escort succeeded with Italian intelligence. Admiral Iachino assembled a fleet of two Littorio-class battleships, five heavy cruisers, and attendant destroyers and set out from Naples.

Throughout the night of September 26 Iachino maintained a southwesterly course. The weather came down with patches of haze over the sea and low cloud. The Italians hoped that during the following day bombers from Cagliari in Sardinia as well as from Sicily would soften up the convoy and its escorts, leaving them scattered and ripe for an attack by the fleet in the afternoon. But Wellington bombers out of Malta laid on a heavy raid of Cagliari that night; parked aircraft were set on fire, bomb dumps blown up, and hangars wrecked. The result was that although the fleet and the convoy had to accept a number of torpedo-bomber attacks, the whole scale of air activity was diminished. The only damage was to the flagship H.M.S. *Nelson*, which was hit on the stem by a torpedo and had her speed accordingly reduced. At 2:30 that afternoon a Malta-based reconnaissance plane reported two battleships, four cruisers, and sixteen destroyers less than eighty miles from the convoy on a converging course. Admiral Somerville aboard the damaged *Nelson* ordered his other two battleships and the rest of his force to steer to engage, and the *Ark Royal* to launch a torpedo-bomber strike. It seemed that for the first time a fleet action in protection of a Malta convoy might indeed take place.

The visibility had been gradually worsening all the day, the thunderclouds of autumn lofting over the Mediterranean and haze lying over the sea. The poor visibility and some confusion in radio communications, combined with a change of course by the Italian fleet, resulted in the Swordfish failing to find them. Meanwhile, Admiral Iachino had become suspicious. He knew that there was an aircraft carrier in the force opposed to him, but radio traffic combined with reports that the Regia Aeronautica had sighted more than one battleship led him to the correct conclusion that he was in danger of falling into a trap. Since he had strict orders not to risk an action unless he had assured superiority of strength, and since he might equally expect an attack at any moment by carrier-borne planes emerging suddenly out of the clouds and haze, he wisely turned his whole force back for Naples. The Swordfish continued to look for him on his last reported line of advance until lack of fuel compelled them to return to the *Ark Royal*. So ended another battle that never was. Admiral Somerville and the heavy ships returned as usual to Gibraltar, leaving the cruisers and destroyers to take the merchantmen through the narrows to Malta. He was confident that the Italians would not risk a night action involving capital ships, and that the convoy's escort could cope with any other surface vessels that might challenge them in the Skerki Channel.

At sunset the cloud and haze cleared away, and a fine moonlit night exposed the ships advancing toward Malta to a number of attacks by torpedo bombers coming both in pairs and singly, with the convoy silhouetted up-moon. They pressed home their attacks with resolution, and it was more by luck than anything else that only one of the ships, the *Imperial Star,* was hit. She was a large merchant ship carrying a very typical mixed cargo for Malta—several hundred crates of bombs, five hundred tons of kerosene, five hundred tons of refrigerated meat, grain, flour, and small-arms ammunition, as well as three hundred passengers. Fortunately for them she did not explode or go down at once, being a well-built modern ship of twelve thousand tons, and they were taken off safely. Despite all the hazards through which the convoy had passed she was the only ship to be sunk, and the battleship *Nelson* was the only other to be damaged.

The following morning the first of the escort entered Grand Harbour in advance of the merchantmen upon whose stores and supplies, troops and technicians, the whole besieged island depended. The news had of course been passed around in advance, those words everyone was poised to hear: "There's a convoy coming in!" Having now lived constantly—every day, week after week, month after month, for over a year—with the pustulous face of war ever present, there was no one who did not feel deeply about what had been endured to bring in those heavily laden merchantmen. And when the advance guard swept in with such panache, how else could they respond?

". . . the whole population of Malta appeared to be lined up in serried cheering masses along the shore, as the cruisers, with guards paraded and bands playing as though returning from a peace-time cruise, passed through the breakwater and up the stretch of sheltered water with which the Mediterranean Fleet had been so long and so intimately acquainted."[2] The golden moment hangs suspended like a fly in the amber of time, still recalled by old men on drowsy harbor evenings and by many others who will never write their memoirs.

Despite the loss of the *Imperial Star,* at least sixty thousand tons of stores reached Malta in the convoy. This meant that, quite apart from military supplies, the seven-month reserve of essential commodities for the island was once more brought up to scale. Kerosene and coal were to remain in short supply, but in all other respects the island could face the winter with confidence. This was just as well because, although no one could have known at the time, it would be nearly ten months before another convoy of any size would reach the island again.

17

Individuals

Obsessed with the campaign in Russia, which was, after all, the fulfillment of his strange dreams and (more than anything else) the purpose of his whole war, Hitler could hardly pay attention to the cries for help from the Mediterranean. Mussolini's war was not Hitler's war, and the Mediterranean was a sideshow. The Führer could not be distracted from the great German crusade—reflecting, as it did, an earlier one carried on centuries before by the Teutonic Knights in Prussia and the Eastern Territories. (He conveniently forgot that it was this same *Drang nach Osten* that had led to the Knights' terrible defeat at Tannenberg and the complete eclipse of their order.) The German High Command, however, could not ignore their commitment in the south and Rommel's persistent calls for some action to be taken to ensure that supplies got through to his desert army. These were reinforced in September by Vice Admiral Weichold, the German liaison officer with the Italian Navy, who informed Berlin that the current situation was untenable and that the Italians were unable to provide adequate protection for the convoys. He asked for "radical changes and immediate measures to remedy the situation, otherwise not only our offensive but the entire Italo-German position in North Africa will be lost."

In effect he was asking for some Luftwaffe squadrons to be redeployed to Sicily. It was clear enough that when Malta had been heavily under attack, the Axis convoys had proceeded without overmuch interruption. Hitler refused to withdraw any squadrons from the East, but he did agree to the diversion of *Fliegerkorps X* from its concentration in Egypt, the Canal Zone, and the desert war, to the protection of convoys bound for North Africa. No units were moved to Sicily, however. All that happened was that convoys from Greece down to Benghazi were brought under the protection of *Fliegerkorps X* operating from Greece and Crete, while those units that were engaged in the desert were given the additional duty of protecting coastal convoys. Far from having any effect on Malta, the result of these orders was merely to ensure that the Luftwaffe in the Mediterranean was spread more thinly over a wider area, leaving the island unmolested except by the Regia Aeronautica.

After their disastrous losses on the short route to Tripoli, west of Malta, it was natural that the Italians would change to the easterly route—through the Messina Straits and then out into the Ionian Sea, making a great curve to keep outside the range of Malta's aircraft before heading south for Benghazi or Tripoli. This was the route normally taken by the fast passenger liners (now converted to troopships), but it was being increasingly used by merchantmen carrying stores and supplies. The route west of Sicily and then along the Tunisian coast had too often proved disastrous for convoys, for the eyes of reconnaissance planes out of Malta (and often the ears of Ultra information) were quick to alert the British to their passage. The longest route was the safest, but it had the great disadvantage that the ships had to pass through the narrow funnel of the Messina Straits, which remained under close observation by submarines and aircraft out of Malta.

In the first week of September two transports were hit by torpedoes from Swordfish in this area; one sank and the other was towed back to Messina, out of commission for many months. A week later a reversion to the western route proved no more helpful. A convoy was attacked by Swordfish at night, then escaped under smoke, but was located again the next day by Blenheim bombers coming in at masthead height. One ammunition ship was hit and blew up, for the high price of three Blenheims. In the dark hours of the following morning the convoy—its route plotted and its destination known—was again attacked by Swordfish, and another ship carrying ammunition was exploded. Rommel's planned offensive to capture To-bruk in September looked further and further away.

For some time, in view of the absence of the Luftwaffe from Sicily and the relative safety of Malta as a base for surface units once more, Admiral Cunningham had been in communication with the Admiralty as to the desirability of reviving Force K. This had been a striking force of four destroyers and one cruiser that had been stationed in the island in April to increase the weight of attacks on the Axis convoys to North Africa. For a time Force K had succeeded admirably, on one occasion catching a convoy off the Tunisian coast and sinking all five heavily laden transports as well as the escort of three Italian destroyers. This was the kind of conclusive action "in the Nelson style" that only a surface force could execute. Submarines and aircraft might sink one or two ships in a convoy, but only warships could sink them all.

The operations around Crete had effectively put an end to any further ships being available for Force K, and intensive minelaying had rendered operations out of Grand Harbour increasingly hazardous. On one of its last expeditions the ships had returned safely to the island, only for one of their number to be mined alongside the breakwater, completely blocking the entrance channel for several days. Circumstances were different now, however, and a surface force operating from Malta along with the submarines, the RAF bombers, and the Fleet Air Arm torpedo-carrying planes (a squadron of Albacores had joined the Swordfish at Hal Far) might be expected to reduce Rommel's chances of mounting an offensive even further. Owing to his numerous commitments, which now included the Red Sea, Admiral Cunningham found himself unable to provide any ships for a new Force K, but the Admiralty had agreed with his conclusions and were preparing to send out from Britain a striking force of two six-inch gun cruisers and two of the best-armed fleet (heavy) destroyers. They would arrive in October, but meanwhile the submarines out of the island were to make another decisive strike.

The preparations for assembling a convoy of almost any size in Italy were almost impossible to disguise, and so long as Malta could mount an efficient air-reconnaissance unit (which she continued to do throughout nearly all the siege), the chances of a convoy getting far without being observed were very slight. In many respects, even though Allied convoys had to traverse thousands of miles from Britain around the Cape of Good Hope, always at risk in the Atlantic to the deadly efficiency of the German U-boats, the British had a better chance of bringing men and matériel unobserved to their forces in the desert than did the Axis powers. It was true that, since the Luftwaffe had been operating in the east, Port Said, Alexandria, the Suez Canal, and the assembly point at the head of the Red Sea had all come within their range, thus increasing the hazards. These were still relatively small, however, compared with those faced by ships run from Italy or Greece. These convoys had to assemble at a few known points, and their destination by sea was always known because of the very limited number of ports in North Africa. The British, once they had got their men and supplies into Egypt, were at liberty to deploy them as and when they wanted. The Axis powers had to take theirs into two ports that were constantly bombed and through waters that were always menaced—by Malta. The conclusion was obvious, but it was not fully acted upon for a few months.

In the meantime the known destination of a particular convoy, as well as its port of departure, played a large part in an ambush that was carefully set up by four of the Malta submarines. It was true that sometimes this information was supplied by Ultra, but on this occasion, as on many others, it was the work of reconnaissance planes out of Malta. They operated with immense skill and almost unbelievable disregard for the earlier established rules of such work, covering ports and harbors almost daily and bringing back from heights of no more than five thousand feet large-scale photographs that rendered futile any attempts at secrecy about naval units and ships assembling for convoys.

Since the disclosure of the Ultra secret, there has been a tendency to overcompensate for the inevitable omissions of earlier war histories by ascribing almost everything to the brilliant intellects and technical abilities of the hitherto unknown "backroom boys." This is an error, and particularly so in the case of Malta. Despite the island's prime position as an intelligence listening post, a large part of intelligence-gathering was done by individuals flying aircraft, operating submarines, or, at a later stage, paddling ashore onto enemy-held territory in canvas canoes.[1] The war as fought from Malta was in itself a particularly individual one, and the very nature of the besieged island gave full vent to the extremely individualistic nature of the British. This was shown in such characters as the quiet, brilliant Scot Wanklyn as well as in other submarine commanders of a wildly flamboyant nature. Every gun battery, every army unit, every ship, and every squadron had at least one or more whose private talents and whose oddities would hardly have fitted them for any kind of promotion in peacetime, but whose unique abilities flowered under the peculiar exigencies of the siege. Since it would be invidious to make an arbitrary selection from such a wide gallery at this remove in time, let one man stand duty for them all—particularly since it was the low-level reconnaissance he introduced to Malta that led to so much coveted information.

"Wing-Commander A. Warburton," says an official history, *The Air Battle of Malta,* "first came to the island at the end of 1940, and specialised in reconnaissance flying, with only short interruption, throughout the period covered in these pages [the whole of the siege]." His friend, A. J. Spooner, the captain of a Wellington operating from Malta, who knew him from early days, describes how "in Egypt [he] borrowed a Beaufighter, stripped it of all armour plate, guns, ammunition etc. installed vertical cameras and flew it to Malta. He dismissed the Baltimore [the official reconnaissance plane] with a wrinkle of his disdainful nose. 'No bloody good. But this Beau,' he said, 'is the fastest aircraft in the Mediterranean. . . . With this I can reconnoitre any place at any time at any height.' He photographed the Italian fleet in their naval base of Taranto in appalling weather from less than a hundred feet. He navigated himself all over the Mediterranean without adequate meteorological services or navigational equipment. He went when they expected him and when they did not. He always came home undamaged, often followed by an armada of enemy fighters. He carried no guns or armour. He refused to fly with regular aircrew. He chose to fly with A.C.2. Haddon and L.A.C. Shirley, their role on board being to change the camera spools and to count aloud the enemy fighters following him. He liked to take his coat off and to assist in servicing his own engines—a task for which he was not qualified. He would fly in almost any clothes provided they were *not* the official ones. A thigh-length pair of sheepskin leggings which he had acquired in Crete were characteristic. Above this he would wear Army battledress with air-force stripes (he was now an acting flight-lieutenant). He preferred an Ascot cravat to a tie. He was proud of his ash-blonde hair, so let it grow to near shoulder length. He had a notoriously grease-stained cap which he used to wear at times—on top of his flying helmet even. Against orders he smoked as he flew. He would take little part in mess life at Luqa, but instead could be found on occasions playing cards with the airmen at the dispersal site in one of the home-made huts there. Yet on one occasion, at a time when most of us had run out of buttons, polish and smart uniforms, he turned up in the mess immaculately dressed in order to meet the new group-captain. He was like that—utterly unpredictable. He lived in Valletta with a charming cabaret artiste, and he drove himself to work in an old car. . . . Although not by nature a normally contented person, I believe that he found himself—and happiness—in Malta. And later, when posted to other Mediterranean bases, he found unofficial ways of returning to the island that welcomed him and appreciated him."[2]

It was air reconnaissance that revealed three ocean liners gathered in the harbor of Taranto. Clearly, a troop convoy was assembling, and since their destination could only be Tripoli—Benghazi was not able to handle them and was even more subject to bombing attacks—it was decided in Malta to lay a trap for the convoy at the "toe of the sock," the approaches to Tripoli itself. Four of the U-class submarines from the island—*Unbeaten, Upholder, Upright,* and *Ursula*—were accordingly stationed along the coast toward Tripoli, starting at a point one hundred miles to the east, where it was known that such convoys usually made their landfall. The *Ursula* was last in the line at the entrance to the swept channel that began thirty miles east of Tripoli; the others were spaced some ten miles apart eastward of her.

Coming from Taranto, the convoy naturally took the expected route. Escorted by five destroyers, the ships steered at high speed through the night of September 16. They were first sighted in the early hours of the following morning by the *Unbeaten,* which was at the end of the line and too far away to get into an attacking position. Her immediate radio report was received by Wanklyn in the *Upholder,* who steered on the surface to intercept. When he came to fire his spread of four torpedoes, his usual skill came into play, but it was reinforced by some good luck for him and *mala fortuna* for the Italians. As two of the liners zigzagged, they happened to coincide across the path of the torpedoes—making in effect, though at different ranges, one target. One liner was hit aft and brought to a standstill, and the other received her death blow. There were comparatively few casualties, however, as most of the troops got away in the boats and life rafts.

Wanklyn finished off the stricken liner the following morning. The third ship, which happened also to be the fastest of the trio, was missed astern by the *Ursula* at the mouth of the swept channel and reached Tripoli safely, the sole survivor apart from the escorts. But at such a moment, when Rommel was waiting for men as well as machines, this was a further insulting blow to his hopes of a desert offensive. As Count Ciano, the Italian foreign secretary, wrote in his diary for October 6: "The supplies for North Africa are becoming more and more difficult. Only twenty percent of the material set aside for September has been shipped and delivered."

The authorities in Malta were well enough aware that the constant run of successes against Axis shipping that was crippling the armies in North Africa would one day invoke the Furies. The Maltese people—artisans, businessmen, and peasants alike—were extremely shrewd and recognized that unpalatable fact. They would not have survived as a separate race in the Mediterranean through all the centuries if they had not been as shrewd as they were tough. While they rejoiced in the damage that the island was causing their enemies, they had felt the weight of that enemy before. As the winter came on with its first downpours of rain, reviving memories of the damp, unhealthy life of the shelters, they felt uneasy as well as hungry.

"Fears of starvation began again as early as six weeks after the previous eight-ship convoy had sustained Malta. There were many who expected some relieving measures in the situation, and no doubt there were some in the way of replenishment of ammunition, petrol, spares and foodstuffs, but any effects there must have been in this respect were certainly not visible."[3] The government, looking ahead, was certainly not going to increase rations with the winter approaching and, in fact, had already engaged a group of experts to report on how to eke out existing stocks. No one knew when another convoy could be expected. Minelaying submarines still brought in their limited and specialized cargoes, and a few merchantmen still ran the blockade alone and unescorted from the western end,[4] but no one could predict when the next large convoy would arrive. The memorandum on "Rationing in Malta" drafted for the government told the leaders little that they did not know about stocks in the island and what possibilities there were for further cuts in the rations. After mentioning that "the rations of coffee, tinned meat and tinned fish are very tight and could not be reduced without further hardship," the memo went on to stress: "Bread is much the most important article of consumption with the people of Malta. . . . it is undesirable that any rationing of bread should be attempted."

As has been said before, bread was indeed the staff of life to the people. Indeed, the crusty Maltese loaves, baked in wood-fired ovens, had long been considered about the best in the whole Mediterranean basin. (No wood had been imported for a long time, of course, but the great beams and fittings from wrecked houses, storehouses, and other buildings as well as wrecked ships and boats were gleaned in these days as if they were gold—to bake the flour.) Adulteration had inevitably set in, and since there was no overall control of the bakers (that was to come), there were many who complained that, apart from the difficulty of getting it, the bread was often heavy and strange-looking through having been mixed with potatoes. These were a problem, too, since Malta had always had to import seed potatoes on account of the climate; if they failed, there was no substitute.

After the first winter rains, the sea around turned muddy. Every crack and fissure in every building was penetrated by the weight of the downpour, and soon all the land began to be feathered with green. Troops familiar with the desert, who knew how the passage of a single rain cloud could revivify seeds that no one would have suspected lay hidden beneath the sand, would have recognized the phenomenon. Every year in October Malta began its second spring—perhaps the best months of the year, coming as they did after the barren summer, when the eyes had ached with the glare of bare earth and rock. Now once again for two months or more wildflowers rose everywhere and the scent of narcissi effaced the dusty smell of summer. The harsh temperatures had dropped to about 70°F. throughout the day, and the sky was a rinsed pale blue.

Though people had not come to terms with the endless oppression of war, they had adapted their lives to accord with it—in a curious way, it was as if peace had never existed. Reality was gun barrels against the sky, the ululant sound of the sirens, the torn buildings and the yellow scars where old walls had had their skin ripped off to reveal the fresh stone beneath. Tattered clothing blew in the breeze, drying on improvised lines stretched out from shelter mouths, and iron pots with little in them sat over makeshift fires made between limestone blocks. People felt hungry but not as yet starved.

News passed by word of mouth quicker than by the savaged telephone system or the slow, carefully controlled information released over the radio. There had been a stir at the harbor mouth, the crunch of the sea under the moving forefoot of a warship. The two six-inch-gun cruisers, *Aurora* and *Penelope,* new to their light-gray Mediterranean paint, accompanied by the two heavy destroyers *Lance* and *Lively,* were entering Grand Harbour.

18

Striking Force

Approached from seaward there was no more imposing harbor in the Mediterranean than that which is justifiably called "Grand." On the right Fort St. Elmo—its guns pointing skyward in those days, a star-shaped bastion built on the site of the fortress that had defied the Turks in 1565—hunched heavy shoulders in protection of the grid-plan city of Valletta behind it. Undulating over the hill of limestone on which it was built, the light shining clear down the mathematical lines of the streets, Valletta's sides were protected by great walls. On the Marsamuscetto side the nineteenth-century spire of the Anglican cathedral made its sharp statement against the flat-roofed palaces and houses of the City of the Knights, the masterpiece of the sixteenth-century architect Laparelli.[1] Though it was called after its Grand Master *Humillima Civitas Valette*—Most Humble City of Valletta—there were those from the seventeenth century onward who maintained that it should have been called "Most Proud." Certainly during this siege, fulfilling its function as a fortress city, it was indeed most proud, and the scars and shattered buildings showing here and there like the gap-teeth of an old fighter did not diminish its grandeur. From Fort St. Elmo the broken iron girders of the viaduct to the breakwater, destroyed in the Italian attack, hung down or pierced the surface of the water where they effectively closed the gap. Behind them the boom defenses of the

149

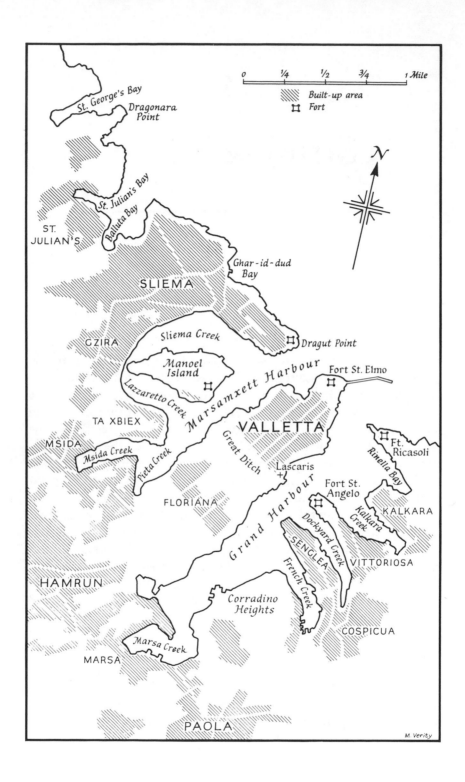

St. George's Bay

Dragonara Point

St. Julian's Bay

Balluta Bay

ST. JULIAN'S

Ghar-id-dud Bay

SLIEMA

GZIRA

Sliema Creek

Manoel Island

Lazzaretto Creek

Dragut Point

Fort St. Elmo

Marsamxett Harbour

VALLETTA

Ft. Ricasoli

Rinella Bay

TA XBIEX

MSIDA

Msida Creek

Pieta Creek

Great Ditch

Lascaris

Grand Harbour

Fort St. Angelo

Kalkara Creek

KALKARA

FLORIANA

Dockyard Creek

SENGLEA

VITTORIOSA

HAMRUN

Corradino Heights

French Creek

COSPICUA

Marsa Creek

MARSA

PAOLA

0   ¼   ½   ¾   1 Mile

Built-up area

Fort

N

M. Verity

harbor sealed it yet again. Spreading back as far as the Upper
Baracca and the Great Ditch beyond (which protected the city from
the landward side) rose the walls of the city that had caused a Turkish spy, visiting Valletta just after it had been built, to report to the
Sultan: "We shall never take this place!"[2]

Opposite Fort St. Elmo and on the left of the breakwater—the
latter completed by the British in 1906 to protect their battlefleet
from the *gregale* (the fierce northeasterly wind of winter) as well as
from potential attack by the new weapon, torpedoes—lay Fort Ricasoli. This late-seventeenth-century fortress had been built to seal
the harbor mouth, providing a complement to Valletta's Fort St.
Elmo. Running out on a narrow strip of land, this was a longitudinal
fort whose curtain and bastions rose sheer from the water's edge
to seaward. On the harbor side, looking over Rinella Bay toward
the village of Kalkare and Bighi Hospital, it displayed one of the
finest baroque gates in the island, with barley-sugar twist pillars at
its entrance. Antiaircraft and shore-defense guns now squatted
where bronze and iron cannon had once gleamed. The end of this
fort and the promontory on Grand Harbour bore the name Gallows Point. As early engravings show, it was here that the bodies of
malefactors once hung, wind- and sun-dried, as a warning to those
approaching Malta's city and harbor and as a reminder to those
leaving. Across Rinella Bay, opposite Fort Ricasoli and at the head
of the next peninsula, stood the large Palladian building of Bighi
Hospital, dating from Nelson's days. It was of little use now in
the siege because it was overexposed to air raids. Further on, across
Kalkara Creek, at the head of the peninsula on which stood the
township of Vittoriosa, was the largest fortress of all, St. Angelo.
This was a giant whose scars bore evidence of many air raids but
that remained as indomitable as when it had been the headquarters
of Grand Master La Valette in 1565. A mile from the entrance to
Grand Harbour, beyond Fort St. Angelo and Dockyard Creek, lay
the fortified peninsula of Senglea, distinguished by its old watch-
towers on which were carved an eye and an ear to denote their
unsleeping vigilance. French Creek, site of the modern drydocks,
was backed by the whale-hump of Corradino. Over half a mile
farther on again lay the Marsa ("harbor"), where this great sleeve
of water ended in tumbledown buildings, small ships, tugs, barges,
and lighters.

All this was not only the arena where the fight was staged but also the base from which issued forth the ships that took the battle elsewhere. It would not be long before the two cruisers and their escorts, now refueling after their passage from Gibraltar, would move out beyond the breakwater, guarded by its two forts, and—like the impossible bull that gets in among the crowd—create havoc outside. The arrival of a new Force K did not escape Axis observation. Coupled with the recent severe losses inflicted by Malta-based aircraft and submarines, the presence of this surface striking force caused the Italian Naval Staff to discontinue—even if only temporarily—all convoys to North Africa. Rommel's complaints were now reinforced by a fact that could not be concealed. The listeners in Malta and the coordinating brains in Bletchley Park knew that such a situation could not be allowed to continue, since it would mean a complete Italo-German breakdown in the desert. At the time he diverted *Fliegerkorps X* to convoy protection, Hitler had also ordered six U-boats to the Mediterranean. Their presence would soon make itself felt, but it was clear that further measures would have to be taken. With the advent of winter on the Russian Front there could be no doubt that there would soon be planes to spare.

The absence of any convoys meant a long wait for Captain Agnew of the *Aurora* and the ships under his command. At last, however, the Italian Naval Staff was forced to bow to the pressure from the High Command. A convoy had to be run through to North Africa to ensure that the army could at the very least stave off the attack the British were clearly preparing. On November 8 a convoy of eight freighters escorted by six destroyers issued out from the Messina Straits, eastward bound toward the coast of Greece, where they would be joined by a further smaller convoy, the whole then turning south for Tripoli. Despite the fact that the convoy was given an air escort throughout that first day, it was sighted by a patroling Maryland out of Malta. This report caused Captain Agnew's Force K to get under way at dusk. In anticipation of any such move the Italians had already stationed a submarine watch on the approaches to Grand Harbour. It must have been inefficiently maintained, however, or the submarines may have been "put down" by destroyers dropping depth charges prior to the emergence of the cruisers and their escort, for Force K steamed out at high speed through the breakwater and headed east without being attacked or reported. In the words of a marine who was aboard H.M.S. *Aurora* at the time: "We sailed in a hurry, in fact some men were still ashore, and the captain of *Penelope* went aboard in a launch just as his ship was going through the boom."[3]

In order to avoid any confusion in night actions the two destroyers *Lance* and *Lively* and the cruisers *Aurora* and *Penelope* fought as one ship. Steaming at twenty-eight knots at close stations, each keeping in the other's wake, they were at liberty to open fire on anything that was not either dead ahead or dead astern of them. As had been seen in earlier engagements, the British were not only highly trained in night fighting (whereas the Italians were not) they also had the immense benefit of radar, which again the Italians did not. The Italian convoy had, apart from its destroyer escort, close support from two heavy cruisers *Trieste* and *Trento* and four destroyers. In theory this force, commanded by Vice Admiral Brivonesi, should have been quite sufficient to cope with anything that the British could bring out, but in the face of the deficiencies mentioned above it was to prove useless.

It was a brilliant moonlit night, and the second convoy, consisting of two merchant ships and two destroyers, was just joining the main body when Captain Agnew picked them up. Reducing speed to twenty knots, he led his ships around to the north of the convoy, silhouetting them up-moon, and turned on a parallel course. There had been a report of other ships astern of him, but he had ignored this to concentrate on his target. These other ships were Admiral Brivonesi's cruisers and destroyers, which he had positioned astern of the convoy, maintaining a patrol on a north-south line to ward off any threat that might develop from the direction of Malta.

Without radar, Brivonesi was dependent on visual sighting, and his lookouts had failed to observe the British slipping between his force and the convoy. Indeed, the first that he knew of the enemy's presence was when there were flashes and explosions from the direction of the convoy, some three miles to the east. Force K, steaming parallel with the convoy and its escorts, came up first with the destroyer at the rear and left it damaged and out of action. Two further destroyers were sunk in the action that followed, the situation being to some extent made easier for the British when Admiral Brivonesi came to the conclusion that the convoy was under air attack and gave the order for all ships to make smoke. The destroyers on

the far side of the convoy from Force K were confused by the smoke blowing over them and to all intents and purposes were put out of the action. Brivonesi discovered his mistake too late when the mast supporting his radio aerial was shot down, leaving him unable to communicate with his squadron.

Meanwhile, Captain Agnew led his ships almost at leisure in the destruction of the convoy, nine ships being sunk and a tanker left ablaze. About an hour and a half after the first sighting Force K turned southwest for Malta. Such was the course that might have been expected, and it was athwart such a course that Admiral Brivonesi should have laid his ships. Inexplicably, he turned to the north to intercept the British squadron. (He and Captain Bisciani in command of the close destroyer escort of the convoy were subsequently deprived of their commands.) The ultimate humiliation was yet to come, when the submarine *Upholder* put in an appearance at dawn and sank one of the remaining destroyers.

The sudden urgency with which Force K had steamed out from Grand Harbour the previous night had made it quite plain to any Maltese in the vicinity of the waterfront that a convoy must have been sighted. Next morning the people were waiting at every vantage point—gun crews in the old forts, men, women, and children thick on the roofs and in the windows of the houses in Valletta, and dense along the shoreline. Their cheers rebounded off the limestone battlements as they welcomed the gray ships. As the marine aboard H.M.S. *Aurora* put it in his letter: "Arrival back in Malta was pretty exciting because the Maltese knew just about before anyone that we had been in a successful action, and they used to line the front and all viewpoints waving and cheering. . . ."

This action, the first of several, was but the shining tip of the iceberg that was sinking the Axis in the Mediterranean. In the previous month, on the night of October 16, sixteen Wellington bombers out of Malta had carried out a heavy raid on Naples, hitting docks, factory buildings, the Arsenal, and a torpedo factory. As well as their normal one thousand-pound bombs, they dropped a number of four thousand-pounders—the first time bombs of this caliber had been used anywhere in the Middle Eastern theater of war. In the same month airfields in Sicily were attacked, as well as roads and other targets on the North African coast, by Malta's Blenheim bombers. And the submarines continued to take their usual steady toll.

The Italian mercantile marine was being destroyed. With under-standable alarm the German Vice Admiral Weichold noted: "In Oc-tober 1941 the African tonnage dropped to 50,000 tons—a third of the monthly average of the past seven months. Of this, almost 63 percent was either sunk or damaged; in the whole month only 18,500 tons of shipping space arrived safely in Libya. . . . In Novem-ber the total tonnage used fell to 37,000; of these 26,000 tons were sunk and 2,100 tons damaged. This was 77 percent—the highest per-centage of tonnage lost and also the remaining 8,400 tons was the lowest monthly delivery. . . . The battle for Cyrenaica (Western Des-ert) was not decided during a month of actual land fighting, but rather by these external factors."

Radar-equipped Wellingtons were used by the RAF working in close liaison with the surface forces, the former preceding the air-craft at dusk in the direction in which a convoy had been reported, the latter picking up the convoy and then guiding the attacking force in its direction, as well as illuminating it with flares on moon-less nights. Sometimes, as has been seen, the convoy was reported by one of the reconnaissance planes out of the island, but there were also other sources of information. Commenting on his liaison work flying one of these Wellingtons a pilot observed: "A typical sortie worked out like this. It would start when the Navy received an in-telligence report from one of their 'men on the pier' that a supply convoy was due to pass through the Straits of Messina or was to leave Naples or Palermo on a certain tide. Naval navigators would then work out where the enemy was most likely to be at various times during their passage to North Africa."[4] The mysterious figure "on the pier," of course, carried a signal for Captain Agnew con-taining information that had been deciphered and construed by those anonymous men and women working in the hidden fungi-vorous tunnels below Lascaris Bastion.

Without radar and without efficient sonar the Italian Navy made a brave effort to get convoys through to the Axis forces in North Africa. If besieged Malta was always deeply concerned about fuel for its ships (doubly so when a surface force was based there) and for its aircraft, the Italians throughout the war were also hard-pressed, being dependent almost entirely on the goodwill of their German partners to see that supplies from Eastern Europe were made available. Often they were not, and the restricted movements of Italian battleships were not always due to the grand policy of keeping "a fleet in being."

Thus, what one writer has termed "Massacre on the Libyan Supply Route"[5] was regularly taking place; a battleship was even brought out to cover one convoy and heavy cruisers for others, while light cruisers were used to run oil through for the Axis air forces and mechanized armies. Even these moves did not always succeed, and late in November of 1941 one convoy escorted by three heavy cruisers, two light cruisers, and attendant destroyers was attacked after leaving the Messina Straits by RAF bombers and Fleet Air Arm Swordfish and Albacores. One of the cruisers was torpedoed during the day and had to return to Messina, and a second cruiser was also forced back after being torpedoed that night by a submarine. At this point the Italians, expecting the arrival of Force K or further air and submarine attacks, recalled the whole convoy. A few days later Force K did indeed strike, and two German ships laden with ammunition, bombs, oil, and other supplies for the Afrika Korps were blown up and sunk as they tried to slip by on the eastern route to Benghazi.

The combination of the onslaught at sea and a fresh British offensive in North Africa proved almost fatal to the Axis in the Mediterranean theater, and if it had not been for the outstanding military talents of Rommel, the Allies probably would have crushed his troops. The British advance on November 18 had caught him by surprise, but he struck east into Egypt to threaten his enemy's supplies. Then, on the news that Tobruk was on the point of being relieved, Rommel turned west again, and after heavy fighting in the desert he succeeded in preventing the junction between the Tobruk garrison and the New Zealand Division—at one stroke keeping the British and imperial forces from the main object of their offensive. Had he had his supplies, armor, and reinforcements, he might have continued his advance into Egypt, cut the British off from their base, and broken through the "soft" defenses of Alexandria and Cairo to reach the Suez Canal.

Such had been his intention, but it was defeated at sea by the air, submarine, and surface naval forces operating out of Malta. Even as it was, Rommel could no longer maintain the land blockade of Tobruk and, reporting that he would have to abandon Cyrenaica, he began to withdraw toward Tripolitania on December 11. His moves could in any case have been anticipated, but little could have prevented a general of his caliber from extricating his hard-fighting forces. By the end of that December Tobruk was finally relieved, after a siege that had lasted 242 days. The closing months of the year had shown that other besieged fortress, Malta, at the peak of its capacity for disrupting the enemy's supply lines, and thus able to view the success of the British forces in the desert to some extent as a by-product of their own efforts. This warm feeling, shared by the islanders, seemed like a cheerful prelude to Christmas, which, austere though it was bound to be, was a longed-for break in the overall harshness of war. But before then, unknown to most, the balance of power in the Mediterranean had already started to change. Hitler had ordered more U-boats into the sea, and *Fliegerkorps II* had been ordered to transfer from the Russian front to Sicily and North Africa.

19

A Hard Winter

Inside a fortress there is a special kind of claustrophobia, an insularity quite beyond that normally associated with islands. The news from the greater war beyond their embattled walls is heard only as a distant rumor, comforting insofar as it shows that the besieged are not quite alone, and doubly comforting when it is about supplies or some damage inflicted upon the enemy that must ultimately weaken his hold upon their position. The news of December 7, 1941, that the Japanese had attacked Pearl Harbor, thus bringing America into the war, was heard first with astonishment and then with a warmth of fellow-feeling. Japan was far too remote to come within the ordinary Maltese's sphere of thinking, but many had relatives in America as they had in other parts of the English-speaking world. No one of whatever rank on the wintry island could possibly understand what the fact might mean in the enormous battle-painting of the war itself, but all could understand that there was now a massive ally on their side—thousands of miles distant, indeed, but construed as a menace to the enemy that besieged them.

About a week before this news came there had been an ominous sign high in the sky over the island—a distinctive twin-engined shape known to all, a Junkers 88 on a reconnaissance flight, something not seen for many months. A few had already been warned that "information" suggested that there might soon be a return of the Luftwaffe to the airfields of Sicily. What the many had long suspected (without access to any secret sources) was about to be revealed.

Something similar had happened nearly four hundred years earlier, when the great corsair and tactician Dragut Rais had arrived on the scene in Malta a few weeks after the attack had begun. The siege suddenly acquired a new direction and force: Guns were sited on Tigne Point, facing Fort St. Elmo to the north, and on Gallows Point (site of Fort Ricasoli) to bombard St. Elmo from the south.[1] The overall strategy of the attack on the island was also drastically reshaped. So it was from the moment that Field Marshal Kesselring took over the command of *Fliegerkorps X* in the eastern Mediterranean, of all the German forces in Sicily, and of *Fliegerkorps II*, under General Lörzer, now transferred from Russia to Sicily and North Africa.

Months before, the blitz on the *Illustrious* had been a kind of "one-off" performance. This had then been followed by heavy raids using massed bombers, in the belief that this would be sufficient to break the will of the island's defenders and above all of its civilian population, as such attacks had done when applied to cities in Europe. But the German and Italian experience in the air had subsequently shown that Malta was every bit as indomitable as London and, because of its nature, presented quite a new problem to Luftwaffe thinking.

The island was, as its defenders boasted, "unsinkable." The civilians in their air raid tunnels had developed a way of living that no one had been able to do in the bombed cities of Europe and the islanders seemed to be completely welded to the British in a homogeneous whole.[2] *Luftflotte 2,* as Kesselring's command was known, was governed by an overall directive issued by Hitler himself, now back in Germany from his advance headquarters on the Eastern Front and able to see the whole scale of the war again from a European viewpoint. First of all, Kesselring's forces were to concentrate on achieving mastery over the sea between southern Italy and North Africa, thus ensuring the passage of convoys between the two. This meant suppressing Malta. Second, they were to prevent the passage of enemy convoys through the Mediterranean. This also meant suppressing Malta.

Although Luftwaffe losses had been extremely heavy in the first assault on the island, air power was again to be used like a bludgeon—but this time with a difference. Instead of staking everything on a few large saturation raids, the bludgeon was to be applied intelligently as well as incessantly. (Something had been learned from the Italian tactics of keeping the defenders permanently without rest or sleep.) The campaign was to fall into three phases. First, the air defenses were to be neutralized by forcing the defenders to expend their personnel and their ammunition. Second, the airfields were to be rendered inoperable and any aircraft caught on the ground destroyed. Third, the dockyards, shipping, harbor installations, and lines of communication were to be destroyed. Until the nuclear scientists succeeded in their morally dubious achievement, no area on earth had ever endured such an explosive power as the one that was now to fall on Malta. It would be fair to say that, but for the quite exceptional nature of the garrison (which includes everyone on the island at the time) and of the men who managed to fight the shattered remnants of convoys through to sustain it, Hitler had a good chance of success.

The lone Junkers 88 had been the portent of things to come. A few days afterward, like an old gage of battle flung down before an opponent, something strange occurred in Grand Harbour.

"Nick Harrison and I were talking in the Castile Square when suddenly we heard a familiar whine. I queried Nick saying: 'Surely that is an ME?' We both turned round in time to see a single ME 190 with a yellow nose, flying down the length of the harbour with its guns blazing, and at enormous speed. Nick, who was an expert at these things, said at once that he thought it was a ME 109F, which was the very latest German fighter. If this were true, it boded ill for the R.A.F. in Malta, as not only was Malta's airfield space largely given up to bombers, but the fighters we had would be outclassed by this type of Messerschmitt."[3]

Things had begun to go wrong for the British long before the appearance of the Luftwaffe over Malta. Despite the objections raised by the German Naval Staff, Hitler had ordered six U-boats to the Mediterranean in September and then, weeks later, a further four. The result of these new dispositions was soon seen on November 12, when the *Ark Royal* was torpedoed by *U.81* and sank some thirty miles east of Gibraltar. This was a grievous loss, coming at a time when two of Britain's carriers were away being repaired from war damage and another was being docked after a grounding. It was the *Ark Royal* that had consistently managed to "feed" Hurricanes into Malta over the previous months. Since Force H no longer had a carrier, the supply of aircraft into Malta dried up, and Force H could no longer escort convoys to the island.

Less than a fortnight later Cunningham's Mediterranean fleet from Alexandria also suffered a disaster. Operating in conjunction with surface forces out of Malta, Cunningham with his three battle-ships—*Queen Elizabeth, Barham,* and *Valiant*—had been "trawling" along the North African coast when *U.331* penetrated their destroyer screen and put three torpedoes into the *Barham.* The old warship rolled over to port, blew up, and sank, taking 56 officers and 812 ratings with her. This was but the beginning of a series of heavy blows to Britain's naval forces that was to change the balance of power in the Mediterranean to an extent not even rivaled by the Fleet Air Arm attack on Taranto in 1940.

Before this turn of the tide became apparent on the island, and before the Luftwaffe had had time to get settled into Sicily, all the signs seemed to point to the continuance of a successfully aggressive future. The harbor-watchers (of whom there were many hundreds) argued from the presence of Force K that the battle was being won, a feeling that was reinforced by the arrival of two more cruisers, *Ajax* and *Neptune,* and the fleet destroyers *Kingston* and *Kimberley.* Of course, the presence of these additional surface forces on the island meant that, while the Axis convoys were even more threatened, the expenditure of fuel doubled. In view of the need to maintain some essential reserve, there was at that time on Malta only enough fuel for all four cruisers and fleet destroyers to make three sweeps of normal range. The only fast fuel carrier available was the *Breconshire,* a converted merchantman that could carry five thousand tons of fuel oil and a certain amount of gasoline. Without her many runs between Egypt and Malta no surface force could have operated, shore installations would have failed, and even the submarines would have been port-bound. To some extent Malta existed and maintained its fighting capability for some time on the slim thread of one ship.

Some good news reached the island in mid-December. Lack of radar and inadequate training in night-fighting techniques had led to another disaster for the Italians on the North African run. Two light cruisers, *Da Barbiano* and *Di Giussano,* had been loaded with gasoline urgently required by the Axis forces in the desert and sent out with a torpedo boat to make a fast run from the west of Sicily down to Cape Bon and thence along the coast to Tripoli. Their departure was observed by Malta reconnaissance, and an obvious target for Force K was presented, but owing to the fuel shortage at that moment no ships could be dispatched. A strike by torpedo aircraft was accordingly arranged, although the chances of finding two fast ships at night were not promising. However, outside of Admiral Ford and his staff on Malta, no one knew that by sheer chance four fleet destroyers, the *Sikh, Maori, Legion,* and the Dutch *Isaac Sweers,* were at that moment on their way from Gibraltar to Malta as replacements for Cunningham's fleet. They would be nearing Cape Bon at about the time that the two Italian cruisers were anticipated in the area. This was the night of December 13.

After receiving a message about the Italian cruisers from Admiral Ford in Malta, the four destroyers began a dash for Cape Bon to try and come up with them. By chance only, after the cruisers had temporarily reversed course to throw torpedo planes from Malta off their track, the destroyers—at action stations, gun crews and torpedo tubes at the ready—encountered them off the dark loom of the Cape. Hit by shell and torpedoes, both of the cruisers were sunk; the Italian torpedo-boat was left behind to pick up survivors.

"The Maltese knew just about before anyone. . . ." Bad news could almost always be contained within a tight group, but good news was always allowed to find its own mysterious source of leakage—from a signalman to a friend, to a Maltese sailor, to a civilian, and so to all the waterfront. When Commander Stokes in the *Sikh* and the three other fleet destroyers steamed in line ahead through the breakwater in daylight on December 14, ships' sirens were sounding on the bright air and the whole population, as it seemed, was out to welcome them. It would be a long time before they would hear anything that again gave them such a sensation of riding the flashing crest of a victorious wave.

On the following day *The Times of Malta,* that unique newspaper, which never missed a day's publication despite conditions that at times few newspapermen could even have imagined in a nightmare, maintained the regularity of its imperial prose-style: "The spectacle as the victorious destroyers entered Grand Harbour, amid the cheers of the populace, which were returned by the bluejackets lining their ships, was one that will not easily be affaced from memory. The ships were welcomed by cheering crowds lining the Lower and Upper Barraccas, St. Angelo and every vantage point. The cheering conveyed a simple message of pride and gratitude, of sympathy and shared resolve, and of appreciation for the heavy blows they are dealing the enemy in the waters around Malta."

Quite often, after sliding out of the dark harbor on one of their convoy hunts, Force K had drawn blank and returned before dawn with nothing to show for their efforts except expenditure of fuel. At other times they made a successful attack in the night, with nothing but flames on the sea to show that the predator had struck before returning to its lair. There had always been the danger of the game-keeper—those battleships used as escorts—or the sharp report of a mine exploding. In fact, it was the danger of the heavily mined waters off the North African coast that had earlier caused Admiral Cunningham to dissuade the Admiralty from asking for any further ventures by the battlefleet in bombardments of the enemy-held ports. He was well aware how quickly one or more capital ships could be lost and how irreplaceable they were under the circumstances of the Mediterranean war.

After the loss of the *Ark Royal* and the *Barham* a further blow to a dwindling Mediterranean fleet was the loss of the cruiser *Galates,* torpedoed and sunk off the entrance to the swept channel into Alexandria by a German U-boat. Also, with the war now breaking over the Far East, the Australians and New Zealanders were wanting to recall their destroyers and frigates, which had been an invaluable part of Cunningham's forces, while the South Africans were asking for their antisubmarine group for the Indian Ocean. These small ships had proved their efficiency many times in the escort of troops and stores along the desert coast and were now needed more than ever in the face of the new submarine threat.

A severe blow was about to befall the British fleet in an operation that involved passing the *Breconshire* through to Malta on one of her invaluable fuel runs that enabled the surface forces to stay operational. Admiral Iachino, who had been covering a convoy to Tripoli with his battlefleet (three battleships, two heavy cruisers, and ten destroyers), wisely refused to engage a British force from Alexandria in a night action, even though the latter had no more than four light cruisers and attendant destroyers. He had turned for home after seeing his convoy near enough to the harbor. That night, however, Wellington bombers and torpedo planes out of Malta attacked Tripoli heavily, and the convoy was forced to anchor outside the port. On receiving this news, Force K, consisting of *Aurora, Neptune,* and *Penelope* with the destroyers *Lance, Lively, Havelock,* and *Kandahar,* dashed south from Malta to try and catch them outside. Some twenty miles east of Tripoli they ran into a moored minefield. In the struggle to help one another and at the same time get clear of the minefield, the *Neptune* was lost with all hands save one, the *Aurora* badly damaged, the *Penelope* slightly less so, and the destroyer *Kandahar* so severely damaged that she had to be sunk. Something that Cunningham had feared might happen to his battlefleet off that dangerous coast had now almost wiped out Force K.

The spectacle of stricken ships limping into the harbor was not new to the island; the dockyard was always busy repairing damaged ships. The Maltese already had the cruiser *Ajax* in hand, out of action because of mechanical defects, and they now had two more cruisers with serious damage that needed dry-docking to repair. All this went along with the permanent normal maintenance jobs on submarines, minesweepers, harbor craft, and any other odd fish that swam within reach of the sheltering harbor. It was now that the underground workshops, fuel lines, and other facilities—many of which owed their existence to the unending labors of Admiral Ford to ensure that the island could repair its damaged ships as well as the hospitals did its wounded men—proved themselves invaluable.[4] They were to continue doing so during the black turmoil of the ensuing months.

Malta had been an island under almost continuous siege since 1940, but it was not until the end of December 1941 that the people learned what "siege" really meant. Hitler's personal Directive No. 38 to Field Marshal Kesselring on the subject of Malta had been not unlike that of the Sultan Suleiman the Magnificent at his Diwan in October 1564. The latter had told his assembled ministers, admirals, and generals that he envisaged the day when "The Grand Seignior, or his deputies, masters of the whole Mediterranean, may dictate laws, as universal lord, from that not unpleasant rock, and look down upon his shipping at anchor in its excellent harbor." For the immediate future, however, he had issued the ultimate directive:

"Those sons of dogs! I say now that, for their continual raids and insults, they shall be destroyed!"

On December 4, 1941, the Luftwaffe appeared again over the island, timing their first raid for the hours of darkness. They brought from Russia a contemptuous fury and a deadly seriousness to the annihilation of this arrogant island. During the next five weeks of the campaign there were 93 daylight air-raid alerts and 120 night alerts. Only two nights were completely free from attack.

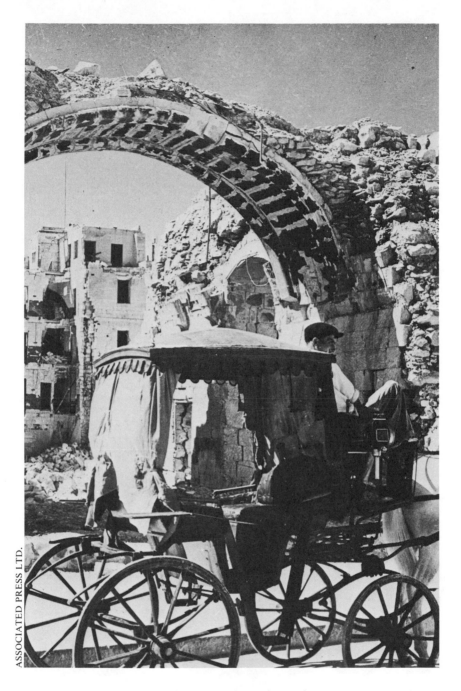

A *karozza* among the ruins

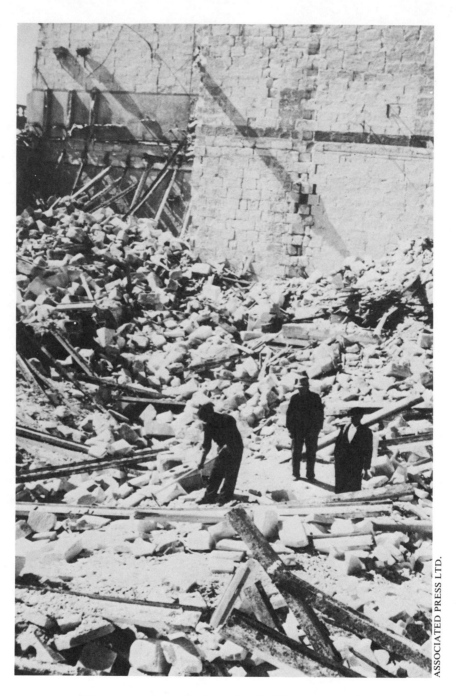

The most heavily bombed place on earth

Land freshly turned by ancient plows

The welcome sun outside the sheltering darkness

A convoy enters Grand Harbor in 1942.

HMS *Ark Royal* torpedoed and sinking

Changing a worn-out four-inch gun on a destroyer

Albacores with torpedoes fly off on a mission.

Farmers and servicemen bring in the harvest.

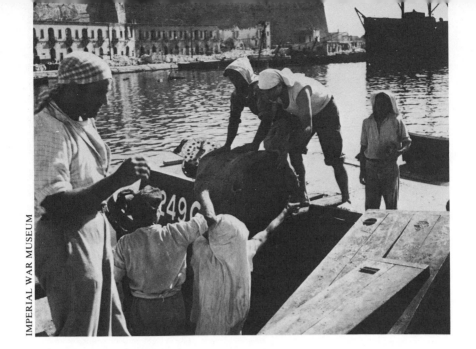

Stores transferred from a lighter to a waiting truck

Interior of a family air-raid shelter

Quarrying new tunnels to enlarge headquarters

Clearing blast debris off and around a bus

20

New Year 1942

Christmas 1941 was probably the most depressing in history. Everywhere throughout the world it seemed that might was proven right and that naked aggression would always triumph. There had been terrible winter seasons in other wars, most notably World War I, but never a time when at every point of the compass there seemed no hope—except for men who had deliberately rejected the cardinal virtues, including hope itself. In the Far East the triumph of the forces that had treacherously attacked the United States seemed to be borne on such a victorious tide that their onrush looked irreversible. The Mediterranean was poised like a fulcrum between Hitler's war against Russia and this new war instigated by Japan. On December 10 the news that the old battle cruiser *Repulse* and the new battleship *Prince of Wales* had both been sunk by Japanese dive-bombers brought a chill to people on an island that suffered every day and night from the high scream and the thunderous roars that the very word portended.

The worst news was the crippling of Cunningham's remaining two battleships in Alexandria harbor on the morning of December 19. Although it was well known that the Italian 10th Flotilla would certainly try to use its small craft against the main British fleet, the precautions taken against them had been quite insufficient. This time, and fully compensating for their failure at Malta, the *Decima Flottiglia Mas* achieved a triumph with their two-man "torpedoes."

The flagship *Queen Elizabeth* and the *Valiant* were both so severely damaged as to be unseaworthy, and the tanker *Sagona* and the destroyer *Jervis* were both severely damaged. This meant that, with the Italian battlefleet increasingly active in the central Mediterranean, Cunningham could no longer oppose it with his own battleships. With the Luftwaffe striking daily and nightly the island of Malta was imperiled as never before.

It was at times like this that a native insularity coupled with the siege mentality served people in good stead. What mattered was here and now—in the immediate vicinity. Other things could look after themselves, and indeed would have to; here was the current raid, here was the tunnel, the air-raid shelter, the immediate family and neighbors. Outside was the dark of the world. It is significant that everyone who has written about those times, Maltese or foreigner, civilian or serviceman, has always commented on the strength that the islanders derived from their faith. In every air-raid shelter of any size there was always a priest, an altar, a lamp burning, and the rites of the Church available. Even in small private shelters there would almost invariably be part of a corner where a statuette, a colored reproduction of a favorite saint or the Madonna, would stand in a small aureole of light—an oil- or candlelit glow that quivered and twisted against the rough-hewn walls when the bombs were dropping. Holy Malta, as the old people had always called their island (paying no attention to the skepticism of some of the young, let alone the cynicism of foreigners), was in itself a very real presence, helped and preserved by the many saints as well as the Holy Family. Apart from the prescribed prayers there were prayers for many occasions, and special ones had been approved by the archbishop for the terrible circumstances of this new war.[1]

Mussolini's fascists, in their endeavor to reclaim their "Catholic brothers from the yoke of the Protestant British," had also maintained that the language of the Maltese was only a dialect of Italian. How many of them would have recognized the following words, said often in those days in the shelters by thousands of young and old?

> *Missierna li inti fis-smewwiet,*
> *Jitqaddes ismek,*
> *Tigi saltnatek,*
> *Ikun li trid Int, kif fis-sema hekda fl-art.*

These are the opening lines of the Lord's Prayer in Maltese. Except for a number of Italian loan words, which then suffered a sea-change and were declined like Arabic, there was as much resemblance in the languages as there was in the temperaments of the people—very little.

Indeed, the temperaments of the races involved in this struggle present an interesting contrast. Even allowing for the many different gradations between individuals, it is still possible to make out a composite picture of attackers and defenders, bombers and bombed. As far as the Maltese were concerned, the instigators of the war were the Italians. This had seemed somewhat unbelievable to many in 1940, although no one in prewar Malta could have been ignorant of fascist attempts to arouse anti-British feeling and to popularize the new regime in Italy. There had been the inevitable disagreements during the interwar period between the British and Maltese at governmental level, and the British had even revoked the Constitution in 1933. There were feelings on which anti-British elements could well play, but at a private level there were so many friendly everyday contacts between the two peoples that, despite the occasional flareups that inevitably happen in garrisons and naval ports, what prevailed was a feeling of rough friendship. Much was forgiven on both sides at times for the sake of a long relationship, which was more like a marriage than that to be found in any other colony.

Against this general feeling had to be set the Italian culture adopted by many of the middle class and more prosperous Maltese, although in the relatively sparse ranks of the old upper class Mussolini tended to be regarded as a vulgar, dangerous buffoon. For the working classes, whether from the dockyard and harbor areas or from the country, Italian fascism had little appeal—except the inevitable one to poor men of any organization or party that promises better things. Comparatively few working-class Maltese spoke anything but basic English, and fewer still any Italian at all. Theirs was a typically Mediterranean culture with North African undertones, deeply impressed over centuries by the influence of the Catholic Church and somewhat less so by the simple pragmatism of British servicemen. Those islanders who had traveled at all—as ratings in the Royal Navy, aboard merchantmen, or even in fishing boats— were well aware that the living standards of the Italian working men were far lower than their own and that the "new" Italians of a fascist persuasion appeared to dislike Maltese and attempted to patronize them.

The Maltese were literally fighting for their country. This stony land of blinding summer light was indeed their own; the glories of their towns and villages, the churches, were now daily desecrated by bombs, which, they remembered, had first been dropped by the Italians; their homes and familiar streets and loved places were threatened as never before in a hard history. The Maltese had indeed a real stake in the war, since they could not bring themselves to believe that people who had killed and injured so many of them and ravaged their country would ever treat them humanely in any occupation. They had long ago cast in their lot with the British, and they did not see (as some postwar Maltese politicians would maintain)[2] that if it had not been for the British presence they would not have been involved in the war at all. Their position was unshakable.

The official Italian position had been stated over and over again by Mussolini and others, and formed the subject of many books. One of these, *Il Mediterraneao,* may do duty for them all: "By the will of the Mediterranean people, by the affirmation of their national independence, the 'British episode' in this sea is finished— that period, during which, for some length of time, they included the basin of this sea in the security system of their imperial communication routes."[3]

The young Italians who formed the officer class of the Regia Aeronautica as well as the army and navy were mostly fascists. How could they not be? The regime had promised them an African empire (though the last of that was now imperiled), and in *Mare Nostrum* (words that, along with *Imperium Romanum,* were unspoken nowadays) had seemed at first, with its fine new ships, to be fulfilling what it had promised. But then disillusion began to rankle at the hearts of the young flying officers; certainly, as far as Malta was concerned, they had lost too many of their own number to feel much enthusiasm for that target, though they continued to show themselves excellent pilots of torpedo bombers against convoys. And, like the naval officers of the 10th Light Flotilla in their explosive high-speed boats and manned torpedoes, they were capable of exploits of dashing bravery. The real trouble was that the aircraft with which Italy had entered the war were obsolescent. Their fighters were not the equivalent even of the old Hurricanes, and their bombers were slow and lacked armor. Worst of all, aircraft production in Italy was not geared for the rate of loss incurred in all-out war, with the result that airplanes had to be husbanded almost as jealously as warships. The Italians wished to swagger with the great, yet they knew in their hearts that the role was beyond them. They had seen the Luftwaffe, its aircraft and its officers (they had also seen how the Germans, too, had been received over Malta), and they knew that they could not emulate them.

As for Malta itself, it was a constant affront. The Italians knew how many planes it had claimed, how many navy and merchant navy men that Scylla of a rock had seized.[4] The fact that the chief of the S.M.G. (Stato Maggior Generale) was apt to repeat, like Cato the Elder some two thousand years before, *Delenda Carthago*— "Carthage must be destroyed"—was not likely to impress them. They were well aware that before an invasion of Malta could even be seriously considered, the combined Italo-German air forces would have to bomb the island into the silence of death. It was not likely to be easy. So far as they had any personal feelings, they hated the English, who had seemed to mock them on the sea and in the air, and they felt an inordinate dislike of the "Arabic peasants" whose obduracy was an insult to their culture and their pride.

The attitude of the Nazis is more difficult to define because the records of those who took part are inevitably few and the consenting silence of postwar years in Europe has been allowed to erase the memory of what was at the time, after all, much publicized as the *Kampf um Malta*.[5] German newspapers and magazines featured many articles and photographs of the Stukas diving like hawks over that strange, shining island, with its streets like dark chessboard patterns, of bomb bays opening to release their tumbling cargo, and of storage and ammunition dumps boiling up in great white clouds.

The first wave of Luftwaffe pilots who had attacked the *Illustrious* and then the island had been borne forward on the complete confidence instilled by past successes. The masters of Europe had nothing to fear, had only disdain for such a humble target as a Mediterranean island defended by a few British and inhabited by peasants. Then their losses had taught them a salutary respect for the word "fortress" and an understanding of its meaning. *Fliegerkorps II,* under General Lorzer and directed from above by Field Marshal Kesselring, came to Sicily with a different outlook on war, and though at that time they still represented a triumphant Luftwaffe, they had no illusions about their current target. Some of them had been in the Battle of Britain, and most had recently been in Russia. One of them, later shot down and hospitalized at Mtarfe, said: "It was great fun fighting the Russians, one being able to destroy usually four or five aircraft in a day. . . . My C.O. has forty victories, and my No.1 on this last flight is a man with twenty-eight victories."[6]

If *Fliegerkorps X* had been unable to destroy Malta, then their successors were determined to prove it could be done. Like most fighting men they lived almost entirely within their own world. They thought little of Sicily, where the winter of 1941–1942 was as cold there as anywhere in Europe—though not as cold as it would be in Russia. (On January 4 Blenheims out of Malta had attacked Castelvetrano airfield and destroyed a number of German planes, the raid being followed up the same night by Wellingtons, which left many more burning and had blown up a petrol dump.) Malta was an airfield and a navy base. It was disrupting the German campaign in North Africa and as such had to be neutralized. Invasion was still considered the real objective, and Operation Hercules was very much talked about, even though there was a tacit feeling among the Germans that their allies would be unable to cope with their side of the bargain. If the latter felt an almost feline distaste for the island, the Germans as the year wore on were to acquire an implacable resentment of it.

The fourth party in this siege, the British, had by now become so much part of the island—from, among many other units, the 2nd battalion of the Devonshire Regiment (which had been there since 1939) to the Hampshire and Cheshire regiments, which had landed from Alexandria in February 1941—that they were as native to the scene as the King's Own Malta Regiment or the Royal Malta Artillery. The one thing they had to endure that the Maltese did not was the absence of mail from home. When mail did get through (sometimes in submarines), it was invariably many weeks late. Anxiety about their families fueled the men's resentment of the war itself. Many of them came from industrial cities, ports, or London itself—places under constant attack. In all those years it was the condition of war and therefore of those who had instigated it that provoked the deepest hatred. No one could actually grasp the loathsome Cerberus-head of this monster, though it was represented by every attacking plane. The men who were defending, from this small, strange island, their own very different and distant one were not in fact weakened in morale by absence from home, but felt an additional vehemence that even their Maltese neighbors at the guns, who saw their own homes being smashed, could hardly feel. More often than not—and this was especially true of those living in pillboxes on the coast or out in country districts—they had already been adopted by local families. They had, in the phrase, "their feet under the table" somewhere—though there was likely to be no more to eat at a cottage table than on an empty packing case at the back of a gun emplacement.

Christmas 1941—the day itself, but only the one day—was again observed by both sides. The holiday in no way resembled the previous year's, however. Everything was much harder, townscapes had changed, and damage and deaths had accumulated. Children's parties were given wherever possible, for rations had been saved, and there was still drink for the adults (rum that mysteriously disappeared from naval stores seemed to turn up in strange bottles all over the island). Getting toys for the children had seemed an insuperable difficulty, except for repainting old ones and passing them from one family to another, but in fact this was one of the more easily solved problems of the time: "Now the hours of leisure of the soldier in the garrison were very difficult to fill. Transport was out of the question owing to the petrol rationing, and the vast majority found themselves stuck in the middle of the country with only five or six companions, living in what are known as Elephant Shelters. The CRA [Commanding Officer Royal Artillery] seized upon this and said: 'The Gunners will make the toys.' The result was the day before Christmas there was a most magnificent collection of toys (over two thousand were on view), all made by the soldiers out of their own local resources. They ranged from accurate scale models of MTBs down to the inevitable Spitfire and motor cars, and included two magnificent forts, complete with model soldiers, made from bully beef tins, and one working model of the interior of a theatre.... The ingenuity that the soldiers had displayed was something to marvel at, and there were very few of the toys that Hamleys would not have been proud to sell in the days of extravagance before the war."[7]

The previous Christmas season had witnessed that rarest of all sights in Malta, a sprinkle of snow over the high ground, but this year was marked by something almost equally unusual, steady rain. After the dark shut down—crisply as it does in that latitude—the blackout, the shelter life, the absence of entertainment, the all-night raids, the hunger, and the cold were almost insupportable. And now, as if the elements themselves conspired, the damp permeated house and shelter and worn winter clothes. In the records of the island those months of 1941–1942 are known as "the Black Winter."

21

Raids and Rain

In the old days when the enemy brought up the great siege guns, manhandling them into position and laying them carefully to concentrate on one weak part of the wall, the besieged knew exactly what to expect. Day after day the bombardment would go on, frightening at first, then monotonous, then frightening again as it became clear that the wall was collapsing. Looking beyond the smoke and the guns the besieged would see what they expected to see—the massing lines of the enemy waiting for the bombardment to lift as a breach opened in the wall. The sight of the ravaged city made the waiting soldiers suddenly spill forward toward the shining prospect of plunder. More often, however, and especially if the besieged were well ordered, as at Rhodes in 1530 and Malta in 1565, the invading troops were met by yet another wall—constructed by the defenders out of torn houses and the remnants of the perimeter.

The chronicles of such sieges tend to make monotonous reading. Except for brilliant and savage incidents, like fireworks against a summer night, they are little more than the sound of the metronome of war steadily beating: "*Monday 18th June:* The bombardment of St. Elmo continued, two further cannon having been added to the battery firing on the Spur. Ceaselessly by day and night, these guns kept up their fire. *Tuesday 19th June:* The new Turkish battery was almost ready. Their trenches had gone so far that our men, drawing water to throw on the breastworks, were now in great danger. So many of them were killed that there was little hope of getting any more water. During the night a small powder-mill in St. Angelo caught fire. It blew up and killed eight men who were working or sleeping there. . . ."[1]

These extracts from the diary of Francisco Balbi di Correggio, a Spanish harquebusier who fought in the siege of 1565, tell us as much, or as little, as do accounts written in 1942: "The sirens sounded and we manned our gun. We did not have long to wait before the heavy AA guns gave us the direction of the first wave of twenty-five planes and as soon as they commenced their dive another twenty-five came in from the opposite direction. Now dust clouds were blowing over from the centre of the city, which had taken the brunt of the attack. We could not see or hear anything above the noise of the world's most formidable barrage; stones were falling, shrapnel coming down like rain and planes dropping from the sky. It was terrifying, and more planes were coming in. We saw very little of this wave because of the clouds of dust which now enveloped us." This latter was written by Bernard Gray, a *Daily Mirror* journalist who had smuggled himself onto the island aboard a bomber from England and who was greeted by an icy Governor-General Dobbie with the words: "We would rather have had a sack of potatoes than you." (Later, in an equally determined endeavor to get himself to Alexandria to join the army in the desert, Gray inveigled a berth aboard a submarine bound for Egypt, but this time he was unlucky—the submarine never arrived.)[2]

The main differences between the earlier siege and the siege of the Second World War were that the attack now came from the air and, instead of curtain walls and bastions protecting the enceinte of a fortress or a fortified township, fighter planes provided the outer defense, and artillery the inner wall. The whole island was now the fortress, although, even as in 1565, the heaviest blows still fell on certain selected points. The account of air raid after air raid can have little meaning to those who have not experienced them. Every raid was as individual as a fingerprint, even though it was directed at the same specific target area. A bad raid, to be remembered and talked about by one person or one group of people, was clearly one where the action was in their vicinity. The overwhelming impression conveyed by all was a hurricane of noise: The barrage itself, as it

were, provided the main scream of the great wind, and the diving
roar, falling bombs, and collapsing buildings were like the height of
the storm, where the hurricane walks through a city, wrecking
houses and streets and wiping out landmarks with a casual hand.

"The towns and villages lay much in ruins. The heavy limestone
blocks of which the houses were constructed were vast heaps of rubble. Whole streets were blocked and areas cut off."[3] And again,
"The once beautiful harbour had become a foul lake of wrecks and
more than ever a dangerous gauntlet to run. . . . Docks, wharves and
store houses were now rubble of cordite grey stone, the once white
stone buildings were scarred, looking like eyeless sockets where
bombs had struck."[4]

The simple record in itself tells everything—and nothing: "On
January 14, 1942, there were 14 alerts in the space of 19 hours, last-
ing in all 9 hours; and on February 7 the Island had 17 alerts within
24 hours." On February 25 the *Times of Malta* (which sometimes
appeared with its edges damaged by fire) reported: "For some eighty
days now there has been a period of almost continuous alerts. With
few respites, days and nights have been enlivened with the sound of
tense air battles, antiaircraft guns in action, and the whistling and
crash of falling bombs." On February 15 the Regent Cinema in
Kingsway, the main street of Valletta, received a direct hit, and an
unknown number of civilians and servicemen were killed.

The world is not contained by facts and figures—that is where the
actuary, the computer, and the mathematician fail us—for numbers
do not contain emotion. Blake drank damnation to Newton for ex-
plaining the rainbow, but the great mathematician never for a moment explained or conveyed what the sight of that tenuous peacock
arc has meant to myriads of human generations on the face of the
earth. Perhaps a few fragments from an unrelated source convey
better something of what was felt by people who were present in the
Great Siege of Malta 1942: "It was something formidable and swift,
like the sudden smashing of a vial of wrath. It seemed to explode all
round . . . with an overpowering concussion and a rush of great waters, as if an immense dam had blown up to windward. In an instant
the men lost touch with each other. This is the disintegrating power
of a great wind; it isolates one from one's kind. An earthquake, a
landslip, an avalanche, overtake a man incidentally, as it were—
without passion. A furious gale attacks him like a personal enemy,

tries to grasp his limbs, fastens upon his mind, seeks to rout his very spirit out of him. . . . He had struck his head twice; he was dazed a little. He seemed to hear yet so plainly the clatter and bangs of the iron slice flying about his ears that he tightened his grip to prove to himself that he had it there safely in his hand. He was vaguely amazed at the plainness with which down there he could hear the gale raging. Its howls and shrieks seemed to take on, in the emptiness of the bunker, something of the human character, of human rage and pain—being not vast but infinitely poignant. . . . The heavy iron plate turned on its hinges; and it was as though he had opened the door to the sounds of the tempest. A gust of hoarse yelling met him: the air was still; and the rushing of water overhead was covered by a tumult of strangled throaty shrieks that produced an effect of desperate confusion. . . . Pieces of wood whizzed past. Planks, he thought, inexpressibly startled, and flinging back his head. At his feet a man went sliding over, open-eyed, on his back, straining with uplifted arms for nothing: and another came bounding like a detached stone with his head between his legs and his hands clenched."[5]

Perhaps Joseph Conrad, writing about a typhoon in another century and another sea, conveyed something like the actuality of being caught in a bad air raid better than any contemporary, let alone columns of statistics. Yet the *fact* of 262 air raids in January and 236 in February is something that one must attempt to understand in order to grasp, however remotely, what that siege was like. Aboard ships under heavy air attack men sometimes jumped overboard—a fruitless exercise, since either the ship would survive and sail on, leaving the man to drown, or the bursting bombs would kill him with their flying metal and the compression of the exploding sea. No one jumped off Malta. True, the island could not sink—although there were some in those days who recalled an old story that Malta was like the head of a mushroom, supported on a slender stalk of rock that would one day become eroded by the constant surging of the sea, so that the head would fall back into the depths from which it had once sprung.

Worse in some ways than the bombing was the wet. Mediterranean buildings, especially in Malta, where they were all of stone, are damp, drafty, and cold in the winter. Built to an open-plan design to accommodate six months of sunshine (four of which are like the torrid zone), with marbled, tiled, or stone floors, Maltese houses are not built to be cozy. Windows and doors dry out and warp over the long summer. The carpenters, often working with indifferent woods, are not highly skilled like the stonemasons, and icy drafts abound. Many a traveler shivering in Seville, Algiers, Malta, Athens, or Istanbul during the winter months has cursed the roseate enthusiasm of travel agents. Malta, exposed to every wind that blows over the central Mediterranean, an island entirely built of stone, mops up the rain and breathes out damp—especially in a winter as wet as that of 1941–1942.

A temperature of 45 °F., which would occasion no concern in a northern country, can produce aguelike shakes unless one is warmly clad as for wintry Scotland. Yet the Mediterranean peoples never seem to be prepared for the winter months, never have adequate winter clothes or proper heating for their houses. They endure the winter as the inhabitants of Britain endure a summer, on the six or seven times a year when the latter get anything approaching the Mediterranean norm. In besieged Malta, where most of the residential areas had by now suffered bomb damage and where those houses fit to be occupied had often lost windows, doors, or other fittings, living conditions were horrendous. Except for some of the grand houses, the Mediterranean *palazzi* to be found in Mdina, Sliema, and other select parts of the island like Lia and Balzan, fireplaces were almost unknown. The shortage of wood and the high cost of coal had always made them almost exclusive to the well-to-do. As has been seen, it was difficult to find wood even for firing the bread ovens, and early in 1942 an organization was set up to collect wood officially from the debris of ruined buildings. By midsummer over twenty tons a day was being collected all over the island. Coal gas for lighting and fires, only found in Valletta and other central areas, soon became unavailable. Electric heaters were practically unknown, and in any case the electricity itself was uncertain, even when it was not completely cut off. Kerosene was the only reliable form of heating and lighting, and kerosene was strictly rationed. In the shelters families slept huddled together to try and escape the all-pervading cold and damp.

The weather, so maleficent to the health and spirits of underfed people, was almost equally damaging to the island's striking role. It was true that the submarines had not suffered badly from the air attacks as yet, and such surface forces as remained (including two cruisers) were still operational, but the airfields had never been designed to carry their current load. Almost constantly under bombardment, they were suffering severely. In the third and fourth week of January 1942, when Rommel was making a reconnaissance in force in the desert and a convoy vital to him was being escorted to Tripoli, 150 sorties were made against the island. The weather limited the enemy's attacks, but it also markedly reduced Malta's air striking power. Gales, torrential rain, and much low cloud persisted throughout January, so that the fighter airfields of Hal Far and Ta Qali became waterlogged, necessitating the transfer of fighters to the constantly attacked and overcrowded main bomber airfield at Luqa. All this meant that during the British Army's final advance in January the number of supporting sorties out of Malta was reduced by at least thirty percent.

A problem that pilots based on Malta had because of the smallness of the island was that if the weather suddenly closed down over the airbases—as it did so often at that time—there were no other landing fields to which aircraft could be diverted. A big island like Sicily had airfields in various places, where completely different local climate and visibility might obtain, but Malta, "unsinkable" though it might be, suffered from the same deficiency as any aircraft carrier alone in the sea. Meteorological information was unobtainable from any source outside the island, which meant that the weather forecasts could cover no more than six hours. The result was that aircraft away on missions often had to be recalled at the threat of any change. Records from that winter show bad weather, lashing winds, and cold rain very often, and at the turn of the year there were violent electrical storms. The same weather that often grounded aircraft in Malta might let through bombers from Sicily, which, having completed their mission, were able to use the cloud cover to make good their escape.

With no battleships to give cover to convoys for Malta from the eastern end of the sea and with no aircraft carrier for the Gibraltar end, it might have seemed that Malta was cut off. But so long as the British army held Cyrenaica and the airfields on that coast, cover could still be provided by planes from North Africa and Malta combined. In mid-January three merchant ships out of a convoy of four managed to reach Grand Harbour. The fourth vessel, which had developed engine defects and had been diverted to Benghazi, was hit in a dive-bombing attack and had to be sunk as she was carrying large quantities of ammunition. A destroyer was also torpedoed and sunk by a U-boat, but all in all the ability to get ships through when the island was under such heavy attack was some encouragement to the authorities as well as to the people on the bastions and waterfront—and was a tribute to the cooperation between the island and the desert air force.

Admiral Cunningham communicated to the Admiralty at the time his belief that "the employment of airforces in maritime operations should provide sufficient aircraft to give us control of the Central Mediterranean where at present we have no battleship. It is vital that the number of aircraft should be apparent to the enemy immediately to hide our weaknesses from him, which, if known, would permit him to establish himself in his objective in such a way that it would be impossible for us to regain our present position." Aware that the invasion of Malta was still a possibility, he was concerned at the drain on his forces imposed by the new requirements in the Far East, especially now that he had no capital ships to deploy against the Italians. "If we fail to deter the enemy's heavy ships during the next months from establishing control of the Mediterranean, he will achieve reinforcements of his forces in North Africa, be in a position to secure Malta and endanger our Middle East forces." Looking ahead in an accurate prophecy he wrote: "Our return route to Europe can be obtained from North Africa and it is in Europe that we must defeat Germany. For this reason we must consider the retention of control of this theatre as our main objective."[6] Retention of control meant retention of Malta, for without the island the whole sea and probably the war was lost.

With Force K reduced to the cruiser *Penelope* and three destroyers, and with the island airfields largely out of action through constant bombing and the heavy weather, the inevitable had been happening on the Libyan convoy route. Escorted on one occasion by the entire Italian battlefleet, and regularly by heavy cruisers and one battleship, the Axis convoys had been getting through, and the Afrika Korps was regaining its strength in fuel, fresh armor, and reinforcements. The British, on the other hand, were now at the full stretch of their supply line in the desert, and the most westerly port, Benghazi, had been so badly damaged by earlier British bombing that it was taking a long time to get it serviceable again. As happened more than once in the desert war, one side built up supplies and threw the enemy back; then in its turn it became overextended; the enemy with shortened lines of communication built up its supplies; and the seesaw shifted once again.

Malta was the pivotal point of this movement, and when, as now, its striking power was almost exhausted, the inevitable could be expected. With adequate fuel and fresh armor Rommel struck in the desert on January 21, and eight days later he recaptured Benghazi. By February 6 the British had fallen back to a line a few miles west of Torbruk, and most of Cyrenaica was lost. This meant that any convoys from Alexandria to Malta must now pass through the corridor dominated by Crete in the north and Axis airfields on the Benghazi hump in the south. Malta was to outward appearances suppressed and, in the face of overwhelming air power and threatened by the only battlefleet in the Mediterranean, might expect an invasion.

22

Awaiting Invasion

In a New Year broadcast to the people of Malta the governor had anticipated likely events by giving detailed instructions of what was to be done in the event of invasion. Church bells, which had previously been rung to indicate the local all-clear signal after air raids, would now only be rung when invasion was imminent. This would be a clear-enough signal to everyone wherever they were, since Malta has hundreds of churches, and none but the stone-deaf could have escaped the clamor of them all sounding together. The streets were to be immediately cleared, and everyone stay at home or at any rate within their own villages or towns.

The protection officers in each area would be kept informed by the central government and would be in local control. The Protection Office Organisation had been set up in 1940, quite separate from the special constables and air raid wardens, and was composed of responsible citizens—very often members of the judiciary or the medical service, and invariably assisted by the parish priests. These officers already had powers to requisition buildings for housing refugees, to order the construction of air-raid shelters, and to exert some control over the distribution of essential commodities through local shops. They were now to be provided with provisions to cope with any immediate emergencies in their districts. As in Britain, signposts and milestones had long since been removed or defaced, and in any case an invader trapped within the Daedalus-type maze of most Maltese towns and villages would have been as lost—and probably as dead—as an unwelcome visitor from the Barbary Coast three hundred years before.

Operation Hercules was indeed being discussed at Axis headquarters and before the spring was out would be one of the subjects of talks between Hitler and Mussolini at the Berghof on April 30. A curious fact about this meeting of the two dictators and their staffs (and one that shows how badly coordinated was the Axis High Command) was that, although there were generals and field marshals present, there were no admirals from either side. Since Operation Hercules was high on the agenda, this seems surprising to say the least, but it may be no more than an indication that Hitler never regarded the assault and capture of Malta as feasible. The Italians pressed for an early invasion, and indeed this was the best moment they could possibly have chosen, since Malta's air force was worn down and the British had no capital ships available to protect the island. (Apart from the remnants of Force K in Malta, Cunningham had only destroyers, three light cruisers, and one antiaircraft cruiser in Alexandria.) However, Malta's RAF bombers, Fleet Air Arm torpedo planes, and submarines had given the Italian naval authorities sufficient respect for the island's capabilities against surface ships without any naval threat being necessary to deter them. Despite all the arguments put forward in favor of the operation, Hitler still regarded it with scarcely concealed mistrust. He could see from the many aerial photographs that the island was quite unsuitable for glider landings, and its massive fortifications—few of them, in fact, later than the eighteenth century except the Victoria Lines—were hardly designed to inspire confidence in a would-be aggressor.

Perhaps Hitler felt that by diverting Luftwaffe forces and U-boats to the Mediterranean theater he had done as much as he could then afford. Let Rommel get his major offensive, code-named Theseus, under way in the desert and then, presuming on its success, there would be time to consider Hercules again. Relying on Field Marshal Kesselring's confidence that "Malta was completely neutralized," Hitler was prepared to come to an agreement with Mussolini that an assault on Malta could indeed take place after Rommel's offensive in the desert, which was designed to begin on May 26. Rommel was eager to continue the advance right into Egypt, but the Italians were more cautious (knowing the difficulties on the supply routes), and a compromise was reached. If all went well, the desert offensive should halt on the Egyptian border before the end of June, after which everything was to be turned against Malta. The preliminary date for the island's invasion was fixed for July 10.

What Hitler principally mistrusted about the operation against Malta was that it must be largely an Italian affair—troops, ships, embarkation points—and thus he had good reason to anticipate failure. The war must be won in Russia. Let the German and Italian air forces continue softening up Malta to such an extent that it was completely suppressed. He was indeed eager to see Rommel in Egypt and to establish that other pincer to the east of his great adversary, but not at the expense of some costly air- and seaborne expedition that the Italians might mismanage. On the surface, however, Italian pride must not be ruffled, and their natural concern about the serious losses to their navy and merchant fleet, occasioned by the British presence on Malta, must be soothed by the promise of future action *after* success in the desert.

The essential fuel supply was still reaching Malta, though a bare minimum, brought by fast single ships like the *Breconshire* and *Glengyle,* but they could only enter or leave during the hours of darkness. The daylight skies were dominated by dive-bombers and fighters from Sicily, the latter having so much confidence now through the lack of fighter opposition that even small villages were terrorized by lone fighters swooping down their dusty streets and spraying anything that moved with machine-gun fire. Then a fleet destroyer, the *Maori,* one of the few remaining to escort the *Penelope* if this survivor of Force K was to provide protection for an incoming convoy, was hit and sunk in Grand Harbour. The submarine base on Manoel Island was under very heavy attack, land mines having destroyed much of the shore facilities and living quarters. The sole fleet minesweeper left in operational order was riddled with machine-gun bullets and could only be used at night. The first part of the Luftwaffe's task—putting the airfields and the aircraft out of action—seemed well on the way.

A minimum of four ships a month had been calculated as necessary to keep Malta functional, a target that had been fulfilled in January but that looked increasingly difficult with almost every day that passed in the following month. In an endeavor to get the *Bre-*

conshire and three empty merchantmen away from Malta during the dark of the moon, and at the same time run in a convoy, Cunningham dispatched the antiaircraft cruiser *Carlisle* and eight destroyers as close escort to three fast freighters on February 12. Not one of the merchant ships reached Malta. With Axis airfields now commanding the whole of the Benghazi bulge, any convoy was almost a full day west of Crete without any fighter protection, and the amount of fighter cover that might be expected from Malta in the last, closing phase of the convoy operation grew thinner by the day. Air attack after air attack on a scale that had never been known at sea before (even during the Battle of Crete) ensured that despite the heavy fire put up by the cruiser and the destroyers, first one freighter and then another would be sunk by the bombers. The last to go, her engines disabled by the explosion of a near-miss, had to be sunk as there was no chance of towing her to Malta before daylight. The only good thing to emerge from this operation was the transfer of the empty ships, including the invaluable *Breconshire*, to the Alexandria force and their safe arrival at that end.

It was hardly surprising that before the end of February new regulations were issued governing the sale of bread and flour. The reason that nothing similar had been attempted before was perhaps the report issued the previous autumn on the whole subject of rationing, which had stressed the undesirability of attempting to ration bread, since it was "the basic diet of the Maltese." The new regulation meant little more than that families might only buy from the one breadseller with whom they were registered, that no other "farinaceous foods" (pastries, cakes, and biscuits) could be made, and that pasta (never so popular with the Maltese as with the Italians) was rationed. This move was, of course, no more than the thin end of the wedge, for it was inevitable that bread rationing would have to be introduced before very long. The current black market and the fighting in queues at bread shops and carts were worse for morale than any rationing could be. Before the end of April Governor Sir William Dobbie was compelled to announce this unwelcome but delayed legislation.

Some wheat was grown on the island, but it was never enough to feed the population, which had multiplied first of all under the rule of the Knights and then exploded under the improved sanitation, health services, and (not to be forgotten) availability of work made possible by the British. In the past, by a special arrangement (Malta being considered as part of the Kingdom of Sicily), the Order of St. John had been able to import grain duty free from that island-granary of the Roman Empire. Often, though, there were bad harvests in the north, and the galleys of Malta raided the Moslem North African routes for grain cargoes—at times even seizing Sicilian ships that were trying to avoid their Malta quota and sell the grain at better prices elsewhere. Famines were not unknown in those centuries, and the word still held a hereditary menace for the Maltese. Under the British, with their ready supply of cheap grain from the Empire, it had been almost forgotten, but it was to be remembered again in this second siege.

Wheat was now being milled "to the highest practicable extraction rate," about ninety-five percent, and was then mixed with maize or barley. We have seen how adulteration with potato flour had already become part of the millers' practice, but the bread as now issued came hard to a people who were used to hot crusty loaves of tasty white bread. (The bread van's arrival in a Maltese village, scenting the air with its loaves straight from the baker's oven, is still one of the great daily occasions in village life.) Now it was becoming dark and tough, and early in May it had to be rationed to under half a rotolo (less than fourteen ounces) per person.

Food was already beginning to occupy peoples' thoughts to the exclusion of almost all else, except self-preservation. Potatoes, after their introduction by the first British commissioner Alexander Bell (one of Nelson's captains) early in the nineteenth century, had become one of the island's principal crops—and in the 1930s had even become a major export. Because potatoes would not germinate in Malta's soil, however, the seed always had to be imported, and the loss of a ship carrying the whole seed crop for 1942 led to an acute shortage.[1] The entire potato crop was then bought by the government and reissued at a low, subsidized price on a ration. Unlike the inhabitants of northern cities during the war the Maltese were not short of vitamin C, but even here, on an island that is normally a market garden for fruit and vegetables, there was very little to be had through legitimate channels.

Whole areas had been taken over by the military, and farms destroyed by bombing. Labor was short because of the call-up of so many young men, and in the spring of 1942 hardly any part of the island was safe for men out in the open during daylight hours. The roaming fighters from Sicily would even come down to sea level and turn and fly up the *wieds,* or rocky gulleys, to machine-gun the cement pillboxes often placed to command their approaches. Peasant-shooting, too, was all part of the day's excursion over Malta.

As the siege grew steadily worse through that terrible spring and summer, even the simplest foods grew as scarce as luxuries once had been. *Soppa ta l'Armla,* widow's soup (so-called because even the poorest peasant's widow had been able to make it with the aid of the small plot at the back of her house), became a gourmet's dream. It consisted of whatever vegetables were available, one egg (dropped in at the last moment just before eating), and a bit of ricotta cheese made from sheep or goat's milk. At this time eggs were almost priceless, one bean could cost a penny, and the familiar herds of goats that were part of the Maltese landscape had sadly dwindled or vanished into the hills and remote hamlets. No longer did they come every morning in their dozens right into built-up areas like Sliema and Valletta, their full bags swaying, up and down the man-made steps and alleys to be milked into cans at the doorsteps. (In Valletta, where some of the houses were many stories high, they had even been taken up hundreds of stairs to the doors of the sick or bedridden.) Pigs and rabbits had vanished—or were guarded with a shotgun—and cats, which can look very like rabbits (once skinned, with head and tail removed), turned up in many a pot. Later in the year the fruit of the prickly pear as well as the carob bean, usually animal fodder, were as sought after as the normally abundant fruit of the island. The weather that year was bad for the citrus trees and, sheltered as so many of them were in narrow valleys or old worked-out stone quarries, they were either ruined by rain or plundered.

One of the curiosities of the siege was the fact that among the imported goods so urgently required in the cargo ships was canned fish, principally sardines and tuna, especially asked for indeed as being "the principal food of workmen." It might have been thought that an island in the middle of the sea could supplement its rations by a little fishing. But, for one thing, no fishing boat could venture out, and there were few enough afloat (most having been sunk at their moorings or destroyed in bombed buildings around the Marsa at the far end of Grand Harbour). For another, there were very few fish to be caught at any time. The Maltese islands, being situated on the submarine ridge separating the eastern from the western Mediterranean, were not near any fishing banks, and the two best fish to be caught in the vicinity, the lampuki and the dentici, were both seasonal. Boat fishing by night was impossible, since the flare or acetylene lamp needed to attract squid or flying fish might also bring enemy aircraft. The water of the Mediterranean, in any case, had become biologically exhausted and too saline ever to support fish like the great oceans. Except in a few places—and Malta is not one of them—the *frutti di mare* that rejoice the traveler are far from abundant, and the swordfish of the Messina Strait and the tuna that annually close the coast of Sicily to spawn do not venture this far south.[2]

Shortage of goats' milk led to increased demand for canned milk, the sweetened condensed milk in particular being very popular with mothers for their children. (The wartime acquired taste for condensed milk never deserted the islanders, and even many years later, when cows' milk was available as well as goats', many still preferred the canned milk in their tea or coffee.) The increasing shortage of local meat and the limited amounts of frozen meat available meant an even greater call for canned meat, principally corned beef. Like most Mediterranean southerners the Maltese were never large meat eaters, but even so the shortage was so acute that no animal was safe unless guarded. A countryman going in his cart up steep Rinella Hill in Kalkara village during an air raid had the misfortune of his horse slipping and falling between the shafts. Being unable to get the horse to its feet and finding no one around, since the people were all in the shelters, he went home on foot to get one of his sons to help him. When they got back, the road was still deserted, with the cart in the middle of it—but the horse had gone. He never expected to see it again between the shafts of any other cart.[3]

Throughout all this period, with the airfields steadily deteriorating despite incessant work on them by British soldiers and Maltese Pioneers, Malta still maintained its other important role as a stopover for aircraft flown from Britain to the Middle East. Night after night, landing often under incredibly difficult conditions, this steady traffic flowed through to build up vital reinforcements for the desert war. Not only fighting planes came this way. That merchant service of the air, the British Overseas Aircraft Corporation, flew in unarmed planes bringing essential supplies to the island and taking out sick and wounded so as to relieve the pressure on the local hospitals. Air Vice Marshal Lloyd, the air officer commanding in Malta at that time, had already signaled his superior in Cairo that the situation in Malta was becoming increasingly serious—continuous alerts, aircraft on the ground being damaged yet again while awaiting repair, and seventeen Wellingtons at that moment undergoing repair and therefore unserviceable for night bombing raids. The Hurricanes, as had always been known, were outclassed by the new Messerschmitts, and though they still fought on without respite, he had to report that the enemy was rapidly achieving air superiority. Lloyd made a most urgent request for some Spitfires. Almost at the same time Admiral Cunningham was reporting to the Chiefs of Staff that unless something was done about the air situation over Malta, and unless the military situation in Cyrenaica improved, it would seem useless to try to pass a convoy through to Malta. The reply he received was that Malta was of such importance as an impediment to the enemy's supply line and as an air staging post to the Middle East that almost any steps were justified to hold it and that "No consideration of risk to ships need deter you."

By this time Cunningham had few enough ships to risk, but the combination of his messages and the air vice marshal's as well as the governor's regular reports on island conditions did have some effect. First of all, a change in the responsibility for Malta, which had previously been divided among the governor and the naval and air commanders-in-chief in the Middle East, now placed all the troops in Malta under the Commander-in-Chief, Middle East. This meant that all three commanders-in-chief now shared the responsibility for the island, thus ensuring a high degree of cooperation among the three services. This was to be very clearly demonstrated in the matter of the next convoy that was run to the island. In addition, Air Ministry at last allocated Spitfires to Malta. Force H in Gibraltar, which still had no modern armored-deck carrier capable of being risked within range of the Axis air forces, was nevertheless augmented by two old prewar carriers, the *Argus* and *Eagle*. On March 7, from a position well clear of the central Mediterranean (slightly southeast of Majorca), fifteen Spitfires were flown into the island. All arrived safely.

An eyewitness remembered: "They came in waggling their wings as if to say 'O.K., boys, we're here.' " The war-torn Hurricanes were up above to cover their landing, forcing away Messerschmitt intruder patrols. The Maltese knew about their coming—probably long before the first shining distinctive shape of the world's most famous fighter was seen heading in from the sea over the island's cliffs. The arrival of the Spitfires had not passed unnoticed in Sicily, and that night all hell broke loose over the airfields. But the islanders had to wait three days before they first saw the new arrivals go into action. On March 10 the superiority that the Messerschmitts had held over the Hurricanes was established over them in their turn. Crowds were out in the streets and on the ramparts again, just as they had been in the early days, clapping and cheering at the dogfights overhead. Two Messerschmitts were shot down, there were two probables, and one damaged. Sixteen more Spitfires were flown in before the end of the month.

In the meantime Field Marshal Kesselring had ordered his chief of staff, Marshal Deichmann, to commence the final all-out onslaught on the twentieth. Everything was to be devoted to the suppression of Malta, regardless of cost in men or machines. *Fliegerkorps X* was even to be diverted from its duties in the eastern Mediterranean and the desert. The hope that the Spitfires brought the islanders was temporary and illusory.

23

Convoy

On the very day that had been set by Kesselring for the all-out blitz to begin, a convoy sailed from Alexandria destined for Malta. There were three fast freighters—the *Clan Campbell* (which had been knocked out of the February convoy by bomb damage), the *Pampas*, and the Norwegian *Talabot*—and the battle-seasoned *Breconshire,* a ship that was by now a household name in the island. The antiaircraft cruiser *Carlisle* and six destroyers formed the close escort, while Rear Admiral Vian in the *Cleopatra* together with two other light cruisers, the *Dido* and *Euryalus,* and four destroyers provided the covering force. In advance of the convoy Hunt-class destroyers carried out an antisubmarine sweep westward toward Tobruk. This type of mass-produced, small destroyer with its six high-angle, four-inch guns housed in twin mountings, and equipped with Oerlikons and pom-poms, was the backbone of many a wartime convoy. In the Mediterranean, where antiaircraft firepower was all-important, they proved their worth over and over again—and were indeed the mainstays of the convoy system.

As evidence of the close cooperation of the three armed services to facilitate the passage of these ships to the island, numerous diversions, feint attacks, and bombing raids were carried out. The army made an advance to threaten enemy airfields in the desert, the Long-Range Desert Group raided landing grounds far back behind the Axis lines, while the RAF attacked airfields in Crete and Cyrenaica to keep aircraft grounded. Fighter cover was provided as far out as possible over the Mediterranean, and the small port of Derna on the Benghazi bulge was attacked two nights running. These diversions all played their part in securing for the convoy and its covering force a most welcome and unusually trouble-free passage through Bomb Alley, the area between Crete and Cyrenaica. One of the Hunt-class destroyers on the sweep ahead of the convoy was torpedoed and sunk by a U-boat in daylight on March 20, but otherwise their progress toward Malta was undisturbed. It was not unobserved, however, for on the twenty-first Junkers transport aircraft flying on a regular route between Crete and Cyrenaica inevitably spotted the undulant wakes of the merchantmen on the clear sea and the crisp wave patterns of the destroyers zigzagging around them.

Not long after midnight on March 22 the Malta submarine P.36 on patrol off Taranto reported that destroyers and heavy ships were leaving the harbor. Admiral Iachino in his flagship *Littorio*—nine fifteen-inch guns and twelve six-inch guns—was putting to sea in company with two heavy eight-inch-gun cruisers, *Gorizia* and *Trento,* the light cruiser *Bande Nere,* and four destroyers. They headed southward to intercept the convoy.

At 8 A.M. on the morning of the twenty-second Admiral Vian was joined by the six-inch cruiser *Penelope* and the fleet destroyer *Legion* from Malta. His force was now complete, and the convoy with its close escort headed for Malta, about two hundred fifty miles distant—the Ionian Sea to the north and to the south the great gulf of Sirte that sweeps the Libyan shore. They were now beyond range of their fighter escort, heavy ships were out to intercept them, and air attacks might be expected to develop at any moment.

In earlier days Vian would certainly have received further sighting reports from air reconnaissance out of Malta—course, speed, and composition of the enemy force at sea. It is evidence of the overwhelming wave that was at that moment engulfing the island that no aircraft had been able to scramble into the sky to follow up the lone report of P.36. The air attacks began at 9:30 A.M., Italian torpedo bombers coming in against the convoy and its escorts. These were carried out at long range and, deterred by the escorts' firepower, were of no great concern, nor were similar high-level bombing attacks. It was later in the day that the Luftwaffe was to take over, and then the sporadic alarms of the morning would be quite forgotten. It was later reckoned that throughout that day one hundred and fifty aircraft in all came into action against the convoy.

Rear Admiral Vian was more concerned about the heavy surface forces that must now be steaming hard to cut him off. He had already made known to his captains that, come what might, "the convoy would proceed to Malta, even if surface forces made contact." The pattern of any action that might follow had been long rehearsed, under various circumstances of wind and weather and the constitution of whatever force might oppose them. Hardly perceived as yet by those about to engage in what was tactically the most brilliant naval action of the Second World War, the wind and the weather were about to take a hand. Far away in the desert a *khamsin* was blowing—the dust clouds rising in front of it—a typical spring *khamsin* that would reach Malta as a strong southeast sirocco.

Shadowing aircraft had never left the convoy out of sight throughout the day, and at 1:30 P.M. one of them dropped a line of flares across the ships' path. This could only be a signal to surface forces—which must therefore have been fairly close at hand. Forty minutes later the *Euryalus* reported four enemy ships in sight bearing northeast. This was earlier than Vian had expected. According to the prearranged plan, the convoy under its close escort immediately turned away to the southwest, while Vian's covering force turned north to lay a smoke screen. "It was blowing a strong breeze from the southeast, which was rapidly freshening, with a rough sea and moderate swell."[1] The wind laid the smoke clean athwart the advance line of the Italian ships.

The four ships sighted were two destroyers and the two heavy cruisers. Out of sight behind them were two more destroyers, the light cruiser *Bande Nere,* and then the *Littorio.* Vian headed his ships in five columns straight for the enemy, while the *Carlisle* and a Hunt-class destroyer laid a smoke screen across the wake of the convoy. At a range of thirty thousand yards the two Italian heavy cruisers opened fire, which Vian's ships of course were unable to return. The black, oily smoke laid by his advancing ships now blew under the strengthening southeasterly steadily in the direction of Malta to the northwest, effectively screening the convoy. After about fifteen minutes Vian's own ships came within range and opened fire.

There was a brief exchange, then the Italians turned away to the northwest. Signaling to the commander-in-chief "Enemy driven off," Vian headed back toward the convoy, which had by now come under heavy air attack from Junkers 88 and Stuka dive-bombers. The Italian withdrawal had been in response to an order from Admiral Iachino. Had the British precipitately followed, they would have come under the guns of the *Littorio*.

Because of its salinity, the Mediterranean "gets up" quickly, and the seas were already heavy. The small destroyers of the escort were washing down as they plunged alongside the convoy, the gun crews soaked through as they kept their weapons on the attacking aircraft, which in their turn were distracted by the breaking seas and the showers of spray that covered the ships. Even the director range finders and the bridges of the cruisers, some forty feet above the sea, were seething with high-flung spume. They were in a better shape than the Italians, though, for they were capable of radar-ranging, whereas the Italians only had optical range finders, which were being obscured as they steamed at full speed to cut off the convoy. At 4:48 P.M. the whole Italian force was once again in sight to the northeast; shortly afterward Vian signaled the commander-in-chief that he was in contact with an enemy battleship, four cruisers, and four destroyers. Even after all these years the feelings of Cunningham and his staff far away in Alexandria can be imagined—one broadside from the battleship was more than the firepower of all Vian's ships combined.[2] According to every canon of naval warfare the covering force should have been annihilated, the convoy and its lightly armed escorts picked off at leisure.

Vian moved out again toward the Italian ships, the thick smoke behind him rolling densely across the face of the sea, driven to the northwest and screening the opposing warships from one another. The Italians on the far side of it could not see their fall of shot, but they could not risk emerging through the dark curtain for fear of what they might find on the other side. Iachino was rightly unwilling to hazard his heavy ships through a smoke screen, on the far side of which enemy destroyers were waiting. On the other hand, the British destroyers and cruisers could emerge briefly from the rolling smoke, fire their guns or torpedoes, and then wheel back again into its protecting cover. They were at full risk during those brief moments when they were in view; in fact, Vian's *Cleopatra* was hit on the bridge by a six-inch shell, and her sister ship the *Euryalus* was near-missed by a fifteen-inch shell that peppered her with heavy splinters.

Admiral Iachino, wanting to get at the convoy without entering the smoke screen, had two options: He could either circle around the smoke to leeward by continuing on his southwest course, or he could drive to windward and come around the smoke at the point where it was thinning and clearing away. At this point the wind was now almost gale force, and if he turned to windward to come around the smoke, his ships would have to batter at high speed into a damaging sea. In addition, with his range finders blinded by spray and his ships possibly having suffered weather damage, he might emerge to find the British waiting. Thus, the Italian commander decided to keep his ships together in a body and work around the smoke screen to leeward from the west. Admiral Vian, however, having considered his counterpart's options, had come to the conclusion that the most seamanlike procedure would be to head to windward and come around the smoke where it was failing. Accordingly, he divided his cruisers and sent *Penelope* and *Euryalus* to keep an eye on the weather gauge.

At about 6 P.M. Admiral Iachino, having almost reached the fraying edges of the smoke to the northwest, decided to stand boldly for the south where the convoy must lie. For nearly half an hour Captain Micklethwait and Captain Poland, in command of the two fleet destroyer divisions, boldly moving out with their ships "like a pack of snapping terriers," raced through the edge of the smoke to fire their torpedoes. At times they seemed to move through a forest of shell splashes as they closed to within six thousand yards on their run-in, their 4.7-inch guns like toys against the eight-inch and fifteen-inch shells that were bursting around them. Two destroyers were badly damaged by near-misses from the *Littorio* during this part of the action, one having her speed reduced to sixteen knots and the other being temporarily crippled. (Both managed later to reach Malta safely.) The *Penelope* and *Euryalus* raced back to rejoin the action and also fired their torpedoes. There were no hits.[3] However, the combination of the British destroyers closing to six thousand yards to attack, a spread of torpedoes fired by the *Cleopatra* crossing the *Littorio*'s bows, and a hit on his flagship by a six-inch shell between his two after-turrets, caused Admiral Iachino to turn away. The wind was now gale force, and night was falling. Without radar, the Italian force wisely disengaged and headed northward. The Battle of Sirte was over.

Despite the many air attacks the convoy had undergone throughout the day, it was still unharmed, and its four ships, dispersed under the orders of Captain Hutchinson of the *Breconshire,* made their own ways at full speed for Malta. Their close escort divided to cover each ship and went with them, while Admiral Vian's force returned to Alexandria to receive a well-deserved welcome. Sirte was a tactical and moral victory that provided a welcome tonic to the British fleet in its reduced state and with increasingly bad news coming from the Far East. The ships that entered Alexandria harbor bore the marks not only of near-misses from heavy-caliber shells but also of damage from the southeasterly through which they had returned. Except for the two badly damaged destroyers, which had gone on to Malta, all ships were still functional.

As the Italians made for home, their morale in no way improved by the day's action, they suffered even more severely from the southeasterly as it roared up astern of them into the Gulf of Taranto. Evidence that Iachino had been wise not to steam at full speed into the gale in order to gain the weather gauge during the action was provided by the damage that his ships now suffered from this quartering southeasterly. Two destroyers foundered, the *Littorio* shipped thousands of tons of water, and the cruiser *Bande Nere* was sufficiently damaged to require dockyard repair at Spezia.[4] (To add insult to injury, as she was proceeding to this northern port, she was torpedoed and sunk by the submarine *Urge* out of Malta.)

If the Italians had not achieved their objective in sinking the convoy, they had nevertheless forced it to make a wide detour to the south, and this was sufficient to prevent the scattered ships from being able to reach Malta at first light on March 23, as had been planned. Malta was now under the full weight of the onslaught that had started on the twentieth and that had not let up despite the bad weather. As Air Vice Marshal Lloyd put it: "Every aeroplane in Sicily seemed to be flying round the island." Despite a lowering dawn aircraft immediately appeared looking for the convoy, and they soon found it. Laboring over the gray sea the ships kicked up masses of spray, and their torn wakes made them easily visible. Their escorts' ammunition had been so depleted during the previous day's attacks that their replies to attacking planes had to be severely limited to the planes that came in lowest and seemed most threatening. From dawn onward all ships came under attack, the veteran *Breconshire* being hit in the engine room and completely disabled when only eight miles off the island. The Norwegian *Talabot* and the *Pampas,* each accompanied by a destroyer, passed through the breakwater into Grand Harbour between 9 and 10 A.M. Despite the fact that there was an air raid in progress—dive-bombers swooping, bomb splashes all around, fighters above engaged in a fiery whirlwind—the people of Malta were out along the ramparts as the savaged ships came in. Both freighters had been near-missed many times, and the *Pampas* had actually received two direct hits from bombs that had failed to explode. The people stood, waving and cheering, as the ships moved down harbor. The fourth ship in the convoy, the *Clan Campbell,* was destined never to see Malta. Hit and disabled in the previous February convoy, then towed to Tobruk and repaired in Alexandria, on this occasion she received the *coup de grâce* some twenty miles offshore. Under air attack since daylight, she was sunk at 10:30 A.M. by a bomb in her engine room. A Hunt-class destroyer stood by her and saved many of those aboard, but the fleet destroyer *Legion* (which had taken part in the torpedo attack on the *Littorio* at six thousand yards) ran out of luck as she steamed to the rescue. Near-missed, she managed to reach Marsaxlokk, where she was beached; three days later, having effected temporary repairs, she made her way to Grand Harbour, where she was sunk in another dive-bombing raid.

The plight of the *Breconshire*—a name that had become synonymous with Malta to everyone in the Mediterranean fleet—was irremediable. All efforts to tow her to Grand Harbour were rendered hopeless by the weather and the depth of her damaged draught. Nearly wrecked on the shoal off Delimara Point in the southeast of the island, she was finally towed into Marsaxlokk where, after being hit yet again and set on fire, she finally rolled over and sank on March 27. Part of her bottom remained exposed, and some of her oil cargo was later saved by fitting valves to it.[5] The outnumbered Spitfires and Hurricanes operating from cratered and ceaselessly attacked airfields had not been able to save her, any more than they or the Malta barrage could save the *Talabot* and *Pampas*. Over three hundred bombers and fighters were ordered down from Sicily to see that no ship remained out of the hard-fought convoy.

The *Illustrious* blitz had been more or less one short action directed against one ship, but now the island and its inhabitants reeled under incessant air attack. On March 26 the *Talabot* was hit, fire broke out, and she had to be scuttled in Grand Harbour because of danger from ammunition aboard. The *Pampas* was also hit and settled on the bottom, with only two of her holds unflooded. Apart from the oil later salvaged from the *Breconshire,* only five thousand tons of cargo reached the island out of the twenty-six thousand tons that had been so hard fought for—in the teeth of the enemy fleet and of incessant air attack. Despite the brilliant naval action in the Gulf of Sirte, despite the subsequent courageous battles to get the convoy through to the island, sea power had been defeated by air power.

24

April Forty-two

To effect the passage of three ships out of four to Malta at that time was a supreme achievement, but to lose the three ships under the island's protection—two of them in Grand Harbour itself—was intolerable. Any claim that the air forces could still provide fighter cover was null and void. It was also very clear that there was something disastrously wrong with the system for unloading ships. The *Talabot* and *Pampas* had been berthed on March 23, but it was not until the twenty-sixth that they were both sunk. Malta was basically a lighterage port; there were no unloading quays for deep-draft ships, and even if there had been, they would by now have been a heap of rubble spilled into the harbor. Merchant ships normally made fast to buoys out in the harbor and were then unloaded by "dumb" lighters towed out to them by harbor tugs. Many of the lighters had now been sunk or damaged, as had the tugs; in fact, one of the causes for the delay in moving the *Breconshire* had been the lack of seagoing tugs capable of getting out to her in the weather that was blowing.

After the disaster of the *Talabot* and *Pampas,* which had lain at anchor for nearly twelve hours before systematic unloading had begun at all—men of the Cheshire Regiment coming forward to help the stevedores shift what they could of the cargo before the ships were sunk—it was clear that if Malta was to survive, more efficient and much faster methods of unloading would have to be devised. In addition, a tighter grip needed to be taken on the whole organization of the island, and above all something had to be done to get more Spitfire replacements. This, as would be seen, was useless in itself unless the organization for their reception and protection (until battleworthy and airborne) was as streamlined and improved as the harbor arrangements had to become.

How many of the inhabitants of today's large cities, who have to live with the acceptance—consciously or subconsciously—of the possibility of their nuclear devastation, can even comprehend, less than fifty years later, what the bombing of London was like in 1940? Uncomfortable thoughts are shuffled out of sight by most people in the same way that they tacitly accept their own mortality. How many of the inhabitants of modern cities would even be able to endure—in their skyscrapers, totally dependent upon an oil-fueled civilization—even one month of heavy bombing at the level of that experienced by London in 1940?

The whole of Malta occupies an area smaller than Greater London. During two months, March and April 1942, the tonnage of the bombs dropped on Malta was twice that dropped on London during the worst full year of the Blitz. During the first half of 1942 there fell such a rain of explosives on that small island that the survivors—children then, or young men and women—cannot even manage to reconstruct it in memory. "The survivors," as Stewart Perowne wrote in 1968 "are curiously reticent. Not that they are not willing to furnish any scrap of information which may be of use to a recorder. On the contrary, they will do all in their power to help him. But there is a psychological obstacle to be overcome. The time really is 'lost,' and it is a hard task to recover it. I feel that myself. After visiting a friend, and going over with him memories of the war, documents perhaps relating to his war duties, I come out into the bright sunlight of Malta at peace, hear the children at play, look down into Grand Harbour from which German and Italian tourists are coming up to admire and to purchase—I find it hard to realise that five minutes ago I was listening to tales of death and destruction, of ruin and survival in this same square, where the flowers grow and transistors howl."[1]

This is because time really is lost to all except a few artists of great stature (Conrad evokes the feeling of fearful disorganization and terror where others "who were there" cannot). As another great artist put it:

> Between the idea
> And the reality
> Between the motion
> And the Act
> Falls the Shadow.[2]

Facts, however little they can really convey, must make their statement. A computer age can recognize them, though not the emotion behind them. During March 1942 there were 275 air raids, 90 of them at night, and during April there were 283, of which 96 were at night. Malta suffered 154 days of continual day and night bombing, whereas the longest number of consecutive days on which London was raided only amounted to 57. In the blitz on the City of Coventry (which gave a temporary verb to the language, "to conventrate") it is reckoned that 260 tons of bombs were dropped. In contrast, 6,700 tons of bombs fell on the towns and installations around Grand Harbour during six weeks of March and April. In the latter month the airfields alone received twenty-seven times as great a weight of bombs as that which fell on Coventry in October 1940. In March 1942 *Fliegerkorps II* flew 4,927 sorties against the island; in April, when *Fliegerkorps X* joined in the attack, 9,599 sorties were flown. Between January 1 and July 24 there was only ONE period of twenty-four hours during which there was no raid.

Except for those who had earlier moved out to the country or had been evacuated (three thousand people had gone to the sister island of Gozo early in the war), the shelter life became the norm for all the inhabitants of Valletta and the Three Cities around Grand Harbour. It was hardly surprising that under the crowded conditions and with growing malnutrition as the siege went on, many health problems arose. Vitamin-deficiency diseases increased, particularly pellagra and ulcerative stomatitis, and there were also cases of rickets and scurvy (something normally unheard of). Trachoma and other eye diseases, not uncommon in an island of dust and blinding light, became widespread. Every type of tuberculosis spread unchecked, as might be expected in those living conditions, reaching a peak—along with everything else—during 1942. (Tuberculosis was also a major hazard for the communications personnel housed in the dank tunnels below Lascaris Bastion.) Typhoid, with all its compli-cations, had been on the increase since the beginning of the war but was to reach epidemic proportions during the summer of 1942. Ba-cillary and amoebic dysentery were its attendants.

All this was inevitable in view of the sanitary problems encoun-tered when masses of people were cooped up under such circum-stances, with house drains out of action and main sewers badly damaged by bombing. The disposal not only of human excreta but also of house refuse remained a problem until well after the siege was over. In the main shelters toilets were installed wherever possi-ble, although the pail system was generally used in houses and pri-vate shelters, where water was unavailable. Refugee centers and public shelters were supervised by hygiene officers, who organized ablution rooms and who saw to it that walls, floors, and beds were regularly sprayed with disinfectants and insecticides.

The typhoid epidemic of 1942 started after sewage escaped from fractured sewers and began infecting cultivated land; in addition, in some areas crude sewage was used to irrigate the fields. Lice, fleas, and bedbugs were common, but scabies was perhaps the worst med-ical plague. Benzyl benzoate for the treatment of scabies was often unattainable or at best in short supply, so the mites spread through-out the island, even among those who were not shelter-dwellers. Many people developed septic sores from scratching, and the combi-nation of acute hunger with the itching of scabies has been de-scribed by survivors as their most permanent memory of the siege.

All these factors, combined with permanent nerve-strain and anx-iety, might have been expected to lead to a great increase in nervous breakdowns and mental illness. Contrary to the expectation of the psychiatrists this was not so, and the behavior of the besieged in Malta was a surprise to the practitioners of this somewhat ambigu-ous branch of medical science. "Before the opening of hostilities it was anticipated that the people would react to the horror and havoc of modern warfare in an exaggerated and abnormal manner. It was consequently forecast that the number of psychiatric casualties would be high and beds for 'cases of war neuroses and psychoses' were prepared in special wards at the Mental Hospital at Attard. Subsequent experience, however, showed that this precaution was unnecessary because the factors that were regarded as being preci-pitants of mental illness did not produce the expected baleful effects on the population. Indeed anxiety for one's personal safety, sudden bereavements, the disruption of family life and the presence of material discomforts and food privation did not react unfavourably on the mental health of the population. Panic and hysteria were absent. A most remarkable feature was the fact that admission to the mental hospital fell to 138 in 1942 from the pre-war figure of 169 in 1939."[3]

As in other bombed cities during the war, the inhabitants of this besieged island adjusted themselves to the increased hazards of living. They had been, in the horticultural term, "hardened off" by the first months of the Italian bombing, so that when the Germans unleashed the full fury of modern war, they were already resistant. (It is a matter for speculation as to what might have been the effect if the Luftwaffe had arrived in force in the summer of 1940.) It is a curious fact, which has been remarked on before, that although the Germans did infinitely the greatest harm to Malta and its life, the islanders' deepest hatred of the people was always directed against the Italians. Perhaps the Germans were too remote, too unknown a quantity, whereas the Italians had broken some familiar bond. In general, people lived only for the day, and a deep-rooted Mediterranean fatalism, older by far even than the Catholic Church, underlay a superficial, reckless gaiety that all newcomers to the scene remarked upon.

Wartime love affairs were not uncommon, and in the atmosphere of *carpe diem* that prevailed it would have been abnormal if they had not been. Yet, in so old-fashioned a society, strictly controlled by the authoritarian Church, such liaisons were far fewer than might have been expected or than were commonplace in, say, a bombed city in western Europe. For one thing, privacy was almost unobtainable; for another, poor diet, physical fatigue, and sleepless nights under bombardment were hardly conducive to sexual desire. Contraceptives were unknown in so strongly Catholic a society, except to those who had deliberately or accidentally fallen outside the faith, and these—except at the level of Strait Street "girls"—were comparatively few.

The Maltese are a handsome race, and the young women—before pregnancies, a starch diet, and a hot climate have swollen them into images of the mother goddess—are exceptionally beautiful. They had a good motive to want to marry British servicemen, because this would bring a guaranteed marriage allowance and, later, a family allowance—benefits unknown in their own society. Such marriages were rejected as far as possible by the British authorities because they knew from peacetime experience how few of them lasted. Within a year or two in servicemen's married quarters back in unfamiliar, gray, and rainy Britain, the wives sought the warmth of their island again, their family and familiar surroundings, and departed together with the children. Being Catholic, there could be no question of divorce.

At every level of Maltese society the strictest distinction was made between "good" and "bad" women, the latter being socially ostracized and, if of working class stock, more or less driven into prostitution. Naturally endemic in any seaport, prostitution had been well known in Malta for many centuries. Indeed, as early as 1565 special arrangements were made to transport the island's prostitutes to Sicily before the siege began. A British submarine captain, arriving on the island for the first time in 1942 and naturally ignorant of the prevailing social distinctions, expressed some wonder at the lack of shoreside romance: "Surprisingly, perhaps, there was little fraternising between the lads and the local beauties, although one or two, after filling themselves with lunatic's broth in a boiled-oil shop did use their rations for a purpose regulations never intended. In the main, however, *l'amour* was kept on a vicarious level by watching highly professional clinches on the ten-year-old films shown at the local cinema."[4]

By April 1942 the submariners on Manoel Island hardly got ashore at all, in the sense of into Malta or Valletta itself. The island's airfields were so damaged that on some occasions not a single plane could get into the air, and often only six fighters were airworthy. To Field Marshal Kesselring it naturally seemed that the first part of his operational plan had been achieved, so that the second—the destruction of all naval ships and harbor installations—could now be pursued. For nearly two months the defense of the island had rested almost entirely on the guns. The British Royal Artillery and the Royal Malta Artillery were stretched as never before by raiders whose confidence was such that for a time they seemed to ignore the losses that they were daily sustaining.

The submarine base was obviously a principal target and, far from being able to find girls ashore or get drunk in "boiled-oil" shops, more often than not the crews of the submarines were compelled either to stay on Manoel Island or aboard their submarines, lying submerged in the harbor. To come in from long days on patrol, having been in action and probably depth-charged on more than one occasion, and then to find that far from there being any rest or recreation one was likely to be confined to an islet under constant bombing attack or serving a duty-spell in one's boat lying on the bottom and constantly being shaken by exploding bombs, was not conducive to a high state of morale. Now was the time when submarine pens cut deep into the rock of Marsamuscetto would have served their purpose. (These had often been discussed before the war, but nothing was ever done about them.) Later, when Fortress Europe came under attack, Hitler was to see that such bomb-proof submarine pens were built for his U-boats, but then the Germans had the advantage of all the technology and labor force of Europe behind them. The submarines *Unbeaten* and *P.36* were both badly damaged while lying submerged off Manoel, their crews managing to escape off the bottom. The minelaying submarine *Pandora*—fortunately, after she had delivered her essential supplies—was caught on the surface and sunk by two direct hits. The *P.39*, badly damaged by a near-miss, was towed to the dockyard for repair, where she was blown apart by a bomb exploding underneath her. A Greek submarine operating out of Malta was also sunk by bombing, and the Polish *Sokol* was so badly damaged that she had to be sent to Gibraltar for repair. It was during April that it became known that Wanklyn and his legendary *Upholder* had been lost with all hands, and a fortnight later her sister ship the *Urge* was mined and sank off the island.

The mining by aircraft and E-boats had now reached such proportions that Malta was practically unapproachable, surrounded as it was by every known type of mine. So long as a passage could be swept through these minefields, Captain Simpson, under whose direction the 10th Flotilla had achieved its astonishing record, had been unwilling to withdraw his vessels. He had pointed out that the flotilla was the only unit left that was able to take offensive action against the enemy's supply lines, and that it "was the only remaining means of preventing the enemy from bombarding Malta by heavy surface forces . . ." By the end of April, however, he was forced to agree to withdrawal because the few minesweepers left in Malta (all damaged) could no longer keep the approaches clear. It was high time. The submarine crews were getting practically no rest between patrols, servicing the boats was almost impossible, and the current losses from mines and bombing could no longer be sustained.

Early in May, when the last of the submarines was withdrawn, Malta was undeniably on its own. The surface ships had begun to leave after the March convoy, when it had become apparent that no corner of Grand Harbour was safe from air attack, the defensive barrage notwithstanding. The cruiser *Aurora* and the Hunt-class destroyer *Avon Vale,* both rapidly patched up from bomb damage, had sailed for Gibraltar. The destroyer *Gallant,* so crippled that she could not be moved, was laid up alongside a quay to be cannibalized for spares, fittings, and metal. The destroyer *Kingston,* overturned by bombing while in dry dock, was later towed to St. Paul's Bay and used as a blockship in the channel between St. Paul's Island and the mainland.

The only ship left in Malta from Force K, the cruiser *Penelope,* survived in an almost miraculous fashion. Damaged and under repair in dry dock, she was attacked time and time again, much as the *Illustrious* had been. Firing her twin four-inch guns while in dock (to the extent of wearing them out by the expenditure of sixty-five hundred rounds in two weeks), she was patched up and patched up again. Finally, on the night of April 28, she managed to slip away and reach Gibraltar. Nicknamed H.M.S. *Pepperpot* for the hundreds of wooden plugs that sprouted from splinter holes in her hull, the *Penelope* had earned her battle honors—curiously enough, in the same place as a predecessor of her name. In 1799 the frigate *Penelope,* one of Nelson's blockading squadron off Valletta, had shot away the main and mizzen topmasts of the eighty-gun battleship *Guillaume Tell,* thus leading to the capture of this last French survivor of the Battle of the Nile.

"April is the cruellest month . . ." The poet's words, untrue in Malta throughout all previous centuries, were accurate indeed in 1942. Wildflowers might still be found on the rocky uplands, but everywhere else there was no spring. A pall of dust and smoke compounded of pulverized buildings, exploding dumps, gunfire, burning planes, and collapsing walls hung over the whole island. Whatever wind was prevailing, a huge yellow dust cloud could always be seen moving away on the lee side of Malta. Sullying the sea, it wavered and turned slowly like a giant spinning-top about to fall.

25

A Volcano in Eruption

In the summer of 1565 Francisco Balbi di Correggio had written that "the island was like a volcano spouting fire. When all of the guns fired simultaneously, the noise and the concussion were such that it seemed as if the end of the world was coming. To show you just how terrible was the volume of noise, it could be clearly heard in Syracuse and even in Catania, one hundred and twenty miles from Malta." In the spring and the summer of 1942 the concatenation of the guns and the bombs, both by day and night, sounded like a permanent thunderstorm rolling away to the south of Sicily. The disruption of the airfields was such, and the state of the few remaining aircraft so dilapidated, that there were several days in April when no fighters at all were airborne in the face of the attackers from Sicily.

"For two months during Malta's long air siege, it was antiaircraft guns alone which bore the brunt of the attack." British gunners together with some four thousand Maltese were ceaselessly engaged at heavy, light, and machine-gun posts all over the island, from the airfields and main defenses around Valletta and Grand Harbour to outposts on the coast and Corradino Heights overlooking the Marsa. In February the heavy guns had to be rationed to only three rounds per raid (firing pointer shots to indicate to the other gunners the direction of the approaching aircraft), and even the invaluable all-purpose Bofor's guns had to be restricted so that no more than 50 percent could be in action at any one time—always excluding those protecting any ships in harbor or specially sited for airfield defense.

By mid-April, when no convoy could be expected, the situation was so bad that both light and heavy antiaircraft guns were limited to fifteen rounds per gun per day. The choice of target out of the dozens presented during a typical raid had to be made with the greatest care before a single round was fired. For the fighter planes that got aloft and were either damaged or had run out of ammunition, a special "safe area" was established over Ta Qali airfield below Mdina: As soon as a Hurricane or Spitfire came into sight low over this area, it was given full coverage by the guns massed around. As it became apparent that the airfields were almost neutralized, the brunt of the attack was borne by Manoel Island and Grand Harbour. Until the submarines themselves were withdrawn, their base naturally became the main target for attack. ". . . it was the Battle of the Guns. There was no gun position more bombed or in a more exposed position than an Manoel Island. I remember once seeing an intensive attack put in against this gun position which protected the submarine base. The bombs were dropped with great accuracy, and a thousand-pounder scored a direct hit on one of the guns. But even as it burst and the whole area seemed to be covered with black smoke I saw four red flashes burst through the haze. It was the last flash of the gun that was hit, but the other three carried on without cessation or hesitation until "the attack was over."[1] During April 102 enemy aircraft were certified destroyed by the guns, and about half this number by fighter aircraft. On April 10 Kesselring wrote: "The serial attack on Malta has, I feel, eliminated Malta as a naval base . . . I intend to carry on with the attack until April 20."

Only one thing, it was felt, could enable the island to carry on any longer—the delivery of more Spitfires. Air Vice Marshal Lloyd wrote: "Malta's need is for Spitfires, Spitfires, and yet more Spitfires." He sent a distinguished pilot, Wing Commander Gracie, back to Britain to tell the authorities at firsthand what the situation was like. Emphasis has earlier been laid on the difficulty of people understanding the conditions of the siege nearly half a century later, but the fact that it needed a fighter pilot straight from the battle to explain to the authorities in London (even though they were in the heart of the war themselves) shows the almost unimaginable conditions in Malta.

The result of all this pressure, and of Governor Dobbie's ceaseless efforts to draw attention to the situation, was a message sent by Winston Churchill to President Roosevelt. Spitfires were indeed available in Britain, but there were no British carriers seaworthy at that moment with the capability of carrying and flying them off. Churchill wrote: "Air attack on Malta is very heavy. There are now in Sicily about 400 German and 200 Italian fighters and bombers. . . . Would you be willing to allow your carrier *Wasp* to do one of these [air ferry] trips, provided details are satisfactorily agreed between the Naval Staffs? With her broad lifts, capacity and length we estimate that *Wasp* could take fifty or more Spitfires. . . ."

Roosevelt replied: "Admiral King will advise Admiral Poland that *Wasp* is at your disposal as you request." This was a good example of the top-level accord between Churchill and Roosevelt and evidence that the latter must have applied the full weight of presidential authority to his request, for Admiral Ernest J. King, U.S.N., had no great love of the British. As Admiral Cunningham was to write later about events in North Africa: "King always had a rooted antipathy to placing United States forces under British command." Furthermore, this operation involving the *Wasp* meant that British planes would be flying off a U.S. aircraft carrier, and the *Wasp* herself would be the first American warship to enter the European theater of war on what amounted to a combat mission. Early in April she sailed up the River Clyde, and preparations went ahead for embarking forty-seven Spitfires. On April 14 the *Wasp* with her precious cargo and her escort sailed south for Gibraltar.

On April 15 King George VI made the unique gesture of awarding the George Cross to the island of Malta—the highest honor, equivalent to the Victoria Cross in military terms, that was his to bestow. The king's citation was announced by Governor Dobbie: "To honour her brave people I award the George Cross to the island fortress of Malta, to bear witness to a heroism and devotion that will long be famous in history.—George R.I."

Medals seem to have little meaning in peacetime, except in the marketplace, but in times of war they possess a special aura, and even to the most cynical or disparaging, their statement remains clear: "I was there—at the sharp end." This acknowledgment by the king that the fight being put up by the island and its people was indeed understood and appreciated did at that moment have an appreciable effect on morale.[2] Many are enduring in battle, some are cowardly, a few outstandingly brave, but only a handful of the few ever receive any acknowledgment. After that earlier Great Siege: "Honours were showered upon Grand Master La Valette by all the kingdoms of Europe. Philip II sent him a jewelled sword and poniard, the hilts of enamelled gold set with pearls and facetted diamonds. *Plus quam valor valet Valette* ran the punning device." But this was the first time that the Maltese people had ever received a medal.

On April 19 the U.S.S. *Wasp* was moving through the Mediterranean to her flying-off position southeast of Majorca, and at dawn the next day the first of her Spitfires climbed into the sky and headed for Malta. Unattacked and apparently unobserved, the *Wasp* turned back for Gibraltar. Out of forty-seven planes that had been embarked forty-six were to reach Malta safely. Unfortunately, however, unlike the *Wasp,* they had been observed.

The recollections of one of the pilots, Flight Lieutenant D. Barnham, echo those of many others who made similar flights during the war: "The clouds have disappeared now. Empty sea stretches in all directions; but soon a disturbance of colour on the horizon grows steadily nearer. From navigational logic it's just where I expected it to be. We change formation as two islands, like autumn leaves floating in the water, grow larger and larger. The steep cliffs of the smaller and nearer, which must be Gozo with Malta lying beyond it, rush towards us. White walls crinkle a hilltop. The small fields are yellow. Blue water in front of my propeller and, as we cross the channel between the two islands, I can see waves breaking on the sunlit rocks ahead. Then we are leaping inland over the island of Malta."[3]

One after another the planes upon which so many hopes were based came in to land, and one after another they were destroyed. When they left the *Wasp,* American Martlet fighters had circled the air above the carrier, providing protection that turned out to be unneeded, but when they came to touch down in the heart of the volcano, there was hardly a plane in the sky to cover them. Picked up by German radar on Sicily, they were no more than fat pigeons to be seized on the ground by the swarm of fighters, fighter-bombers, and dive-bombers that now descended. On that first day over three hundred planes flew missions down from Sicily. Within seventy-two hours not one of those Spitfires was airworthy. Most had been destroyed on the ground within an hour or so of touching down.

The causes of this disaster were several, but principally it was the condition to which the airfields had been reduced after more than two months of almost continuous bombing. Stone bays, or pens, in which to park an aircraft the moment that it landed, were broken down, runways were heavily cratered, antiaircraft defenses were overwhelmed, and crash tenders and gasoline tanks and pumps destroyed. There was the added fact that repair facilities were inadequate, technicians worked off their feet, and workshops themselves bombed out of existence. Furthermore, although the ground crews and repair specialists were familiar enough with Hurricanes after years of working on them and were expert at cannibalizing crashed machines and using the spares, or even fabricating their own from bits and pieces of scrap, they were more or less completely untrained in the Spitfire. As the Air Officer Commanding wrote later: "I also wanted at least 200 spare engines. We couldn't run to an aircraft factory for help (the few Hurricane spares we had were useless), and the only answer was another convoy by sea."

A successful operation had ended in total failure, and it was not difficult for those outside the battlefield to point to a great similarity between this new disaster and the one that had befallen the March convoy. On both occasions the supplies had reached the island, but nearly all had been lost through the inability of the recipients to protect them or to get them safely unloaded. The fact was that everything in the island—communications, fuel supplies, transport, essential stores—was breaking down or worn out. Malta had become to a great degree what was implied by the term often used for individuals in those days—"bomb-happy." Akin to the state known as shell shock in the trenches of the First World War, it was not so much a failure of nerve as a deadening of nerve, almost an indifference and, indeed, an inability to concentrate effectively. Inadequate diet, lack of sleep, and permanent tension through bombing had taken their toll. Quite often deafness had resulted from bomb blast or gun fire. Both the garrison and the islanders were more or less reduced to a zombielike state: Work was still somehow carried out, but the people lacked the energy, the drive, and the initiative that comes with physical health.

The destruction of the Spitfires and the daily evidence that Malta was offering almost no opposition, lying supine under the raids, gave Field Marshal Kesselring good reason to think that his objective was attained. The submarines had been withdrawn from the island, the bomber squadrons had long gone (the British could not even protect their airfields), and no surface ships had been in evidence for many weeks. Malta could therefore be termed "neutralized." Demands were being made on him for the transfer of some of *Luftflotte 2* to the Russian front (now opening again after a winter that had savagely surprised the Germans), and more planes were also needed in the desert, where Rommel's Operation Theseus was scheduled to begin toward the end of May. Convoys were passing easily through to North Africa, and reserves of fuel and armor were building up, now that no submarines, surface ships, bombers, or torpedo aircraft operated out of Malta.

After Rommel achieved success in the desert, Operation Hercules could take place, but already it had begun to look as if it would not be needed. Kesselring was confident, but there were some doubts, particularly among the Italians, that the island was as harmless as it appeared. They feared its recuperative powers and, judging from the activities of the antiaircraft guns and searchlights during their night raids, they reckoned that it was still far from safe to risk an invasion. They could hardly believe the propaganda broadcast over their own radio at the time of the award of the George Cross: "This is but one more preposterous deception by the British Government. Had not our unfortunate Maltese brethren been under the heel of British domination, which is being forced on them under the threat of guns and bayonets, we have no doubt as to how the Maltese would behave." They remembered the reception that the Maltese had accorded their surface forces off Valletta, and they feared that iron-bound rocky coast.

At the very moment when for every possible reason it seemed as if the island would be unable to hold out much longer, inexplicably— to the defenders—the pressure began to ease. "One afternoon when the sirens went, instead of low-flying Junkers, five "Black Crows"— as the gunners called the multiengined Italian bombers—appeared. They flew at an immense height in precise formation, just as they had flown before the Luftwaffe took over. The Germans had had to transfer some of their strength to other fronts; they also needed time for resting and servicing their aircraft. On 29th April there were 220 sorties against the island; on 30th April there were only sixty-eight. These attacks were directed mainly against stores, lines of communication and civilian targets."[4]

Throughout all these weeks the army had been working along

with civil defense and in every variety of activity to try and keep the island operational. Among their many tasks had been constant labor on the airfields—the boring, frightening (constantly under attack), and repetitious work of filling in bomb craters, rebuilding aircraft pens around the fields, and helping the gunners patch up the defenses of their heavily bombed positions on the perimeter. The soldiers and the Maltese Pioneers were the men-of-all-work of the island, and now their efforts were especially devoted to ensuring that the next delivery of Spitfires did not meet the same fate as the last. Along the Safi strip, a kind of taxiway designed to move aircraft between Luqa and the airfield at Hal Far (largely built by the army), at Luqa itself, and at Hal Far and Ta Qali, the soldiers worked day and night to repair damage and to build new dispersal pens. Together with the air force ground staff they had to see that each one of these pens was a completely self-contained unit, where a recently arrived Spitfire could be made 100 percent ready for combat within a matter of minutes. Wing Commander Gracie, who had been sent back to London to explain the immediate need for fighters on the island and who had himself flown the first Spitfire off the *Wasp*, was in charge of the reception committee preparing for the next arrivals.

The easing of the air offensive happened at just the right time for the defenders—a reminder, perhaps, to all who are engaged in besieging a fortress that the time to slacken one's fire is not five minutes to midnight, nor midnight itself, but five past. (Kesselring, perhaps through force of circumstances, had made exactly the same mistake as had Mustapha Pasha in September 1565, when "the daily slackening of the Turkish fire . . . had raised the defenders' spirits at a moment when all had been resigned to death.") Although no one could have foretold it during the hot summer of starvation that lay ahead—the worst months, as they were to seem to many, of the whole war—the tide had lipped as far up the rock as it would go. It would hang there for a long time, seemingly irreversible, before its slow retreat would be noticed by the survivors, whose handholds on the slippery rock would seem at that time to become daily more tenuous—even as an outside observer could see that they were saved.

26

A Change of Balance

It was a spring of many changes. The first and greatest was hardly even observed by most—the slight relaxation of the Luftwaffe bombing of the island. The second, which was felt by all, was the departure early in April of Admiral Cunningham to Washington, to head the Admiralty delegation there and to be the representative of the First Sea Lord on the Combined Chiefs of Staff. No more suitable man could have been chosen for this all-important role in Anglo-American cooperation, which was to lead to the winning of the war.

Cunningham himself was loath to go, particularly since he was leaving the Mediterranean at a time when his fleet was practically nonexistent. Like Nelson, he was "an old Mediterranean man," and he had fought, usually with an outnumbered fleet, a sequence of battles that put him in the same class as his great predecessor. He had also conducted a whole maritime strategy that the latter had never been called on to do. He had known this sea as a young commander in destroyers during the First World War, had served in it in many capacities between the wars, and had established himself in the past three years as the greatest fighting admiral that Britain had had since the victor of the Battle of the Nile. A quiet Scot with a bourgeois domestic life, he was in many ways the antithesis of his famous predecessor, but it is certain that if anyone had benefited by reading Southey's *Life of Nelson,* it was he and not his Italian opponents. Apart from being an extremely skillful seaman, he was conversant with modern techniques but had avoided the trap of becoming enmeshed in technicalities. An able administrator, he was also more than able to cope with the politico-strategic problems that engaged so much of the time of a modern commander-in-chief.

Like Nelson himself (and many other great commanders as far back as Drake), Cunningham had learned the business of war in small ships when young, but he had not become imprisoned within that panache of youth and had evolved into one of the most mature and greatest sea captains of all time. He had known Malta in his youth, middle years, and as commander-in-chief, and one of his last messages before relinquishing his command was directed to the Vice Admiral, Malta: "The record has been magnificent, and I heartily thank every officer and man who has taken part, not forgetting those who have had the less spectacular, but none the less exacting task of maintaining and bringing back into action our ships and aircraft to the discomfiture of the enemy. . . . The very extent of the success of the forces based on Malta has led to a ceaseless battering of the fortress, but one has only to think of the air effort that the enemy is diverting to this purpose to realize that this is but another of the services that Malta is rendering.[1]

He was succeeded by Admiral Sir Henry Harwood, the victor of the Battle of the River Plate, a dogged commander whose persistency would be tested to the utmost in the coming months. Curiously enough, although Cunningham suspected that he would probably never see the Mediterranean again, he was to return some seven months later to find that the tide had indeed turned. This great reversal of affairs had been largely brought about by Cunningham and the men who served under him in the hard and sometimes seemingly hopeless years 1940–1942.

The third main change, and one of profound importance to everyone in Malta, came on May 8, when General Sir William Dobbie relinquished his position as governor of the island to General the Viscount Gort V.C.[2] Until then Lord Gort had been governor of Gibraltar, and prior to that he was the general who had managed to salvage the army during the desperate days of Dunkirk. In his farewell address to the people of Malta the Cromwellian Dobbie thanked them for all their kindness to him and his family during recent years, then commended them to "put your trust in Almighty God and seek to honour Him in all your ways." Dobbie was not only physically ill but was as worn out as the island. He had been there since the beginning and had become in many people's eyes the embodiment of the same virtues that had once been displayed by the great La Valette. His involvement with the people had been total, as many accounts confirm, and it was to some extent this identification with the sufferings of the ordinary Maltese that had exhausted him. His successor arrived comparatively fresh from Gibraltar upon a worn-out garrison and people much in need of reinvigoration.

Gort's reputation as a fighting man was confirmed by an array of medals that few could match. The holder of Britain's highest award, the Victoria Cross (from the First World War), the Distinguished Service Order, the Military Cross, and nine Mentions in Despatches, John Standish Surtees Prendergast Vereker, sixth Viscount Gort, arrived at the nadir of the island's fortunes. By his example and simple decency Dobbie had held the morale of the island together through the worst of times, whereas Gort, arriving just before the upturn began, was with the aid of his fiery and self-disciplined nature to see it to the moment when the pale light in the east had become recognizable as the dawn.

General Dobbie did not know, as he left, that within twenty-four hours a successful second mission by the *Wasp* and the *Eagle* would deliver sixty-one Spitfires to the island. These aircraft were not destroyed on landing and soon began to turn the balance once more in favor of Malta's survival. The depression that had afflicted the whole island, from servicemen to the inhabitants of remote villages, after the loss of the *Wasp*'s first Spitfires was lifted. From 1 A.M. onward on May 9 sixty-one Spitfires out of sixty-four that had been embarked flew in from the two carriers lying invisible far to the west. A typical May morning in that part of the sea, cool, but with some dew presaging temperatures in the seventies at midday, heralded their arrival—an engine sound now familiar, recognized as friendly, coming in over the cliffs from the sea. This time there were no mistakes, no incompetence due to fatigue, and no unpreparedness due to "bomb-happy" exhaustion.

"The turn-around of the Spitfires was accomplished in six minutes in some cases on 9th. May, so thoroughly rehearsed were the arrangements. When the enemy came to bomb them on the ground, he was met and attacked by them in the air. The infantry contributed essential manpower to carry out this plan. Each Spitfire was met and directed by a runner to a dispersal pen, which was a self-supporting unit. Owing to the shortage of petrol bowsers and the number of aircraft to be refuelled simultaneously, a supply of petrol was put up in tins for refuelling by hand. These tins, together with oil, glycol, and ammunition, were waiting in each pen. Two airmen, assisted by soldiers, fell upon each Spitfire as it reached the pen. The moment their work was done a Malta pilot took over the machine, though in some cases newly arrived pilots went straight into action."[3]

Throughout that day the pilots, ground crews, and relief pilots lived in their pens. Food and drink were brought to them, while dispatch riders and signalmen maintained communications between the widely dispersed aircraft. So fast was the turnaround that many of the Messerschmitt 109s that had taken off from Sicily the moment the presence of the British aircraft had been detected did not find sitting ducks, as before, but alert hawks already circling in the sky above them. One of the British pilots later described how, after arriving at Ta Qali, "I immediately removed my kit, and the machine was rearmed and refuelled. I landed during a raid and four 109s tried to shoot me up. Soon after landing the airfield was bombed but without much damage done." During that day there were nine air raids, but the results were very different from those of the previous raids. By nightfall eight enemy planes had been confirmed destroyed as well as eight probables (disappeared over the sea and therefore unrecorded); many others were reported heading for Sicily damaged. The same pilot concluded his memories of that first day: "The tempo of life here is just indescribable. The morale of all is magnificent—pilots, ground crews and army, but it is certainly tough. The bombing is continuous on and off all day . . . living conditions, sleep, food and all the ordinary standards of life have gone by the board. It all makes the Battle of Britain and fighter sweeps seem like child's play in comparison, but it is certainly history in the making, and nowhere is there aerial warfare to compare with this."[4]

Everything built up to a climax with the arrival at dawn the following day of the fast minelayer H.M.S. *Welshman* from Gibraltar. Lord Gort bringing fresh enthusiasm and initiative from the top, the Spitfires bringing hope at a moment when it had become thin indeed, and the *Welshman* bringing much-needed supplies (ammunition, spare engines, spare air crews, many other small essentials, as well as several tons of mail for the garrison)—all had arrived at more or less the same time. The combination acted somewhat like a booster shot in the arm to a patient hovering between life and death.

Something else that the *Welshman* brought with her was a consignment of chemical smoke-making compound for use over the harbor when ships were unloading. Drums of this chemical, generating a white haze so thick that some of the attacking pilots later reported "fog over Grand Harbour," were in use within a short time of the ship's arrival. As with the Spitfires, so with the *Welshman*—there was no repetition of the *Talabot* and *Pampas* disaster. Army teams were waiting at her berth before the ship had even entered the harbor, and unloading by crane and human chain began the moment that her lines were ashore. (A jetty had been specially cleared for her reception in French Creek, and a dense antiaircraft barrage—"a cone of steel"—had been designed to cover the whole area.)

When the inevitable raids developed—the heaviest coming shortly before 11 A.M. with twenty Stukas and ten Junkers 88s escorted by Messerschmitt fighters—the three services were all in a combined operation at the same moment. The army gunners took over, as it were, from the army stevedoring parties, the *Welshman*'s crew were at their guns, and the RAF in Hurricanes and Spitfires were in the sky above. The attacking planes were forced to bomb more or less blind through the smoke, but even so the *Welshman* was dangerously near-missed, so that large lumps of her unloading jetty were blown onto the ship. By luck or (as the devout would have said) through the power of prayer, the ship was never hit during her day in harbor. All her stores were safely unloaded and swiftly transported by prearranged routes to safety. That same evening, preceded by the last operational minesweeper in Malta, H.M.S. *Welshman* left for Gibraltar, damaged from her fourteen-hour stay in the most dangerous harbor in the world, but with her mission accomplished and still able to steam at over thirty knots. During the course of the day's air battles, in which Spitfires flew 110 sorties and the Hurricanes fifteen, fifteen of the attackers were destroyed by aircraft and eight by the guns, with many probables. Only three Spitfires were lost.

Before the *Welshman* left Grand Harbour she refueled, taking on only three hundred tons of oil. Her captain reckoned that would be enough with what he already had to see him back to the western end of the Mediterranean. There were then only two thousand tons remaining in the island's underground bunkers. The shortage of oil, like the shortage of food, was not something that could be alleviated by the upsurge in morale. Unless a large convoy could be brought into the island before the end of June, Kesselring's optimistic reported to Berlin on May 10 that "the neutralization of Malta is complete" would be justified. Cutting off supplies of food and oil would accomplish what the sustained blitz of the past three months had failed to do.

On an island like Malta the pattern of events can often be seen more accurately than in the greater world because it is a microcosm. Things present, as in a test tube to the trained observer's eye, evidence of what may be expected under given conditions on a world-wide scale. In 1942 Malta exemplified the plight of an oil-dependent society when it is cut off from its essential source of energy. Even the crane, the one survivor on the jetty where the *Welshman* had been unloaded, was dependent on power generated by oil. Most of the island's wells could no longer be pumped because of shortage of oil. Other public utilities were also powered by oil. The constant cuts in electricity were caused not only by cables being destroyed by bombing but also by the rationing of fuel. Even the electric power necessary for hospitals was affected. In fact, the toll of war was being increasingly felt in the shortage of almost everything needed by surgeons and nursing staff working in dreadful conditions with too many patients to every ward.

Transportation on Malta had long been reduced to a mockery. Service transport had been severely rationed (one of Lord Gort's immediately visible messages to the community was his using a bicycle instead of the governor-general's official car when on his rounds of Valletta), and the whole island was coming to a halt. Such tugs and small-powered craft as remained unsunk needed oil to carry out necessary harbor work, as did minesweepers (when there was more than one operational). Without minesweepers no convoy could get into the harbor, and the escorts that might accompany any convoy would need refueling before making their way back to Alexandria or Gibraltar.

The Malta War Diary, which states that subsequent to the arrival of the Spitfires "such casualties were inflicted on the enemy that daylight raiding was brought to an abrupt end," erred as gravely in its optimism as did Field Marshal Kesselring in his. Although daylight raids did indeed decrease, particularly those on Grand Harbour (where there was almost nothing left to bomb), the conditions in which the people lived during the month of May were in many respects worse than those they had endured in April and March. Hunger and disease were by now taking their toll, although no one died of starvation. The communal feeding kitchens (later renamed victory kitchens), the first of which had been established in January, grew in number until in May there were some forty of them in twenty-three different localities. These facilities provided for all who were registered with them either "one hot dish consisting of meat and vegetable stew" *(kawlata)* or a meatless soup *(minestra)*. There was only one meal per day, which might be taken either at midday or in the evening. Many of those without homes or without cooking facilities, as well as the unemployed or the unemployable, made regular use of these kitchens, although the quality and the quantity of the food were always a major source of complaint. Subscribers to the victory kitchens had to register for them every week. By mid-May they were feeding four thousand, but by the end of the year over 170,000 were registered with them. This was not a tribute to their organization or to their cooking but to "the gradual depletion of the stocks available in the Black Market . . . and the fact that available supplies which could be legitimately obtained were gradually reduced."[5] Ships like the *Welshman* and her sister ship the *Manxman,* which continued to make their high-powered dashes into the island, and minelaying submarines converted to carry cargo, did not bring food—except small bulk items like powdered milk—but ammunition, fuel for the fighter planes, spare parts, and other essentials for the weapons of war. Without the latter Malta would undoubtedly be invaded, but without a convoy with food the people would starve.

The Axis commanders had not put aside plans for Operation Hercules but merely held them over until Rommel successfully completed his attack in the desert. Intelligence gathered by Ultra kept General Auchinlack in Egypt acquainted with Rommel's intentions and also reported the steady arrival of his armor. (The German armor, as was seen when the campaign finally opened, was numerically less than the British but was superior in firepower and in desert-worthiness.) Reconnaissance aircraft out of Malta reported that fresh airstrips were being laid out near Gerbini Airfield in Sicily. As the three bomber airfields already in existence seemed adequate for the planes available, and as this new activity was observed at about the time that the Luftwaffe had begun to withdraw some of its planes, only one interpretation was possible. These new fields were not, as had been first assumed, satellite airfields for the existing bomber force but were designed to accommodate a large number of gliders and their towing planes for an airborne invasion.

Troops were already in training up at Livorno in the north of Italy, where some features of the coastline resembled those of Malta, and plans were well advanced for the transport of German and Italian troops by German navy landing craft as a follow-up to the airborne attack. An armored unit of captured tanks from the Russian front had been set aside for the operation, and three Italian parachute battalions were ready and would soon be joined by a German parachute division. In all, the invasion would involve about thirty-five thousand troops. Given the fact that the British no longer had any surface ships, submarines, bombers on the island and had no battleships or aircraft carriers at Alexandria, it was quite possible for the Italian Navy to provide adequate cover during the first phase of the operation.

The arrival of the Spitfires on May 9, followed by further Spitfire reinforcements on May 18, somewhat altered the picture. But planning for the invasion and the allocation of men and matériel did not cease for some months to come. It was rather like Operation Sealion, the projected invasion of Britain itself. So attractive was the idea in certain quarters that it was hard to relinquish it. For the government of Malta, for the service chiefs, for every serviceman and civilian, it remained a nightmare that would take a long time to dispel. Their fears were soon intensified by the success of Rommel's spring attack in the desert.

27

Bread of Adversity

Even in the quiet places where there had been a spring that year, it was over by May. The thermometer began its regular, steady climb up to the plateau of the nineties (in the shade), where it generally rested until mid- or late September. No one looked forward to the summer. The war was now eternal. There were children born just before or at the beginning of the siege who could remember nothing but the shelter life, the sound of guns and bombs, their mothers' protective arms when dust fell shaking from the roof, and the smell of all the people crowded together.

All depended now not on Malta but on the battle that was about to break out in the desert some hundreds of miles to the south. Under permanent daily attack, the island had ceased to exert its pressure on that decisive area, which must inevitably explode. Refueled, reequipped, and rested, the Italo-German armies now faced with confidence the British defensive line drawn up from Gazala to Bir Hacheim. Rommel was well aware that the 8th Army had also had time to rearm and to prepare an offensive, and he was determined to get his blow in first. His previous advance, designed as no more than a spoiling measure, had won him a lot of ground, and he now aimed for Tobruk. Axis convoys to Tripoli and Benghazi were running almost unmolested, except by submarines from Alexandria, and a recent reorganization, whereby the German Navy had taken responsibility for the shipment of supplies eastward to the small port of Derna, had resulted in such an improvement that he felt his confidence soar. The Luftwaffe together with the Regia Aeronautica had complete air superiority over the desert and over the sea itself, while Malta was apparently eliminated as a menace to his continuing flow of supplies. Rommel's aim was not to attack the British forces head on but to move around to the south, encircling them and cutting them off from their supply lines.

On May 26 the Battle of Gazala opened with Rommel's forces making their expected move and being anticipated. The far end of the British line, at Bir Hacheim down in the desert, held firm against a superior force, the Free French conducting a superb defense. From the very beginning, however, the superiority of the German tanks was evident. Better protected, more heavily gunned, and in the final analysis more desert-worthy than the British armor, these tanks tipped the scales. The battle that had begun on Rommel's initiative was one that Churchill had been pressing General Auchinleck to open ever since February, while Auchinleck had constantly argued that his forces were not yet ready and not yet sufficiently well equipped to take the initiative. Churchill's insistence on an early engagement in the desert was largely prompted by his concern about Malta, for he was well aware that the island could not hold out much longer unless it was revictualed, refueled, and ammunitioned. So long as Cyrenaica, and especially the threatening Benghazi bulge with its airstrips controlling the eastern passage to Malta, was in Axis hands, there was no chance of getting a convoy through from the Alexandria end of the sea. Pressured by delegates sent out by the prime minister, Auchinleck had held out for a date in mid-June or at the very least the end of May, but in the event he had been forestalled by Rommel's advance. Auchinleck was proven right—the British forces were not yet fit to match the German—but what at the time seemed the greatest of disasters turned out in the long run to be the saving not only of Malta but of the whole British war effort in the desert.

Four weeks after the battle had begun, Rommel switched his tactics from the attempt at encirclement and struck north. The German armor, brilliantly used by a master of warfare, broke through and opened a passage to Tobruk. On June 20 Rommel launched a massive assault on the garrison using every element of his bomber force,

from high-level Italian Capronis to Junkers 88s and Stukas employed for what they had originally been designed—heavy artillery
in front of an infantry advance. Tobruk, so long a thorn in the side
of the Axis forces and so long a besieged companion to which Malta
had looked with affectionate regard, fell the following day. Poor
local command, poor morale among the garrison—these and many
other charges were later made as the reason for the collapse of this
all-important fortress. One fact remains inescapable: If Tobruk had
been defended as Malta had been for so many months, it would not
have fallen as it did.

Rommel, ever an optimist, was overjoyed by the collapse of the
garrison and port that seemed to open the way into Egypt. The British were in retreat to take up new positions on the Egyptian frontier,
and with the marked superiority of his armor, as shown in the recent
battles, he only needed to punch a hole through the demoralized
line ahead of him in order to win the great prize. Rommel's ebullient nature was well enough known to the German High Command; it was for this reason that General Paulus had been sent to
North Africa in April 1941, shortly after Rommel's arrival, to for-
mulate a strategy known and acceptable to Berlin. Now, within a
month, Rommel had achieved the whole object of Operation Theseus, and his well-justified satisfaction was crowned by immediate
promotion to field marshal. Hitler also felt the backwash of this triumph, coming as it did at a moment when the war in Russia had
entered a more drawn-out phase than he had anticipated, and when
the Allied bomber raids on Germany were beginning to remind the
conquerors of Europe that Britain was still unconquered. This spar-
kling shower of rockets from the desert war could not help but increase his regard for a general who had always been one of his
closest adherents.

Rommel's speedy triumph had gained him vast quantities of captured stores, ranging from thousands of tons of provisions to nearly
fifteen hundred tons of gasoline, whole ammunition dumps, and
thousands of serviceable vehicles. (If Malta had ever been captured,
there would have been exploding dumps all over the island, with
nothing left for the victors.) In view of this sudden accession to supplies, Rommel felt that all restrictions on his movements should be
lifted. According to the May 5 directive of the Italian *Comando Su-
premo* (to whom all Axis forces in the desert were subject), however,

he was to hold back from any further advance so that the whole Italo-German war effort in the Mediterranean could be transferred to Operation Hercules—the invasion of Malta. But, standing in shattered Tobruk, looking at the battered waterfront made famous in so many war photographs, at the blue harbor, beautiful despite its shattered wrecks, the prisoners of war filing past in their thousands, and his own Afrika Korps *soldaten* triumphant around him, Rommel felt with Brutus:

> There is a tide in the affairs of men,
>   which, taken at the flood, leads on to fortune;
> ... On such a full sea are we now afloat;
>   And we must take the current when it serves,
> Or lose our ventures.

More prosaically, but with the same enthusiasm shining through, Rommel happily bypassed Rome and communicated directly with the German Supreme Command: "The morale and condition of the troops, the quantity of stores captured and the present weakness of the enemy make it possible for us to thrust onwards into the heart of Egypt. Therefore request that the Duce be prevailed upon to remove the present restrictions on my movement and that all troops now under my command be placed at my disposal to continue the offensive."

Hitler was at once disposed to agree with his new field marshal. He felt the run of the tide, too, and it seemed to dispose of the awkward matter of invading Malta, about which he had always felt uneasy. At the German Supreme Command it seems to have been agreed that "with the capture of Tobruk the situation is completely changed. The conquest of Malta is no longer necessary." Although it was still at times discussed, the invasion of Malta was dropped forever.

There was still a great deal of argument from the Italians that Operation Hercules should be pursued. They knew very well that the supply lines were fully stretched (because of the previous heavy losses of their merchant marine) even with Malta apparently suppressed. Rommel was now at the far end of a long desert route, and even with Tobruk available as an unloading port, the Italians were not optimistic—unless, of course, he should sweep into Egypt within a matter of weeks. Mussolini himself was seized by the drama of the moment (and also perhaps by the happy fact that his forces would not be called upon to fulfill their obligations in Operation Hercules). While Hitler, with his indifferent health improved by this good news, was already turning back to his preoccupation with the iron realities of Russia, Il Duce saw a vision that exceeded any other in his operatic life. Verdi's *Aida* had first been performed in Cairo in December 1871, but he envisaged a production that for massive ensemble, richness of production, and magnificence of local color should transcend even that master's musical imaginings. At the end of June he flew to Derna, a white charger following in another aircraft, to await the moment "when he should make his triumphal entry into the Land of the Pharoahs."

The fall of Tobruk, which Churchill wrote "was one of the hardest blows of the entire war," was thus to prove in the end a turning point because it saved Malta. At the time, however, Rommel was unquenchable in his enthusiasm. With his headquarters now at Sidi Barrani, inside the borders of Egypt, and with Alexandria only about two hundred miles away, he met with Kesselring and the Italian Marshal Cavallero for a conference. What concerned Cavallero particularly was the length of the Axis supply line, especially in contrast to the British at El Alamein, who had a short supply line and were already regrouping in strength. Despite the fact that he had been able to pass Mersa Matruh, Rommel was soon to find he was faced with a strong defense line and a resolute enemy.

At El Alamein, only sixty miles from Alexandria, with the glittering prize of the great harbor and city within his grasp, Rommel was held. While Mussolini dreamed of a triumphant entry into Alexandria and then Cairo, and the ebullient young field marshal seemed to hold the riches of the Nile Delta and the ribbon of the Suez Canal within his hands, General Auchinleck was able to hold him and launch provocative counterattacks. As one of those working at Bletchley Park at the time wrote: "It was Ultra which enabled General Auchinleck in North Africa to fight Rommel and his Afrika Korps like an elusive boxer, bobbing up where Rommel least expected him. . . . It was Auchinleck's skill that brought Rommel to a standstill at the very gateway to Egypt."[1]

Another factor in the exhaustion of the Axis armies at this moment was that Malta, knocked unconscious as had been thought, struggled to its feet. The addition of more Spitfires to the island's arsenal meant that the weight of air attack from Sicily, which had been believed sufficient to keep the island suppressed, was not enough.[2] Before the close of June Marshal Cavallero was forced to ask for a transfer of planes from North Africa to Sicily to maintain the assault. Rommel's inability to crack the British defensive line at Alamein early in July was partly a result of the fact that he no longer had air superiority in the desert.

One of Governor Dobbie's last actions in Malta had been to send a signal to the War Office concerning the island's food, ammunition, and fuel situation. It had not changed for the better over the ensuing weeks. Combined with the disastrous news of the fall of Tobruk and therefore the unlikelihood of any further convoys getting through, his successor Lord Gort knew how slight were Malta's chances of survival. Before he had arrived to take over as governor, he had had time to digest Dobbie's account of the supply position:

"(a) Wheat and Flour. No material cuts seem possible as these are staple foods. Present stocks will, with care, last until early June.

"(b) Fodder. Issues already inadequate were recently cut; stocks will now last until end of July.

"(c) Minor foodstuffs. Meat stocks are entirely exhausted. Most other stocks will last until June.

"(d) White oils. Aviation fuel till mid-August; benzine until mid-June; kerosene till early July.

"(e) Black oils. We have only 920 tons of diesel oil (5 weeks' supply) and 2,000 tons of furnace oil, all of which will be needed for fuelling H.M. ships now in dock. The black oil position is thus becoming precarious, and very urgent action appears necessary to restore it.

"(f) Coal. Welsh coal will last only until end of May . . . other grades until mid-June.

"(g) Ammunition. Consumption of ack-ack ammunition has greatly increased in the recent heavy raids . . . and we have only 1½ months stocks left. . . ."

Dobbie had requested a convoy not later than mid-May and had been informed that there was no chance at all of a convoy during that month. More Spitfires arrived, flown in from carriers in the western Mediterranean, but Gort, familiar within a day or two of the actuality of dust and dereliction and near-starvation by which he was surrounded, knew that only a substantial convoy could save the island. Churchill had written to the chiefs of staff, "We are absolutely bound to save Malta," and remained determined on this whatever else might befall. He had known the island's importance from the very beginning of the war, and despite all his other myriad preoccupations, he never faltered in his determination. Like Cunningham, he had always realized the role Malta could play—in the uncertain future—in any assault on Hitler's Europe.

Not one convoy but two were planned for mid-June, the earliest date by which suitable merchantmen and warships could be gathered at both ends of the sea. This was to be the most massive effort yet, with seven merchantmen escorted by a battleship, two carriers, cruisers, and destroyers from Gibraltar (Operation Harpoon), and no less than eleven merchantmen with seven cruisers and twenty-eight destroyers from Alexandria (Operation Vigorous). At the same time, profiting by the cover provided for the Harpoon convoy, the minelayer *Welshman* with her specialized stores would slide through from the west. The convoy from Alexandria would have no capital ships, since none were available due to the demands of the eastern fleet. Its only "heavy cover" was provided by the old *Centurion*, for a long time a wireless-controlled fleet target ship and now mocked up to look like a new battleship. (It was hoped that she would at least draw much of the attention of the bombers.)[3] Since Malta was by now almost entirely mined in, and there could be no certainty as to how many of her own minesweepers would be seaworthy to sweep in the convoys, four fleet minesweepers together with six minesweeping motor launches sailed with the Gibraltar convoy.

At this time, just prior to Rommel's advance in the desert, the Italian Navy with its capital ships and heavy cruisers dominated the central Mediterranean, while the Luftwaffe controlled the skies. It was to be expected that the convoy from Alexandria would meet with heavy bombing in the area between Crete and the Benghazi bulge, but the appearance of the Italian battlefleet, with the battleships *Littorio* and *Vittorio Veneto* together with two heavy cruisers, two light cruisers, and twelve destroyers, was beyond the fighting capacity of the Alexandria covering force. On June 15 both this convoy and its screen were ordered back to Alexandria. So the whole of this, the largest convoy never reached Malta. The convoy from the west fared slightly better. Even though its passage involved an action in the Skerki Channel between British destroyers and a force of Italian cruisers, two merchant ships, the *Orari* and the *Troilus* (as well as the *Welshman*), managed to reach the island and unload.[4]

The threat posed by the Italian battleships had been sufficient to turn the scales against the eastern convoy, but it was the weight of air attack that really prevented any of the ships from being ventured through to Malta. Most of the escorts had fired off so many shells that they were practically without ammunition. The toll taken by the bombers included four merchantmen sunk and two merchantmen damaged, while the escort, which also underwent submarine attacks, had three cruisers damaged, three destroyers sunk, two corvettes damaged, and one torpedo boat sunk. The cold statistics for Operation Vigorous from Alexandria reveal at the end: "Tonnage of Cargoes landed—NIL." Harpoon from Gibraltar had four merchantmen sunk (including the American oiler *Kentucky*, the most important ship in the convoy), one merchantman damaged, two cruisers damaged, one destroyer sunk, and one destroyer damaged. If it had not been for the *Orari* and the *Troilus* reaching Grand Harbour and being promptly unloaded of some twenty thousand tons of flour and ammunition (an appropriately divided package), the island must have fallen, for no other convoy could possibly be put together until August.

The Italians rightly claimed the turning back of the convoy from Alexandria as a signal naval victory. So indeed it was, in the sense that the threat of their battlefleet out of Taranto had been the final blow that had determined Admiral Harwood to recall the convoy and its escort. The debit side for the Italians was one heavy cruiser, torpedoed by an aircraft out of Malta and later sunk by the submarine *Umbra*, and the *Littorio*, which was hit by one bomb and one torpedo. Invisible as yet on that debit sheet was something that would prove of immense importance in the future. The operation of the Italian fleet against the western convoy, and the battlefleet against the eastern, had reduced their oil reserves to such a degree that they would never again be able to take the sea in force. Hitler's optimism about the great oil fields of Russia coming within his grasp was to be disappointed, and from then on the oil fields of Eastern Europe would be called upon as never before to fuel the German war machine. The Italians found themselves excluded from most of this oil supply.

The sight of the *Welshman* and the two merchantmen unloading in Grand Harbour could not ease the acute sense of desperation that rapidly spread throughout the whole island. No one could conceal the news that two convoys had been destined for their relief and that this was all that had been fought through. True, it was better than March, when nothing at all had arrived, but this was now June, and memories of the two terrible months of April and May lay like a great weight on everyone's heart. The loss of the *Kentucky* meant that the oil and kerosene situation was acute. Fortunately, it was now summer, and despite the sufferings that the sun brought, it meant that heating was relatively unimportant and that the damp, disease-ridden shelter life could be somewhat put aside. The fact that the two ships contained a cargo divided between flour and ammunition did at least mean that the island could eat and fight for a little longer.

General Gort and the deputy governor of the island, Sir Edward Jackson (known to all since he had been in his post since the very beginning), both broadcast to the islanders. They made no attempt at concealment. Italian propaganda to the contrary, the Maltese were not a submissive people "held down by British bayonets" but equal and enduring partners—and even more, since this was their own island that they were defending. Gort could promise them nothing more than "further privations," and Jackson elaborated: "We received about 15,000 tons of stores from the two ships which arrived. That is something, and certainly a help, but it is a very small part of what we had hoped for." He told them that there would unavoidably be further restrictions in the rations, and he concluded: "Our security depends, more than anything else, on the time for which our bread will last."

It had come down to that, as it had always done in all sieges throughout history—bread.

28

Heat of the Day

Malta is always a dusty island. Just as all singular places on the planet invariably have a distinctive smell, so Malta's smell on the sea air to the visitor by boat is dry, old, and dusty. Even in places as remote as the Mnaidra temples on the western coast, when the sun flares over an empty sea as the watcher waits for the green flash at sunset, the scent is very old, older somehow than even the sands of Egypt. Those who knew it in the summer of 1942 all recorded the same overwhelming impression—the dust. The thousands of powdered dwellings, the bombed-out airstrips, and the torn roads contributed to the perpetual feel of it on the skin. Even the harbor—its surface foul from sunken ships and oil slick—was powdered with dust. The quaysides eddied with it, scraps of old dirty paper blowing on every errant puff of wind, broken doorways opened like sightless eyes upon the ruin of fallen roofs, old lost lives, sad fragments like a wheel from a broken toy, torn wallpaper rustling in a sun-dried corner—and dust. It was in the food, on the surface of the water in an old enameled drinking mug. It gritted between the teeth over the rough-torn piece of bread, valued now as no one could ever remember valuing bread before.

With the dust there were insects. Eye diseases were on the increase, and the dust exacerbated the sores where scabies sufferers had been unable to stop scratching. So dry did the island seem that it might have been thought that it was impossible for mosquitoes to breed. Yet the *nemus* was everywhere—zithering out of bomb craters, out of dead houses where excrement lay, from broken water pipes and the beehive-shaped cisterns shattered beneath old ruins. Not only houseflies and bluebottles, mosquitoes, and gnats exulted, but sandflies, productive of short but high fevers and a slow recovery, seemed to thrive on war. Indeed, was not the great Prince of Darkness known from millennia before as "Lord of Flies" and "Lord of Dung"? Like most Catholics the Maltese were little familiar with the Old Testament, but there must have been some among the priesthood who recalled the mysterious words of the Preacher in Ecclesiastes, suggesting that they were living in the days, "when they shall be afraid of that which is high, and fears shall be in the way, and the almond tree shall flourish, and the grasshopper shall be a burden, and desire shall fail: because man goeth to his long home, and the mourners go about the streets."

Valletta, that perfect example of a planned capital and fortress combined, was a ruin. The city, which Sir Walter Scott had described as "quite like a dream" and of which Disraeli had said that it "equals in its noble architecture, if it even does not excel, any capital in Europe," had been devastated in the terrible raids of April. The narrow streets were still blocked with rubble, fast though demolition squads and soldiers labored to clear them. The destruction of this famous city and its suburb Floriana could only be laid at an embittered attitude on the part of the attackers, many of whom preferred to drop their bombs on the precision of these noble streets rather than face the hell of Grand Harbour, whose installations and whose ships were their real and intended target. The ancient university, the *Sacra Infirmeria* (the great hospital of the Knights, one of the first ever built in Europe), the famous palace, St. John's Co-Cathedral (a monument to the Age of Chivalry), all were hit, as well as six of the auberges (the magnificent palaces of the various Tongues of the Knights), and inevitably a number of fine baroque churches. The Victorian Opera House, redolent of upper-class splendor and display, was destroyed along with much of the squalid but vivid Manderaggio area of the poor.

It was noticeable that the fury of the onslaught on the island's capital increased as the attacks on the dockyard areas and the airfields began to lessen. Like the "Baedeker raids" carried out on Britain in the later stages of the war, the destruction of Valletta was largely prompted by the fury of frustration.

"Everywhere one looked," wrote Weldon, "one could see nothing but desolation and rubble. In particular was this so if one walked to the top of the ramparts and looked down some of the streets. It was then that one realized the extent of the damage. Malta's buildings are made of very solid blocks of stone and it takes a direct hit to destroy a house. The traveller arriving at Valetta might, at first, think that the damage was comparatively slight, but let him just walk to one high vantage point and look down and he will see that almost every building is nothing but an empty shell. That alone will show the intensity of the bombing. It was estimated at one time that there were a million five hundred thousand tons of debris in Valetta and Floriana alone. In the whole island over fifteen thousand buildings had been destroyed, amongst them seventy churches, eighteen convents or monasteries, twenty-two schools, eight hospitals, ten theatres . . ."[1]

In this fly-blown, dust-ridden landscape, a southern hell such as Dante Alighieri hardly envisaged, the scale of human suffering was deeper than that found in other cities under attack during the Second World War. Although the casualties were far less than might have been expected due to the nature of the island, the condition of being shelter-bound was almost without end. Days, weeks, months, and even years passed in which men, women, and children (but particularly the latter two) were forced to spend a large part of their lives underground—undernourished and often in ill-health. A Reuters correspondent in Malta, who took shelter in one of the beehive-shaped cisterns beneath Valletta during a major raid, described with the vividness of a newcomer a situation that had become familiar to the inhabitants: ". . . the air was filled with the crash of masonry and the uncanny swirl of blast. The building above was hit. Clouds of dust penetrated the shelter, smothering and half-choking the shelterers with dust, mostly women with babies and young children. Some of the children were terrified and cried, but their mothers open-eyed and stupefied, calmly dipped their handkerchiefs in a pail of water kept in the shelter for the purpose and put them over the mouths and noses of the babies. Then hugging their youngest to their bosom they muttered a silent prayer. . . . After a short lull another wave of bombers came over. The lights in the shelter flickered and the blast lifted the skirts of women and children as it swept through. One of the next stick of bombs brought down more of the buildings overhead. A shower of masonry and debris burst in through the emergency exit, immediately followed by a dark cloud of dust and cordite that spread throughout the shelter until none could see the other. Mothers looked up expecting to see the dome of the well give way. All were temporarily deafened by the noise. In this unreal scene figures only faintly visible through the pall of dust moved as if in a trance."[2]

Over the whole island indeed the great Dante might have seen, carved deep in the limestone rock, the words of his vision:

> *Per me si va nella città dolente,*
> *Per me si va nell'eterno dolore,*
> *Per me si va tra la perduta gente . . .*
> *Lasciate ogni speranza, voi ch'entrate.*

But hope was the one thing that they did not lose. Something else that emerged quite decisively from the war and that, as has been seen, was a matter of some surprise to the psychiatrists, was the ability of people to withstand situations of great peril, pain, suffering, and terror without succumbing to what are termed "nervous breakdowns." Such problems appear to be more common under the daily stresses of peacetime—or of the condition known as peace in the great industrial communities of the West. The incidence of breakdown among African or Asian people or among peasant communities in general has never been properly studied—for obvious reasons. Among the physically softer, better fed, more self-indulgent citizens of the world one expects that the least endurance will be found. In this matter the people of Malta showed a remarkably high degree of stability—beyond that called upon in those days in great cities like London and Berlin, since they were required to endure air raids for a far longer time, and on rations that were about half of those available to the citizens of London, for instance. The temperance and frugality common among Mediterranean peoples had been bred into them by centuries—indeed, millennia—of being required to exist on very little. It was these qualities, among others, that enabled the besieged to survive under conditions that, one has reason to think, the inhabitants of modern megacities could not endure.

The great French historian Fernand Braudel has pointed out an important distinction between Mediterranean man and the northerner: "The truth is that the Mediterranean has struggled against a fundamental poverty, aggravated but not entirely accounted for by circumstances. It affords a precarious living, in spite of its apparent or real advantages. It is easy to be deceived by its famous charm and beauty.... In fact, Mediterranean man gains his daily bread by painful effort. Great tracts of land remain uncultivated and of little use. The land that does yield food is almost everywhere subject to biennial crop rotation that rules out any great productivity.... There is one visible sign of this poverty: the frugality that has never failed to impress the northerner."[3] This frugality had amused British soldiers and sailors in Malta in days of peace and continued to amaze them (and outside observers) during the war.

It is significant that in the many British firsthand accounts of life in Malta during the siege an almost constant theme is the shortage of food and drink. The accounts by Maltese, however, tend to refer to the subject only when it became—as in July and August 1942—a matter of near-starvation. On June 20 the government had to announce cuts that Sir Edward Jackson described over the radio as "a far greater privation than any other . . . a far greater hardship than any you have had to bear hitherto." Among the rations for a family of five were four tins of corned beef, four tins of fish, and four boxes of matches *per month.* The daily bread ration per person was fixed at three-eighths of a ratal (under fourteen ounces). The daily calorie intake was now 1,500 (as compared with 3,000, regarded as a daily minimum for a man "leading a moderately active life.")

After the failure of the June convoys to bring in more than two ships to the island's relief, government calculations were that on the present reduced rations the island could just last out until the end of August. Its fighting capacity was immensely improved by the arrival of the Spitfires, which resulted in a decline in bombing raids, particularly during the day. By mid-July the minesweepers had managed to clear the entrance channel to the island, and before the month was out the submarines were able to return. The first to arrive was the *Unbroken,* shortly followed by the *Ultimatum* and the *United,* until there were nine in all operating from the island. August, the first month in which the revived underwater route became available again for the fortress to hit back at the besiegers, was marked by the sinking of over forty thousand tons of shipping on Rommel's supply route. This was of course all to the good as far as the war effort was concerned, but it did not alter the fact that Malta would starve to death unless a supply convoy could get through.

The air raids continued to be noticeably fewer, and to the astonishment and relief of the people there were a number of raid-free nights during July. At the same time, Beaufort torpedo-bombers together with Beaufighters joined the island's forces in a new striking capacity. The diversion of some of the Luftwaffe from the desert to renew the assault on Malta did not meet with the success expected, and in the first ten days of July over a hundred enemy aircraft were shot down. Unknown to the besieged the long-term Allied prospects for the whole Mediterranean war looked better than ever before— even if they had known, it would have done nothing to alleviate their condition. For them it was enough if one day succeeded another in this moonscape of dust and deprivation, where even the slackening of the bomber offensive had as yet meant very little. But the signs on the horizon were so favorable that, for those in the know and capable of taking a long-term view of things, the outlook for Malta was brighter than it had been for nearly a year. Of course, this was always provided that a convoy could be fought through to keep the people and the garrison alive.

First of all, Rommel was held in the desert at Alamein. His troops were themselves suffering from water and food rationing, and ammunition and fuel were in short supply. At the same time the British, with their short lines of communications, were growing stronger almost daily and their air force, reinforced by new types of aircraft from the United States, was not only achieving parity with the Luftwaffe but was on the way to becoming dominant. Far away from the wasteland of Malta in July, an Anglo-American agreement was reached in the middle of that month laying plans for the invasion of French North Africa in October, to be combined with a great offensive in the desert by a massively reinforced British force equipped with American Sherman tanks and 105mm self-propelled guns.

On August 2 Lord Alanbrooke stopped off at Malta on his way through to Egypt. He was determined to tell Lord Gort of the imminent events that would make all the difference to Malta and his role as the island's leader. He knew, as he put it, that Gort was in a depressed state and suspected that "his depression had been increased by the fact that he insisted on living on the reduced standard of rations prevailing in the Island, in spite of the fact that he was doing twice as much physical and mental work as any other member of the garrison."[4] So, early in August, Malta's governor learned that the whole Mediterranean situation would be changed by October, but he could communicate this to no one else—and he still had to try and ensure that his command would last beyond the end of August. He was told that a convoy of exceptional size was planned for the middle of that month.

During July two minelaying submarines, the *Parthia* and the *Clyde,* reached Malta with essential stores, while the *Welshman* made another of her lightning dashes from Gibraltar. Fifty-nine more Spitfires, ferried to a flying-off position by the *Eagle* in two expeditions, reached the island safely. Almost imperceptibly the balance was changing. But this certainly could not be felt in the palms of their hands by those who manned the guns or who looked out the windows of their stone cottages over the hot and barren cactus-land of July and August.

29

Preparations

Once the buildup of Spitfires on the island had been achieved, the whole situation was irrevocably changed. It was something that the Luftwaffe had been wise to try and prevent, but it was the success of the new reception arrangements (more important than almost anything else during this crucial period) that ensured the new climate of confidence. Air Vice Marshal Lloyd, who had seen the island through its worst days and into the new era when fighter protection was once again assured within the flying limits of Malta, relinquished his command in mid-July to Air Vice Marshal Sir Keith Park. The latter, even with his experience from commanding a well-known fighter group during the Battle of Britain, had been forewarned that activities over Malta made even that famous conflict seem comparatively simple. The whole of his new command was an airfield in the front line, with practically no rest and recuperation areas available and no cessation from the sound of battle when enemy raiders approached with the slow, steady buildup of fighter aircraft that could cope more than adequately with the Messerschmitt, Park was able to alter the whole basis of the island's defense. No longer was Malta able to do no more than desperately defend itself with overworked pilots and undergunned and overworked planes. It was now possible to take the fighter offensive. And this fighter offensive would lead the way, with the new bombers and torpedo-carriers that were reaching the island, for the offensive that would shatter the Axis shipping route to North Africa. Since intelligence confirmed that Luftwaffe squadrons had been withdrawn for service in Russia, and since the brief offensive at the end of July had been easily contained, now was the time to put the attackers from Sicily on the defensive. It was sweet revenge for what the island of Malta had suffered over the past six months and more. Rather than waiting for the raiders to come—all that had been possible when there had sometimes been no more than six airworthy fighters for the defense—the Spitfires now met them far out from the island. Improved radar, and training in its use by experts out from Britain, played its part in what amounted to the counterpuncher going on the offensive.

In a special order of the day Air Vice Marshal Park acknowledged the debt to the past but instilled a new outlook for the future: "During the blitz in the Spring, the enemy was so vastly superior in strength that our day fighters were practically forced on the defensive. Under these conditions it was inevitable that Royal Air Force personnel on the ground and civilians should undergo severe bombing daily. . . . Our day fighter strength has during June and July been greatly increased, and the enemy's superiority in numbers has long since dwindled. The time has now arrived for our Spitfire squadrons to put an end to the bombing of our airfields by daylight."[1]

Aggressive tactics became the keynote, with the Spitfires sweeping skyward as soon as a tremor on the radar screens indicated activity over Sicily. The squadron at stand-by had to be off the ground within two minutes, the squadron at immediate readiness within three minutes, and the squadron at readiness within five minutes. The Regia Aeronautica rarely came by daylight over the angry beehive to the south, and the obsolescent Stukas (still deadly on the Russian front) had given place to the Junkers 88s, which themselves could no longer triumphantly ride the Maltese sky without heavy fighter escorts. The enemy to the north, baking on the sun-scorched airfields of Sicily, could only venture fighter sweeps over Malta. Now, fighter against fighter, they no longer had the almost contemptuously hard edge that they had held before over patched-up Hurricanes and exhausted pilots.

Aware of the large convoy that was being planned, and aware that it would be months before the passage to the island could be rendered safe for convoys, the Air Vice Marshal cautioned his crews against easy optimism: "All fighter formations are warned that the enemy will probably reintroduce bomber formations whenever there is an important operation in the Malta area. Because our Spitfires, using the forward plan of interception, have recently stopped daylight raids does not mean that only fighter sweeps are likely to be encountered over or near Malta in the future."[2] He knew that in mid-August the Axis would switch every available plane to attacking a convoy on which the island entirely depended if it was to survive for the rest of the month.

Nearly four centuries before, toward the end of the long hot summer of 1565, the defenders of Malta had noticed that the assaults against them were beginning to lose their ferocity, and there were even signs that some of the troops had to be driven to the attack. Something similar was noticed over Malta during 1942 (the reluctance of the Regis Aeronautica had been so long noticed as not to be worth comment). Even the Luftwaffe fighters that now came down on gadfly raids, dropping a few bombs and strafing, were a far cry from those that in earlier months had almost leisurely cruised low over the island—let alone he who had "flown his gage" down Grand Harbour at the beginning. An increased use of anti-personnel bombs revealed some desperation on the part of the attackers. The new tactics of engaging the enemy over the sea meant that many more pilots were coming down by parachute off the island, and Malta's air-sea rescue service in their high-speed boats were constantly on call from their base at Kalafrana in the south. Injured Germans began to outnumber the soldiers and air-men of the defenders in Mtarfe Hospital, and a great change in their morale was noted from the easy self-confidence of the springtime attackers. One gunner from a Junkers 88, echoing as it were some earlier Turk, later said of Malta: "We were always being driven to it."

As in the unhappy occupied Europe of the New Order, so in besieged Malta, only one thing thrived during the war—the black market. In London, in Paris, in Berlin, in Rome, and equally in Malta, the natural cupidity of man could not be erased, and the same circumstances that brought out the qualities of heroism, sacrifice, and self-abnegation also produced a black market in everything. Because supply ceases demand does not cease, and when the demand is not so much for luxuries but for all the basics of life, the competition to supply it increases in ratio to the price that can be obtained. Malta, dependent on imports for every form of manufactured goods, lacked everything from clothing to razor-blades and soap. Secondhand clothing, clothes stolen from bombed houses, old shoes, belts, shirts, linen of every kind, there was not a thing of the most ordinary household use that had not acquired under siege conditions a value far beyond normal comprehension. Naturally, the real black market existed in food, from any form of meat to bread, eggs, and even vegetables. As a result of the government policy of buying up a large part of the green vegetables, onions, and potatoes for use by the victory kitchens, the armed services, and the hospitals, there was little left over for the private suppliers, the *pitkali* who sold from baskets or carts direct to the public. The foundations of many small fortunes were inevitably laid by farmers large and small in Malta and Gozo during the siege, but particularly during the desperate summer of 1942, when starvation was very close and the island was only a few weeks away from surrender. Jail sentences and heavy fines, followed by increased jail sentences and heavier fines—nothing could possibly extirpate the root of this trouble, the desire to survive.

In Pwales Valley in the north of Malta, and especially in Gozo, farmers thrived on visits by night from *pitkali* and individual citizens eager to make some money or to keep their families alive and healthy. Daytime ferries from Gozo could be inspected, but by night individual boats made their way across to Malta from the agricultural and relatively untouched island to the north, forming a steady chain of private enterprise that no public authority could possibly break. Archbishop Caruana himself denounced the black marketeers over the radio, but there were few who would not face possible future penalties for sin rather than accept the real and imminent danger of starvation. Among the interminable catalog of shortages, there was one that meant a great deal to the thousands of servicemen on the island—the absence of any beer, due to lack of fuel to maintain the breweries in working capacity. Less important than solid food, beer had nevertheless remained the one luxury of the day—and there had been little enough of it even when it had been available. Many months before, the normal exercises and marches undertaken by the troops to keep them fit had been discontinued, and in their place now were compulsory rest periods or, as they were known, sleep parades. In order to conserve their energy for their duties, as well as not to make them more hungry than they already were, the troops were required to lie down and rest at set times.

In July 1942 the Germans were right when they said *"Malta ist sturmreif"* (ripe for attack), but by then *Operazione C3,* Operation Hercules, had been called off and the organization almost entirely disbanded. Furthermore, the island's capacity to strike back as well as to attack locally had been immensely increased not only by the new Spitfires but by the return of the bombers and submarines. The minesweepers that had come through from the Gibraltar convoy in June had been able to carry out sweeping duties under protective air cover during the day, although E-boats still made their minelaying runs by night. The battle against the island's being completely mined-in was to carry on for many months. The swept channel to Grand Harbour required never-ending attention, for it was only down that passage that any relief ships could reach the island.

Everyone was interdependent under the conditions of the siege in a way that would never be comprehended in peacetime life, but that was visible and tangible in a locked-in island. From fighter pilot to officer-in-charge of the minesweeping party on the afterdeck of a motor launch or minesweeper, from gun crewman in St. Elmo to decoder in the tunnels behind Lascaris Bastion, from water-pumping-station mechanic to air-raid warden, through all the gamut of life (from women having babies in underground delivery centers to the old people breathing the last familiar dusty air as the priest bent over them), Malta was a microcosm of the world continuously at war.

To keep the island alive until such time as the survivors on this Promethean rock could receive substantial help, the minelaying submarines from Alexandria continued to bring in such essential small-bulk cargoes as were needed—medical stores, kerosene, bags of mail, powdered milk, armor-piercing shells, and fuel. The *Cashalot,* the *Porpoise,* the *Rorqual,* the *Osiris,* and the *Urge* were among those that kept this slender lifeline open while the preparations went ahead for a major relief. This was something it would be impossible to conceal once it had entered the Mediterranean, and against which the Axis would hurl every available aircraft, submarine, surface ship, and destructive device.

Operation Pedestal was planned to pass a large convoy through from the Gibraltar end of the sea. The experience of the Vigorous convoy from the eastern end in June had shown that, so long as all the coast to the south (as well as Crete to the north) was in Axis hands, it was impossible to run a convoy from Alexandria. The assembly of a large convoy—fourteen ships in all were to be made available—almost inevitably meant that it would be sighted passing through the Straits of Gibraltar and that, once into the Mediterranean, it would soon be found. The acceptance of grave losses from air attack was understood from the first, and the possibility that the Italians, under pressure from the Germans, would make some move with their fleet had always to be considered. A heavier fleet escort than usual therefore had to be provided, with battleships to cover the journey as far as the Skerki Channel, with an escort of modern cruisers and destroyers going through to Malta.

The heavy escort was provided by the two sister ships, *Nelson* and *Rodney,* each of thirty-four thousand tons with nine sixteen-inch guns and twelve six-inch guns. Vice Admiral Sir Neville Syfret, a South African, flew his flag in *Nelson,* being the officer in command of what was called Force Z. With him would go an aircraft carrier squadron under Rear Admiral Lyster, in the new *Indomitable,* together with the 1939-built *Victorious* and the old *Eagle.* A total of forty-six Hurricanes, ten Martlets, and sixteen Fulmers aboard the carriers would provide fighter cover. With this main escort would be the three fast 5.25-inch antiaircraft cruisers, *Charybdis, Phoebe,* and *Sirius,* and fourteen destroyers. As close escort to the merchantmen were the heavy cruiser *Nigeria* (Rear Admiral Burrough) together with the similar *Kenya* and *Manchester,* the antiaircraft cruiser *Cairo,* and eleven destroyers. Designated Force X, it was their task to cover the convoy through to Malta after Force Z had turned back at Skerki. Separate from the main force of Operation Pedestal, but designed to take place at the same time, the carrier *Furious* with a destroyer escort was to fly off thirty-eight Spitfires as reinforcements for Malta. As backup to the fleet there were two fleet oilers with a corvette escort, a deep-sea rescue tug, and another salvage vessel.

All in all, this was the largest naval operation ever set in motion in the Mediterranean, until that time, and its objective was to pass the fourteen-ship convoy through to the starving island. Thirteen of the fast, modern merchantmen carried the usual mixed cargo for Malta—flour, ammunition, and gasoline in cans. This combination of food-fuel and war-fuel was a direct statement of the island's needs. No one on board any ship could have the comfortable feeling that they carried harmless goods alone, since all were almost equally burdened with a highly explosive mixture on the most dangerous convoy run in the world. The fourteenth ship, the *Ohio,* was a large tanker, pure and simple, a new ship from the Texaco Oil Company. She had been loaned for the occasion to the British, was manned by British seamen, and commanded by Captain Mason of the Eagle Oil & Shipping Company. American-owned but also American-manned were two general cargo ships, *Santa Elisa* and *Almeria Lykes.* The remainder of the convoy comprised some of the finest and fastest British merchantmen then afloat. The *Port Chalmers* headed the list, in which the convoy commodore, Commander Venables, flew his broad pennant, followed by the *Wairangi, Waimarama,* and *Empire Hope* of the Shaw Savill Line, the *Brisbane Star* and *Melbourne Star,* of the Blue Star Line, the *Dorset* of the Federal Steam Navigation Company, *Rochester Castle* of the Union Castle Line, *Deucalion* of the Blue Funnel Line, *Glenorchy* of the Glen Line, and *Clan Ferguson* of the Clan Line.[3]

Although no attempt was made this time to pass a second convoy through from the eastern end of the sea, a cover plan was devised whereby Admiral Harwood would mount a dummy operation from Alexandria in company with Admiral Vian from Haifa. A total of five cruisers, fifteen destroyers, and five merchantmen would sail as if bound for Malta, and then on their second night out disperse and turn back. It was hoped that this would tie down some of the enemy and possibly cause dissension among the Italian Navy as to the choice of targets. Meanwhile Air Vice Marshal Park in Malta was to hold in readiness a torpedo-bombing force in case the Italian fleet might be tempted to leave Taranto. The rest of Park's air forces, including over 130 fighters, were kept for support of the convoy. Six British submarines from Malta would be on patrol west of the island in case the Italian fleet should try to interfere in the region of Pantelleria, while two were on patrol to the north of Sicily.

Even if intercepted radio messages had not given them an inkling that a large British operation was afoot in the western Mediterranean, any actuarial Italian staff officer could have foretold that Malta must soon receive a convoy or surrender. German and Italian bombers, dive-bombers, and torpedo planes were assembled on the airfields of Sicily and Sardinia along with fighter aircraft and reconnaissance planes. In all, some seven hundred aircraft were put on duty as reception committee for any convoy that came within range. Eighteen Italian submarines were on patrol, one off Malta itself, eleven in the Narrows, and six spread between Algiers and the Balearic Islands. Three German U-boats were also stationed in this approach area, where the whole body of the escorting fleet might be expected. Off Cape Bon in Tunisia E-boats and Italian MTBs lay in wait, while in the same area a new minefield had been laid where the British might not expect one, since it was part of a swept channel that had previously been kept clear for Axis convoys running to Tripoli. Three heavy and three light cruisers together with ten destroyers were held in waiting to intercept the convoy south of Sicily.

Operation Pedestal began with the assembly of the convoy off the mouth of the River Clyde on August 2, 1942. Upon it Malta would stand or fall, and upon it directly and indirectly depended the fate of millions.

30

Nine Days to Santa Marija

The convoy moved south through the Bay of Biscay in three parallel columns. All hands had been told their destination on the first morning at sea, and from then on they had not been surprised at the degree to which the convoy was put through its paces. The Royal Naval and Maritime Regiment gunners manning the antiaircraft weaponry aboard the merchantmen were aware that ships had more than doubled their normal wartime quota—several Oerlikons where one or two were normally sufficient, and heavier AA guns as well as machine guns and rockets. The crews were endlessly at exercises. The ships themselves were also regularly engaged in tactical maneuvers—altering formation, reducing and increasing speed, and making emergency turns. On either side of the convoy went their constant escort companions, and astern the heavyweight shoulders of the great ships rose and fell as they headed south.

On August 6, when the convoy was well on its way and other units of the fleet were standing by at Gibraltar or on passage to join them from Freetown in West Africa, a great many more people went to church in Malta than was normal. Special prayers were offered to Our Lady as well as to St. Paul, patron saint of the island, while other local saints of special devotion in different parishes were also remembered. A few days earlier the archbishop had sent a circular to all parish priests, ordering a novena to be said in preparation for

ITALY

15°

35°

Messina

0800
13 Aug.
Unbroken

Attendolo &
Bolzano
torpedoed

Catania

C. Passero

1900 12 Aug
4 Italian cruisers
8 destroyers

13 Aug

Safari

Palermo

SICILY

Comiso

MALTA

1600
13 Aug

Noon
13 Aug

11 Aug

Trapani

2345 11 Aug
2 Italian cruisers

Malta Channel

E-boat attacks

9
8
7

Lampedusa

80

20

0800
13 Aug

Skerki
Bank

5

C. Bon

6

Pantelleria

0400
13 Aug

Sousse

DJERBA

10°

Kelibia

1600
12 Aug

4

3

Bizerta

100

2

Tunis

Noon
12 Aug

19

0800
12 Aug

Bone

Tripoli

15°

SARDINIA

Cagliari

36

10°

MINORCA

5°

MALLORCA

IBIZA

2000
11 Aug

Bougie

40°

Noon
11 Aug
1942

1

Algiers

5°

250 Miles

Submarine

7 Waimarama sunk.

8 Ohio damaged.

9 Ohio damaged.
Dorset damaged,
later sunk.
Rochester Castle
damaged.

Line of air attack, showing
number of aircraft

5 Nigeria damaged,
Cairo & Clan Ferguson
sunk. Empire Hope
damaged, later sunk.
Brisbane Star, Kenya
& Ohio damaged

6 Almeria Lykes, Wairangi,
Glenorchy & Santa Eliza
sunk. Manchester
damaged, later sunk.
Rochester Castle
damaged.

0   50 100 150 200 250

19

1 Eagle sunk

2 Deucalion damaged,
later sunk

3 U-boat sunk

4 Indomitable damaged.
Foresight sunk.

M.V.

the feast of "the Assumption of the Blessed Virgin Mary, Mother of God, into Heaven." August 15, the Feast of the Assumption, is normally a major *festa* of the summer, that season of fireworks, illuminated churches, gaudy stalls selling ice creams, almond and honey *helwa,* Turkish delight, images of saints, fruit, pile upon pile of colored sweets, and iced lemon and orange drinks—all under bright electric bulbs or hissing kerosene flares. Since seven parishes in Malta and one in Gozo are dedicated to Santa Marija, this is one of the most widely celebrated summer *festas.* Of course, there had not been any outdoor festivities since the war had broken over the island. The order from the archbishop for the special novena conveyed not only the gravity of the hour but suggested something unusual—some hoped-for form of deliverance, perhaps? The faithful were requested in their prayers to ask that "God the merciful may shorten the time of this scourge and grant us His Help ..." The children were exhorted to receive Holy Communion, and on Santa Marija Day itself all the faithful were recommended to do the same.

On the night of August 10 the convoy entered the Straits of Gibraltar. The weather was fair though foggy, as so often in that area. There could never have been any concealment of the passage of so large a convoy, even if some of the fishing vessels in the straits had not had Axis agents aboard them, even if plain-language communications between carrier-borne aircraft had not been inevitable in earlier routine practices, and even if there had not been an Italian naval agent in Ceuta across the straits from Gibraltar. Questions were later asked in the House of Commons about bad security over the destination of the convoy, but security involving so many items that had to be handled by so many dockers and involving so many ships was always an impossibility. Any large convoy at that time bound for the Mediterranean could only be bound for Malta.

On the morning of August 11 the entire convoy with its many escorts, its two battleships, and its three aircraft carriers was steaming through a travel-brochure Mediterranean, the fourteen merchantmen in the center now in four parallel columns. Early that morning, some sixty miles south of Ibiza in the Balearic Islands, they had been sighted, ineffectively attacked, and reported by the Italian submarine *Uarsciek.* The entire waiting line of Axis submarines, torpedo boats, bombers and torpedo bombers, and the Italian fleet units had all stiffened for action. Among those waiting in the line

ahead was the *U.73,* a German submarine commanded by Lieutenant Rosenbaum, an old Mediterranean hand who had nearly lost his
boat in a bombing attack off Tobruk. In his patrol position off Algiers he was alerted by the steady thrumming sound of the advancing convoy. Skillfully evading the outriders of the fleet and diving
beneath the destroyers (possibly profiting from one of those cold
layers that were the bane of Mediterranean sonar operators),[1] Lieutenant Rosenbaum maneuvered himself into a firing position. He
had before him one of the very targets that the U-boats had been
specifically ordered to try for—an aircraft carrier he had already
identified as the *Eagle.* He fired at a range of five hundred yards,
and his full spread of four torpedoes, set to run at twenty feet, hit the
old veteran along her port side. In less than eight minutes the *Eagle*
had sunk, some two hundred men going down with her. The *U.73,*
taking advantage of the confusion as destroyers raced to pick up
survivors, made her escape as skillfully as she had made her kill.
The convoy executed an emergency ninety-degree turn as gravely as
if on a fleet exercise, while destroyers depth-charged all those errant
echoes that occur on such occasions. Four of the *Eagle's* fighters
were in the air at the time and were able to land safely on the two
other carriers, but so early in the operation, and long before the
need for them had been felt, some 25 percent of the air cover had
been lost.

The convoy and its escort were now steaming on their inevitable
line of advance, expected by the waiting submarines. Throughout
that afternoon, while the destroyers worried away at contacts, with
erratic pillars from depth charges foaming against the picture-postcard blue of the sky and sea, the convoy made seventeen emergency
turns. Torpedo tracks were seen, but there were no further repeti-
tions of that submarine commander's dream—the death of an aircraft carrier. The other U-boats that had been spread to the north of
Algiers lay in wait for the convoy as it neared the Narrows, but they
achieved nothing further to record in their log books.

As the ships edged up into the shadow-line that spread out con-
centrically from the airfields of Sardinia, they came within range of
bomber and torpedo bomber. During the afternoon high reconnaissance came over, just to confirm the convoy's course and composition. Only the heavy antiaircraft guns of the *Nelson* and *Rodney*
opened up on these aircraft, which were out of range of all lesser

calibers. The spotters made back again untouched for Cagliari and Decimomammu while the ships surged on through the stillness and heat, where sky and sea merged in the northerner's dream of the Mediterranean sea. At dusk, as the fighters were being struck down below for the night, the raiders came in—Heinkel torpedo planes and Junkers 88 dive-bombers. They had to fight their way through circles of firepower—destroyers, cruisers, carriers, and battleships— an immense storm of metal that tested the nerves even of seasoned pilots. As the convoy made an emergency turn, torpedoes tracked vivid through the phosphorescent sea, bombs erupted against the darkening water, and the roar and the whine combined with flak startled the darkness. The evening star was effaced by tracer, and four planes came down burning into the sea. The ships stood on again—no casualties.

Later that night Beaufighters out of Malta struck against the airfields on Sardinia, but all was quiet near the convoy. Shadowing aircraft stayed with the ships throughout the dark hours, reporting their course and speed, never leaving them, so that they could be effectively met at dawn. At 6 A.M. Martlet fighters swept up off the *Indomitable* and cut two of the shadowers out of the sky. Wednesday August 12 was certain to prove a noisy one on the gently undulating sea, for the convoy was now only about seventy miles south of Sardinia. If the bombers from Malta had not destroyed planes, hangars, and fuel dumps in the airfields there, the first attacks would have been heavier. As it was, eight Junkers 88s were shot down in the first raid just after 9 A.M. by Hurricanes and Martlets already up to greet them. This reception aloft was matched by the gunfire below, and such planes as did break through dropped their bombs ineffectually before heading for safety in the north.

The morning was full of U-boat alarms, one apparently determined attack being put down by two destroyers working in conjunction on the port side of the screen. All waited for what was surely being prepared for them—the really big raid of the day, the *grande battue* of the twelfth. It had indeed been carefully prepared, involving over one hundred aircraft of various types as well as a number of new weapons. High noon, with the August sun blazing over a sea wrinkled only by the ships' passage, saw the five waves of the main attack from the Sardinian airfields launch themselves against the convoy. The first move was made by ten Savoia bombers escorted by Macchi fighters and fighter-bombers. It was designed to break up the convoy formation by an ingenious new weapon, the *motobomba,* a torpedo dropped on a parachute and designed to run in a circle or on an eccentric course. This weapon was hazardous indeed when dropped only a short distance ahead of a convoy in formation. But in this case the Savoias and their escorting fighters were detected well in advance, the convoy's Martlets and Hurricanes were vectored in their direction, and the convoy itself, as soon as the descending parachutes were observed, executed a ninety-degree turn. It thus neatly sidestepped the irrational torpedoes. The fighter-bombers that accompanied the first wave (designed to distract the outer screen of the destroyers) were again met by carrier fighters, and the attack, alarming only because of its mysterious weaponry, petered out.

The second wave consisted of over forty torpedo planes approaching in two groups, one from each side of the convoy (a convoy that, in theory, should have been disrupted and suffered casualties from the *motobombas*). Most of the attacking planes were met far out by Hurricanes and Martlets, causing them to drop their torpedoes at ineffectively long range. Those that approached closer met the full firepower of the fleet—the immense air bursts from the sixteen-inch guns of the *Rodney* sounded like thunderclaps. During this hurricane of shot and shell over a tranquil sea the convoy faultlessly executed two emergency turns, and such torpedoes as came within range passed harmlessly by.

As the torpedo bombers were retiring, the first German raid developed with a formation of dive-bombers attacking the *Nelson* and the *Rodney.* Both giant ships were narrowly missed—their fourteen-inch armor plate was impervious to fragmented bombs—while the antiaircraft cruiser *Cairo,* also near-missed, emerged with disciplined guns shouting through the pinnacles of spray. The dive-bombers achieved a success on one of the merchantmen, the *Deucalion,* which was leading the port wing of the convoy. Hit by one bomb that passed right through the ship, she was so severely damaged by other near-misses that she fell behind the convoy and, escorted by a destroyer, turned toward the North African shore. Dive-bombed again later in the day, she was still under way at dusk (hoping to reach Malta on her own) when she was found by torpedo planes. One hit was sufficient to touch off the gasoline and kerosene aboard her.

Hardly had the crew abandoned ship than the *Deucalion,* veteran of a previous Malta convoy, blew up with an ear-shattering explosion—the first of the convoy to be lost, and a sinister portent of the night to come.

Italian ingenuity in the meantime tried again where direct action had failed, and a pilotless plane, loaded with explosive, was launched under radio control from a Cant seaplane.[2] Intended for one of the capital ships, the robot's control malfunctioned, and it carried on over the sea to reach the land and explode in North Africa. Last, two Reggione fighters (much resembling Hurricanes) followed in some Hurricanes as they were landing on the *Victorious.* Accepted as friendly by the gunners, each dropped a large bomb. One just missed the bows, but the other fell square on the flight deck, where it would have done immense damage had it penetrated and almost as much if it had exploded among the parked planes. To the general astonishment on board and the justified anger of the Italian pilot, the bomb fragmented without exploding.

Throughout the long, hot afternoon, as the convoy and its escort drew nearer to the Sicilian narrows, one submarine alarm succeeded another. Midsummer warm-water conditions in the Mediterranean were notoriously bad for sonar operators, and there were so many reports of contacts that eventually Rear Admiral Burrough ordered the convoy escort to drop depth charges routinely every half hour on either side of the convoy to discourage prowlers. Real enough, however, was a torpedo track seen at 4.40 P.M., followed by a periscope sighting; in the ensuing depth-charge attack the Italian submarine *Emo* was damaged but managed to escape. On the other side of the convoy, and almost at the same time, the Italian *Cobalto* was forced to the surface by depth charges and then rammed by the destroyer *Ithuriel.* Her survivors were taken prisoner.

Throughout the blindingly hot day, when the proverbial egg would have sizzled on any exposed metal surface, every member of every ship's company, whether carrier, destroyer, battleship, or merchantman, had been ceaselessly at action stations. Submarines could retire to reconsider another attack position, the bombers could withdraw and be replaced by other planes with fresh pilots, but the carrier pilots—like the gun crews, the sonar ratings, the stokers, and the entire complement of convoy and escort—had to remain permanently at their posts. Tired and blistered by heat, the armada turned at last toward the Skerki Channel—the beginning of the approaches through the concentric rings of the inferno at the heart of which lay the island of Malta.

So far the fleet had lost the *Eagle* and the *Deucalion,* while the *Ithuriel* had retired to Gibraltar with damaged bow. The *Victorious* had been hit but not seriously, and many other ships had been near-missed but suffered only slight damage. Even allowing for the fine defense put up by the carrier-borne aircraft and the accurate gunnery of the fleet, it had to be conceded that, in view of the weight of attack thrown at them, they had been lucky so far. The great testing ground lay ahead, as they came within range of the Luftwaffe airfields in Sicily and entered the narrows, where submarines and undoubtedly E-boats were bound to lie in wait. There was also the danger of an attack by surface ships from Sicily. It was at this point, as the evening came down, that Force Z, the battleships and carriers and other units, had to leave and turn back to the west. But before that happened there came one last daylight raid of Stukas coupled with torpedo bombers fresh from Sicily that gave a bitter foretaste of the future. The raid was not unexpected, for radar and reconnaissance aircraft had for some time been reporting planes gathering around the edges of the convoy, visible here and there, then thickening—waiting.

It was a perfectly coordinated combined attack by Savoia torpedo bombers and Stuka dive-bombers that overwhelmed the defenses and broke through, achieving the first major air success of the whole operation. As in that earlier convoy to Malta, when *Fliegerkorps X* had effectively cripped H.M.S. *Illustrious,* so now amid the general maelstrom of Savoias attacking with torpedoes, fighters peeling off in defense of their bombers, and the thunder of the fleet's antiaircraft guns, a group of Stukas dropped down in perfect sequence, taking the *Indomitable* as their target.

No two accounts of confused actions between sea fleets and air fleets ever agree, for the good reason that everyone concerned is totally concentrating within his own sphere of action. For each there is only one particular cone of light and noise and danger that exists. The historian's distant eye, examining the information, can piece together no more than flecks of color, as when a pointillist painting is seen too close up to coalesce into a coherent whole. The *Victorious,* near-missed several times, was hit by three bombs on her flight deck and flared with gasoline fires. Aircraft began burning, and her aft elevator was put out of action. The carrier could no longer receive her own aircraft when they needed to return from the air battle, so they had to be redirected to the *Indomitable,* now overburdened with aircraft and the only carrier left operational out of the three that had set out from Gibraltar. No other ships were put out of action by the Stukas, but the screening destroyers lost one of their number to the torpedo bombers as the *Foresight,* her whole stern blown away, shuddered to a halt. With her motive power gone and too damaged to be towed, she had to be sunk as the convoy moved on.

The dark was coming down, the raid was over, and Force Z had come to the end of its protective role. Admiral Syfret was well aware, as he turned back to the west, that the worst could only lie ahead for the Malta-bound convoy. His heavy ships, those powerful pieces on the great chessboard, had been ventured as far as possible, but he could at least leave Admiral Burrough with his three cruisers and twelve destroyers in possession of a convoy out of which only one merchant ship had been lost.

As the convoy prepared to enter the Skerki Channel, that narrow passage of deep water between invisible sandbars (a place ideal for the skillful submariner to lurk, where sonar transmissions were confused by the irregularity of the bottom) they had to change formation and become a long double line. Well-drilled though they were, it was inevitable that this major changeover for convoy and escort led to some degree of loss in their organized progression. At 7:45 P.M. the first ship to enter the channel, at the head of the port column of ships, was the cruiser *Nigeria,* Admiral Burrough's flagship. A minute later the antiaircraft cruiser *Cairo,* leading the starboard column, followed her in. Behind them the others, closing up into their two columns, followed their leaders over the darkening calm sea, where Lieutenant Renato Ferrini of the submarine *Axum* had already noted: "It is flat calm [and] the feather of the periscope is conspicuous even at minimum speed." At 7:55 P.M. he fired his full spread of four torpedoes from the bow tubes. At almost the same moment another Italian submarine, the *Dessie,* had also fired. Within a few minutes the darkening waters were lit by brilliant flashes and split by the thunderous roar as the *Nigeria* was hit amidships. The *Cairo* was hit aft and had her screws blown away, while the convoy's only tanker, *Ohio,* was hit amidships.

In a moment all coherence of convoy and escort was lost. The

Ohio came to a temporary halt, thus causing the *Empire Hope* behind her to go hard astern in order to avoid collision. Other ships were turning independently to comb torpedo tracks, while the destroyers, were racing to give help—and adding to the confusion. The fact that the two column leaders, the *Nigeria* and *Cairo,* were torpedoed was bad enough, but the fact that the *Nigeria* was Admiral Burrough's flagship meant a temporary loss of control. The *Cairo* was also the only specifically antiaircraft cruiser in the escort, while she and the *Nigeria* were the only two ships fitted with fighter-direction equipment for controlling fighter aircraft from Malta. Against the flames and rending sounds of metal giving away, shouts and agitated figures visible here and there in leaping fires and the drumming roar of the *Nigeria* blowing off steam, the well-timed last aircraft raid of the day came in out of the east. They had the disordered convoy silhouetted against the last pale afterglow of the vanished sun. The carrier fighters had been struck down aboard the *Victorious,* which was well on her way back to Gibraltar. To add to the confusion, during the attack by Junkers 88s and Savoia torpedo-bombers, a formation of long-range Beaufighters arrived from Malta, only to receive an irregular and irrational fire ("If it flies, shoot it!")

Lieutenant Puccini in the submarine *Alagi* now put in an appearance and fired his bow torpedoes "at a cruiser"—undoubtedly hitting the *Kenya* and possibly a merchantman at the same time. Certainly, during this combined submarine and air attack, the *Kenya* was hit in the forefoot, narrowly escaping two other torpedoes, while the *Brisbane Star* and *Clan Ferguson,* both hit either by submarine or aerial torpedoes, came lurching to a halt. The ammunition on the latter went up with a shattering roar and she disappeared. The *Empire Hope,* hit by one of the dive-bombers, caught fire and had to be abandoned. The *Nigeria,* it was soon established, was so badly damaged that she would only be a liability if she continued with the convoy, so Admiral Burrough was reluctantly forced to transfer his flag to the destroyer *Ashanti* while his cruiser limped back to Gibraltar. At the same time Captain Russell in the *Kenya,* not knowing what had happened to the admiral, signaled that he had taken command. Then his own ship was hit in the bows, but it was established that she could still maintain a fair speed. Russell hastened to the head of the convoy even as Admiral Burrough was transferring to the *Ashanti* to take over again. Some time after Lieutenant Puccini had made his attack and disengaged to settle on the bottom, he decided to surface again to see if he could establish what all the random explosions and high-speed propeller noises he had heard above him signified. At 9:13 P.M. he came up, looked around, and noted: "The horizon between bearings 180° and 240° is a continuous line of flame from the burning, sinking ships." And a little later: "A burning ship blows up."

The *Ohio,* meanwhile, which had come to a stop with a great hole torn in her side, had by a masterwork of seamanship been got under way again and, with bulkheads shored up, was making her way slowly after the convoy. The *Brisbane Star* had also got under way, but her master realized that he could not catch up and turned to hug the Tunisian coast in the hope that he could make his way independently to Malta. (This was something he finally managed to do, in an epic voyage distinguished even in a convoy that had enough such epics to keep writers busy for years.) Cohesion had now left Force X, as some masters made their way alone or accompanied by one or other of the destroyers. One small body was still sailing as a group. This consisted of two fleet destroyers with their minesweeping sweeps streamed (it was still thought that some of the losses might have been due to mines) followed by the two cruisers *Kenya* and *Manchester* and two merchantmen, the *Glenorchy* and the American *Almeria Lykes.*

After the attacks by the aircraft and the submarines it was the turn of the fast motor torpedo boats—the E-boats—which had been waiting quietly, their engines stopped, lolling on the easy swell off the great bulk of Cape Bon. It was ideal weather for their work—moonless, but bright with starshine—and no young lieutenant in command of one of those powerful boats (the dash and élan of a Spitfire afloat) could have imagined a more perfect night for a convoy attack. As the ships began to draw close, the hunters, invisible against the dark loom of the land, one by one began to spring into attack. The quick cough of the engines starting was followed by that dark and powerful roar as their engines hurled them at the oncoming ships. Two Italian boats sprang toward the cruiser *Manchester,* and two torpedoes left her immobilized—to be scuttled the following day. Everywhere now the night began to be lit by tracer fire, an occasional searchlight beam, harsh cracks from the ships' main armament, the old-fashioned hammering sound of pom-poms, spraying crackle from Oerlikons, and the intermittent tracer and stammering of Italian Breda all-purpose guns. This was indeed revenge for so many ships sunk by the British in the Cape Bon area. The American *Almeria Lykes* went down, most of her crew being taken off by one of the destroyers. After the *Glenorchy* was hit, her crew, all except the master, abandoned ship. (She sank the next day, Captain Leslie going down with her.) E-boats also claimed the *Wairangi*, while the American *Santa Elisa*, damaged by bombing the previous day, now succumbed to a torpedo that set fire to her gasoline cargo, which then ran into her ammunition, which in its turn exploded.

The *Rochester Castle* had made as many as eleven emergency turns to evade attacking E-boats, but she finally ran out of luck and was hit by a torpedo forward. Fortunately, the bulkheads held, and she was able to stay with the surviving ships as, almost all order lost, the survivors plodded east toward the dawn.

It was a dawn for which they prayed—and which at the same time they feared. All the flash and roar and scattering of fire and shells and the inexplicable explosions of the night were so much the worse for occurring in the middle watch, the graveyard watch, where darkness, tiredness, and confusion added to simple human fear. But with the dawn they could expect the bombers. Although they knew they were within range of some kind of long-range protection from Malta, they knew that they were too far away for secure fighter cover. They had also seen how, even under an umbrella of fighters from the fleet, nothing could stop a determined torpedo plane or dive-bomber.

Admiral Burrough aboard the *Ashanti* had a further grim preoccupation at dawn on August 13. He had heard from Malta the previous evening that a reconnaissance aircraft had reported six cruisers and eleven destroyers steaming south through the Tyrrhenian Sea. Although he had been reinforced from Force Z by two destroyers and a light cruiser, the *Charybdis,* he was otherwise left with only the damaged *Kenya* and seven destroyers should the Italians decide to complete the destruction of the convoy. There was not much of it. Astern of him trailed the *Melbourne Star* and the *Waimarama,* then the damaged and most important ship of all, the *Ohio,* and behind her again the *Dorset* and *Port Chalmers.* (He did not know that in the waters off Tunisia to the south the *Brisbane Star* was fighting her solitary battle to reach the island.) Nor did he know that the threat posed by the Italian cruisers had vanished.

31

Miraculous Relief

During the night of August 12–13, while the convoy had been fighting and sinking off Cape Bon, the Italian cruisers had indeed been heading around the northwestern point of Sicily to intervene on the following day. Their destination obvious, their course and position observed, Malta had dispatched Wellington bombers to illuminate them with flares and attack during the night. Although none of the Italian ships were hit, their Naval Command was concerned. Since their position was known, they would certainly be attacked by torpedo bombers from Malta at daybreak. The commanders were further confused by signals that they picked up from the British planes (deliberately made in plain language) which suggested that Liberator bombers were also being dispatched to attack the cruisers.

All of these problems, coupled with the fact that the Regia Aeronautica, under pressure from Kesselring to provide every plane for the destruction of the convoy, had informed the Navy that no fighters would be available for the protection of their ships during daylight hours, led to the recall of the cruiser squadron. While they were retiring to the north on the morning of August 13, they were intercepted by Lieutenant Mars in the submarine *Unbroken* in the vicinity of the Lipari Islands. Two of them were torpedoed, a heavy and a light cruiser being so badly damaged that they were never repaired to take any further part in the war.

If Admiral Burrough could have been spared this worry, nothing could spare him and the ships under his protection from the weight of air attack that was soon to fall on them. They were some two hundred miles from Malta, southeast of the Italian island of Pantellaria, but they had no means of communicating with the Beaufighters from Malta when they did arrive nor of directing them, since both the cruisers with VHF direction sets had been lost. At 8 A.M. the first wave of Junkers 88s came in, and the *Waimarama* took a direct hit. She disintegrated with an ear-splitting roar, and the sea around her ran like a blast furnace with flaming aviation fuel. The *Melbourne Star* following close astern of her was deluged with flaming debris, fire and giant pieces of iron raining down all over her. Engulfed in flames, her own paintwork burning, the *Melbourne Star* steamed through the explosion while over thirty of her crew, convinced that it was their own ship that had blown up, leaped over the side. Most of them, together with two or three tragically burned survivors who had been hurled from the exploding *Waimarama*, were rescued from the blazing sea by the destroyer *Ledbury*. The *Ohio*, next in line behind the *Melbourne Star*, was also showered with burning fragments, starting a fire in her deck cargo of kerosene, which her crew fought with superhuman fervor—for no one expects much future in a tanker that has already been torpedoed and is now on fire.

The *Ohio* was inevitably the main target for the next wave of dive-bombers. Although they did not score any hits, some of her forward plating was buckled. To add to the damage, part of one of the planes that had been hit by gunfire crashed aboard. The *Rochester Castle*, also near-missed and damaged, caught fire, but this was brought under control; although deep-laden from the tons of water rolling about below decks, she also managed to struggle on. The *Dorset* was left crippled, and the *Ohio*, near-missed again by half a dozen bombs (Stukas were attacking on this occasion), finally ground to a halt. Admiral Burrough sent the destroyers *Bramham* and *Penn* to stand by the two vessels. In the roar of the attacks, crash of guns, thunder of exploding bombs, and bursting boom of water falling aboard the ships from near-misses, there was no time to remember that it was the thirteenth of the month.

The destroyer *Port Chalmers*, the convoy commodore's flagship, had come unscathed through bombing raids and torpedo attacks, but she nearly met her end when one of her paravanes (mine-cutting devices streamed from each bow) suddenly began to vibrate in a sinister manner. This happened shortly after a further attack by Italian torpedo planes operating at long range, some of them launching *motobombas*. When the ship was stopped to investigate and the starboard paravane hoisted out of the water, it was seen that they had "caught" a torpedo. There was only one thing to do—lower it into the sea again, back away, and then slip the paravane when a suitable distance had intervened. As the *Port Chalmers* eased away astern from the taut, thrumming wire, there was a huge explosion (probably when the torpedo at the end touched bottom), and the ship shook as a fountain of water burst off her bows. No real damage was done, however, and she rejoined what was left of the convoy. There was now only the *Port Chalmers* herself, the *Rochester Castle* and the *Melbourne Star* left in the main body, the *Ohio* far behind with a destroyer standing by, and the *Dorset* also immobilized with another destroyer at hand. The Hunt-class *Ledbury* had been sent back to look for the cruiser *Manchester* (it was not known that she had been sunk), and after a fruitless search she too came to stand by the *Ohio.*

The small group of three merchantmen with their escorts and the cruiser *Kenya* (which had suffered an engine-room fire after another dive-bombing attack) now came within the cover of the short-range Malta Spitfires. The minesweeping squadron from Malta came out to meet them, and Admiral Burrough could now withdraw to Gibraltar with what was left of his Force X, handing over his remaining charges to the island's protection. The *Ohio* still wallowed uneasily some seventy miles away, but the *Dorset* had taken another dive-bombing raid and, despite the gunfire of the protecting *Bramham*, had been hit by a stick of bombs. Far away, almost forgotten, the *Brisbane Star,* after outwitting the French authorities in Tunisia and playing hide-and-seek with a U-boat, was still making progress. She had yet to make her solitary dash from the Tunisian shallows to Malta by night, hoping that the island's protecting aircraft would remember her existence on the following morning—before the enemy found her.

In what seems, from a suitable distance, the comfortable eighteenth century, the great jurist Sir William Blackstone wrote: "The royal navy of England hath ever been its greatest defence and ornament; it is its ancient and natural strength; the floating bulwark of the island." It was to the limestone bulwark of another island that the minesweepers and motor launches now preceded the three survivors of Operation Pedestal. At 6 P.M. under an evening sky when Fort St. Angelo glowed like a ruby against the light, one by one *Melbourne Star, Rochester Castle,* and *Port Chalmers* came through the breakwater, past the ancient forts, into the stained and devastated harbor. This time there was no panache. These were indeed survivors, and as always, the people were there in their thousands wildly waving and cheering. Yet this time there was something different in those voices that echoed round the ramparts. A large convoy had been expected, the radio had been full of it, and everyone knew that only a large convoy could save them. And then the ships . . . the very metal of them looked tired, their paintwork was blistered—one was so low in the water that under normal conditions she would not have been allowed to sea—and the scars, the torn metal, the bullet holes and the sides savaged by bomb splinters. And there was no tanker. Everyone knew that there had to be a tanker, for oil was as important as bread, that was understood by now. The governor-general, Lord Gort, was there to salute them, and there was even a small band playing. Santa Marija! Yes, the convoy had arrived. But only three ships—and there was no tanker.

At about the time that they made for their unloading berths, where soldiers and dockers waited, where transport was ready the moment that lines could be got ashore, at about this time the *Dorset* sank. At the same time the three destroyers *Penn, Branham,* and *Ledbury* were all standing by the crippled *Ohio.* They had just got way on her, so delicate and precarious a movement of her shattered and torn sides that it seemed like a breath on the water. And then there came another air raid. One bomb fell under the tanker's stern and yet another went down into her engine room, where it exploded. For the second time the *Ohio's* crew were taken off. It seemed unlikely that the ship could live.

Throughout that night the stores streamed ashore into Malta, the transport moving off by specially allocated routes to storage dumps far from danger. No raids had developed over this convoy once it had reached the harbor. The cover of Spitfires above the island had been complete (no less than 407 sorties by Spitfires and Beaufighters had been flown as soon as the convoy had come within range), and the only sound of aircraft engines overhead was friendly. Some crew members from the ships went ashore, only to find no bars, no cafés, no signs of life. They had been used to coming into battered ports in Britain, where at least there was always some form of entertainment—pubs, certainly, with beer even if no spirits and cigarettes. This was like landing on the moon. They had not previously understood what the word "siege" meant. When they went back to their ships (those who were not found berths ashore), they would not be disturbed by the clatter of machinery, the trampling of feet, the creak and groan of winches unloading, unloading, unloading. Oily, saltwater-skinned, dirty in dirty clothes, they slept out their nightmares far beyond the reach of dreams.

Out in the Mediterranean the still August weather, with hardly a cat's-paw of wind stirring the sea, remained friendly to the *Ohio* throughout the night. While her own exhausted crew lay where they dropped, heads pillowed on lifebelts in the attendant ships, the officers and men of the *Penn* and the Malta minesweeper *Rye,* later joined by the *Bramham* and *Ledbury,* struggled with the interminable problem of trying to tow a vessel that under any normal conditions would have been sunk. By morning they had her moving again, the *Penn* lashed alongside, the *Rye* towing from ahead, and the *Ledbury* acting as stern tug to try and keep her pointed in the direction of Malta. The *Ohio*'s master, Captain D. W. Mason, who had been without sleep for the past three days and nights, reported that he thought his ship might last a further twelve hours. She had less than three feet of freeboard and was slowly settling by the head, but he now had three destroyers, two minesweepers, and a number of motor launches around him. They were producing sufficient power to move the ship and keep her from sinking—but, as he estimated, not for very long.

The same night that had seen the great tanker slowly come to life had also been kind to Captain Riley in the *Brisbane Star.* He had managed to lose his shadowing U-boat in the Tunisian shallows at dusk and had headed north for Malta, making between five and nine knots—as much as could be expected, since the bows had been blown open in the torpedo attack off the Skerki Bank on the night of August 12. When he raised the old lionskin of the island in the daylight hours of the fourteenth, with a circle of Spitfires perpetually renewing itself over his head, and when his ship came in through the breakwater pushing an awkward sea ahead, where her shored-up forward bulkhead did duty as a bow, there were almost as many tears as cheers among the crowds. The torn ship seemed like a monument to the whole convoy. Although well down by the head, and with her forward holds flooded, most of the *Brisbane Star's* cargo was intact. Unloading began immediately.

That same morning the *Ohio* with her cluster of ships (the whole curious pattern of them spread like a broken flower head on the sea) was pushing slowly with eccentric wake in the direction of Malta. Despite the Spitfire patrols Junkers 88s made a final determined effort to deny the island that oil, more important than ever now that some bread had got through in the other ships. The Luftwaffe's dive-bomber pilots were brave and determined as ever, accepting the fire put up by the *Ohio* herself and her watchdogs of destroyers and minesweepers, but when the Spitfires got among them, their attacks were broken up. Three of the bombers still got through, although only one of them came close enough to all but sink the ship. His thousand-pound bomb landed just off her stern, and the explosion buckled her plates, causing her to heave forward on a great wave, and parting the tow. The sage of the Ohio has been often told (though, alas, no poets were around to do it justice),[3] of her last twenty-four-hour fight, avoiding minefields while destroyers and shore batteries put down submarines lying in wait for her, of how finally she came around the south of the island. Countrymen and women, gunners and children, watched with agonized concern as what seemed like a raft of ships struggled along the island's coastline. The Great Siege of 1565 had never witnessed anything as desperate and strange as those last miles of the *Ohio,* when Malta's hopes were suspended, so it seemed, on a bubble of air—or a prayer. For it was on August 15, the very day of the Festa of Santa Marija, that the last and most valuable of the ships struggled into Grand Harbour. Torpedoed, bombed, with parts of a bomber still on her deck, she was nursed down the harbor to be berthed alongside the sunken auxiliary tanker *Plumleaf* at Parlatorio Wharf. Her cargo was intact but, even as she was berthed, she began to settle on the bottom. Her decks had been almost awash for a long time. It had been that close a thing.

32

"We Shall Never Take You!"

The arrival of the four merchant ships, damaged though they were, and the survival of the tanker *Ohio* did indeed ensure the salvation of the island. It did not mean the end of the siege. The ultimate result of the expensive Operation Pedestal was to enable Malta to stay in the war. For the high price of thirteen ships sunk—nine merchant ships, one aircraft carrier, two cruisers, and a destroyer—and one aircraft carrier, two cruisers, and one destroyer damaged, the Royal Navy and the Merchant Navy had indeed saved Malta—but only just. Some thirty-two thousand tons of general cargo had reached Grand Harbour together with gasoline, fuel oil, kerosene, and diesel fuel—enough to give the island about ten weeks more of life beyond the existing stocks of only a few weeks. It was immediately recognized by the Axis that "the supplies which got through in this last convoy have assured an effective resistance by the island for some time to come."

No further attempts to neutralize Malta were contemplated, at least for the present, and the Regia Aeronautica and the Luftwaffe were diverted to the defense of their own convoys to their forces in North Africa. Operation Pedestal, though tactically disastrous, was transformed by the participants in it into what proved a strategic triumph, wrung out of appalling losses by the endurance, courage, and seamanship of the masters and crews of merchant and naval ships alike. As always, the national poet had summed it all up centuries before:

Out of this nettle, danger, we pluck this flower, safety.

After the relief of 1565 Balbi described in his diary how the soldiers and sailors went ashore, "to see the enormous damage to our battlements. These were so ruined that even the oldest veterans were astonished." This was to be the reaction of all the many thousands who came to Malta in the later years of the Second World War.[1] A further entry in Balbi's diary was unfortunately not to prove true for the survivors of 1942: "Now that the fleet had arrived, all of us who had been in the siege ate well, for there were supplies enough for all, even though they were costly." He adds, though, what was certainly true enough of this occasion also: ". . . during the siege, a fowl had cost two ducats (and even at that price they were rare to come by), while an egg had cost one *real* and a half. As for the other luxuries, I do not bother to mention them for they could not be obtained for any sum of money."

About the only improvement in food supplies that occurred after the arrival of the August 1942 convoy was that the bread ration for males between sixteen and sixty was slightly raised. During 1942 infant mortality, normally low on the island, significantly increased, while for the first time since records had been kept in Malta the population declined by nearly two thousand.

The principal effect of the Santa Marija convoy (as it is called to this day) was a great uplift of the spirits, coupled with the morale-boosting knowledge that they had all been as near to the end as could be faced by men and yet still endured. For several months they would still be dependent upon essential stocks being maintained by the steady turnover of fast minelayers like the *Manxman* and of minelaying submarines chuntering in at night—but on nights that were now, as often as not, raidless. From the moment that it was seen how no air attacks had developed during the unloading of these five prayed-for ships, from the moment that they had been seen entering Grand Harbour with a shield of Spitfires held shining over their battered hulls, a wave of confidence had surged through the watching thousands—to be transferred to others all over the island. Hunger had not gone away, but the knowledge that ships could now arrive and be protected meant that more ships would come in due course, and the will to endure was sustained to see them through.

The island of Malta was a legend now in the world, but it had been a legend in this sea long before. During the sixteenth century, after that first great siege, its example had been held up to the Greeks of the Aegean, who were at that time suffering severely under the ravages of the Ottoman Turks. Someone somewhere in Cyprus (at least the ballad is attributed to that island) had first framed the words designed to give men hope:

> "Malta of gold, Malta of silver, Malta of precious metal,
> We shall never take you!
> No, not even if you were as soft as a gourd,
> Not even if you were only protected by an onion skin!"
> And from her ramparts a voice replied:
> "I am she who has decimated the galleys of the Turk
> And all the warriors of Constantinople and Galata!"[2]

The words were true once again, only they spoke now to the whole free world.

The evidence of the convoy was soon to be seen in the increased activity of the island—an activity that swiftly reflected Rommel's calls for reinforcements and help at the end of his long supply line in Egypt. It was not so difficult for him to obtain men, for these were ferried across to North Africa in regular flights by Junkers 52 transport planes, but above all fuel, and then tanks, guns, armored cars, and every form of transport could only come by that same old sea route, threatened once again (and now as never before) by the island in the middle of the Middle Sea. Mussolini had long returned to Italy, bitterly disappointed of his Napoleonic triumph in Egypt, and the war-torn and much-diminished Italian merchant fleet was again called upon to run the gauntlet laid down by the submarines, bombers, and torpedo planes of Malta. It was now the turn of the German field marshal in the desert to lament "the frightful hardships in the heat and desolation of our positions."

Submarines and torpedo-carrying Beauforts escorted by Beaufighters were now unleashed upon that supply line at the end of which the harassed Axis forces were scarcely able to cope with the spoiling attacks launched by the British desert army, which was building up for a great offensive toward the end of the year.[3] It was no longer a question of "How many days to Cairo?" but of whether Rommel could even hold his enemy's attack when it came. His own supplies were being sunk on the sea route and being destroyed on the coastal roads. He complained of how "the R.A.F. had shifted the main weight of its activity to our lines of communication between the African ports and the front, where they were shooting up our transport columns and sinking one barge and coastal vessel after the other."

At the same time the British, with their long but relatively secure supply line, were beginning to profit by the immense American industrial expansion. New guns, tanks, and aircraft were now arriving regularly by sea in Egypt. Meanwhile the bulk of German arms and armaments were being eaten up by the Russian campaign, and what reached the Axis armies in the desert was only a trickle by the time it had survived the crossing past revived Malta, the unloading in the desert ports, and the journey on roads regularly harassed by the RAF. The route by the western coast of Greece through the Ionian Sea was no longer safe for Axis transports, since the long-range Beauforts and Beaufighters were able to reach them. Merchant ships had to be diverted on a tortuous route through the Corinth Canal and down through the Aegean past Crete. Rommel by this time was a sick man and would have been replaced—at his own request—if a suitable panzer general could have been found. There was none available and so, beset by worry and ill health, he continued at his post. His sanguine nature had led him to feel after the fall of Tobruk that Egypt was within his grasp. It was an understandable dream that had beckoned him, but he had known the reality early in 1941 when he had told Berlin: "Without Malta, the Axis will end by losing control of North Africa."

That control was finally lost in October 1942 at Alamein. Largely contributory to the Allied victory was the toll that had been taken over those late-summer and early-autumn months by the aircraft and submarines operating from Malta. Transport after transport had gone down, and tankers—as important to Rommel's army as the *Ohio* had been to Malta—sank blazing into the sea before torpedoes and bombs. Yet the island that dealt out this destruction was itself once again on the verge of starvation. Despite the continuance of the stringent rationing (the slight increase in the bread issue was soon found to have been a mistake) there was at the time of the breakthrough following upon El Alamein less than a two-week food supply for the garrison and the islanders, while the gasoline supply was so low that there was under one week left for offensive operations by the aircraft. To ensure that the planes flew and the submarines continued in their patrols Malta had been taken even further to the limit of "The Target Date" (the date for its surrender) than in August, when the Santa Marija convoy had arrived.

On October 11, at a time of the greatest shortages and starvation in the island, Field Marshal Kesselring made a last desperate bid to paralyze Malta and take the pressure off the Axis armies in the desert: He managed to assemble some three hundred German and Italian bombers in Sicily for a major onslaught. This meant transferring some aircraft from North Africa, which in itself weakened the defense and protection of Rommel's forces. Although the total number of aircraft mustered at the Sicilian airfields, including fighters, was something like six hundred, Malta could now put up one hundred Spitfires and a number of Beaufighters in its own defense. The raids lasted through nine days and were among the heaviest of the whole war. The number of civilian casualties in the island was especially heavy this time, because the bomber formations, broken up by the British fighters, inevitably dropped their loads over civilian areas rather than on military targets, now heavily protected by antiaircraft guns that were no longer limited in the ammunition they could use, as they had been in the terrible days of the spring.

"In many ways," wrote Colonel Weldon in his memoirs of the siege, "this last onslaught must have been the severest trial of all to the Maltese. It came after a long period of comparative inactivity by day when, perhaps, they might have been forgiven for thinking that the days of sudden and violent death had departed and gone. As it was, the full force of this attack struck them when they were almost at the lowest level of their powers of physical resistance. The prolonged starvation had begun to leave its mark and it is much easier to be brave if one has a full stomach."[4]

The townships of Qormi, Tarxien, and Rabat (outside the old capital Mdina) all suffered badly in these raids, and it was noticed—as some evidence of the attackers' desperation—that a large number of antipersonnel bombs as well as incendiaries were dropped by high-flying bombers. The first killed some harmless civilians, but the second, as the Italians had found out during the first days of the war, had little or no effect on limestone houses that were as enduring as the island itself.

The principal aim of this renewed attack was to damage the airfields and to submerge the island's striking power at a time when all-important convoys were being sent through to enable the Afrika Korps and the Italian forces to withstand or counterattack against the advancing British. On balance, the raids were a failure. The bomber losses were well over one hundred for the loss of thirty defending fighters, many of whose pilots parachuted to safety. At the same time the air offensive against the Axis shipping routes never faltered, and during this same month of October 40 percent of the supplies destined for Libya never reached there.

With the swing of the pendulum in the desert, Malta, which had been so largely responsible for it, could itself expect to reap some reward. Operation Stone Age, the passage of four merchantmen from Alexandria escorted by five cruisers and sixteen destroyers, took place in November. One old friend of Malta, the cruiser *Penelope,* was damaged by torpedo bombers during the passage, but despite these attacks all four ships and their escort entered Grand Harbour safely. The last part of their passage had been run through a November gale—conditions in which three Spitfires were lost and the island took on its wintry aspect under lowering clouds. But in this small island alone in the sea, gray weather never hangs for long, and the driven clouds parting revealed the sight of the first peaceful relief to reach Malta since the siege had started over two years before. There was the cruiser *Euryalus* with her Royal Marine band playing on the quarterdeck, the four undamaged merchantmen, the Hunt-class destroyers jinking around outside the breakwater, and the flashing wheel of fighters permanently overhead. The crowds that had cheered and waved for bomb-battered arrivals even when Grand Harbour itself had been under heavy attack were now free to indulge in real rejoicing. Although it would be months before full rations could be restored, even more months before the physical effects of the past would wear off,[5] and even years before the island could be restored to anything approaching its former peacetime state, yet the people knew at the sight of those four slab-sided merchantmen unloading, untouched, in their harbor that the siege was really over. There would still be occasional air raids in 1943, when the island would see the gathering of the armada that was to overwhelm Sicily and begin the restoration of Europe, and true peace was some years ahead, but the island's longest and most devastating siege was raised.

Although the bells could not yet be rung, the people might still have echoed the words written by the harequebusier Balbi on September 8, 1565, when the bells of the conventual church of St. Lawrence had sounded out once more over the shattered harbor: "I do not believe that ever did music sound so sweet to human beings. It was three months since we had ever heard a bell which did not summon us to arms against the enemy. That morning, when they rang for Mass, it was at the same hour that we had grown used to expect the call to arms. All the more solemnly then, did we give thanks to the Lord God, and to His Blessed Mother, for the favours that They had poured upon us."

Notes

CHAPTER ONE

1. For information about Hitler's reaction to Mussolini's declaration of war I am indebted to David Irving, *Hitler's War* (New York: Viking Press, 1977), and in particular to the chapter "The Warlord at the Western Front."

2. Peter Elliott in *The Cross and the Ensign: A Naval History of Malta 1798-1979* (Annapolis, Md.: Naval Institute Press, 1980) has much useful information about Malta in the interwar years and its first preparations against aerial attack.

3. There are numerous accounts of the first day of Malta's aerial bombardment. Lieutenant Colonel H. E. C. Weldon, R.A., in *Drama in Malta* (London: Gale & Polden, 1947), recorded his impressions from the point of view of a serving artillery officer on that day as well as in the subsequent stages. Joseph Attard in *The Battle of Malta* (London: William Kimber, 1980) has given us his account of a young boy growing up during those years.

4. For the number of aircraft involved during these raids and similar information during the course of the siege I am indebted not only to the British records but to Mariano Gabriele, *Operazione C3: Malta* (Roma: 1975). This book also contains detailed information about the preparations by Italian military and naval forces to invade the island, Operation Hercules.

5. Casualty figures vary from one account to another. Stewart Perowne, *The Siege Within the Walls* (London: Hodder and Stoughton, 1970), takes his figures from "A young amateur statistician, Mr. Michael Galea, [who] has compiled from official records a list of every single civilian victim from this first day until the last raid in April 1942. (The last alert was sounded on 28th August 1944)."

6. See Ernie Bradford, *The Great Siege: Malta 1565* (New York: Harcourt, Brace, 1961).

CHAPTER TWO

1. There are many books about every aspect of the Maltese archipelago, for the history of these small islands comprises the history of the Mediterranean. Among the most comprehensive is Brian Blouet, *A Short History of Malta* (New York: Frederick Prager, 1967). Sir Harry Luke, *Malta* (London: George Harrap, 1960), presents a sympathetic picture of the island and its political and economic problems by one who was lieutenant governor of Malta from 1930 to 1938. (See the select bibliography of books about the island and its part in World War II at the back of the book.)

2. P. Brydone, F.R.S., *A Tour through Sicily and Malta in a Series of Letters to William Beckford, Esq., of Somerly in Suffolk* (London: W. Strahan, 1773).

CHAPTER THREE

1. Here and where indicated throughout, the quotations from Admiral Cunningham are taken from his autobiography, *A Sailor's Odyssey* by Admiral of the Fleet Viscount Cunningham of Hyndhope (New York: E. P. Dutton, 1951).

2. Ibid.

3. Ibid.

4. Francis Ebejer in his novel *Requiem for a Malta Fascist* (Malta: A. C. Aquilina, 1980) has vividly recaptured the atmosphere of the prewar years and of the siege itself seen through the eyes of a young Maltese growing up under British colonial rule, the shadow of Mussolini, and the massive aerial bombardment.

5. Despatch of the Secretary of State for the Colonies on the Language Question, August 16, 1934.

6. Sir Harry Luke, op. cit., deals at length not only with the language question but other social and political matters of the period.

CHAPTER FOUR

1. For this information I am indebted to Stewart Perowne, op. cit. Mr. Perowne, although not himself present during the siege, knew Malta well for many years, both before and after the war. His account is largely based on the reminiscences of friends and acquaintances whom he interviewed in later years.

2. Cunningham, op. cit.

3. The brief account of this action is based on Admiral Cunningham's dispatch of April 27, 1948, to the *London Gazette*.

CHAPTER FIVE

1. A. E. Housman, "Epitaph on an Army of Mercenaries," *Last Poems* (New York: Henry Holt, 1922).

2. Brian Blouet, op. cit., writes: "On the first day of the Italian campaign against Malta the Gladiators brought down an enemy aircraft, and although one of the four was quickly damaged beyond repair the remaining three continued to make a considerable nuisance of themselves and were soon nicknamed Faith, Hope and Charity. . . . Some measure of the Gladiators' effectiveness is given by the fact that Italian airmen operational over Malta estimated the strength of the defending fighter force at 25! How many aircraft Faith, Hope and Charity ac-

counted for is in doubt as in the hectic battle conditions it was rarely possible to confirm a kill. One Gladiator pilot was credited with six victories in one month and awarded the Distinguished Flying Cross early in June 1940." The partially rebuilt skeleton of Faith (the only survivor) has been preserved in Malta, as have some of the arms and armour of the Knights who in their time had fought to preserve the island from invasion.

3. Cunningham, op. cit.

4. George Hogan, *Malta: The Triumphant Years* (London: Robert Hale, 1978).

5. Jeremy Boissevain, *Saints and Fireworks: Religion and Politics in Rural Malta* (New York: Humanities Press, 1965).

6. Weldon, op. cit.

7. Cunningham, op. cit.

8. Ibid.

CHAPTER SIX

1. Joseph Micallef, *When Malta Stood Alone* (Malta: 1981).

2. The one word *Is-Silg* in Maltese serves to cover snow, hail, and ice. Literally, *Ilma maghqud,* congealed or frozen water.

3. Ian Cameron, *Red Duster, White Ensign* (London: Frederick Muller, 1959).

4. Cunningham, op. cit.

CHAPTER SEVEN

1. Weldon, op. cit.

2. Cunningham, op. cit.

3. Joseph Attard, op. cit. An invaluable account from an islander's point of view.

4. Ibid.

5. Weldon, op. cit.

6. Quoted in *The Air Battle of Malta* (London: His Majesty's Stationery Office, 1944).

7. Ibid.

8. Cameron, op. cit.

CHAPTER EIGHT

1. The full story of the Italian involvement in the war as far as it related to Malta, as well as the planning of the invasion that never happened, is to be found in Mario Gabriele, op. cit., which is valuable in presenting the other side of the picture as well as that presented by the British and Maltese historians and diarists.

2. Eric Brockman, C.B.E., *Last Bastion. Sketches of the Maltese Islands* (London: Darton, Longman & Todd, 1961).

3. *The Times of Malta* was admirably edited throughout the siege by the remarkable Miss Mabel Strickland, O.B.E. The daughter of Lord Strickland, she profited by her father's perspicacity in seeing the necessity for deep air-raid shelters long before the war. Although his counsel had gone unheeded by the authorities at the time, he had provided for his own newspaper an almost bombproof

headquarters carved out of the rock. The newspaper continued to be issued daily under Miss Strickland's direction throughout the war, even when most of Valletta lay in ruins round about.

4. Quoted in Joseph Micalleff, op. cit.

5. A full account of this action can be found in Captain S. W. C. Pack, *The Battle of Matapan* (London: B. T. Batsford, 1961) as well as in the account given by Admiral Cunningham in his autobiography.

CHAPTER NINE

1. F. W. Winterbotham, C.B.E., *The Ultra Secret* (New York: Harper & Row, 1974). The breaking of Enigma as first told in Group Captain Winterbotham's book revealed one of the last great secrets of World War II. All previous histories to one extent or another need to be reviewed in the light of this revelation. Subsequent books enlarging upon the subject have included Peter Calvocoressi, *Top Secret Ultra* (New York: Pantheon Books, 1980). The United States being a more open society than the United Kingdom, somewhat similar American successes in breaking Japanese ciphers before and after Pearl Harbor have long been public knowledge. The absence after so many years of a great deal of Ultra material in the Public Records Office in Britain has been commented upon by others.

2. The writer spent some months of 1951 in his sailboat in the old boat pound of the Knights of St. John, where some of their galleys used to be housed. It lies behind Fort St. Angelo and the old city of Birgu (Vittoriosa). Opposite it, right under the towering rock on which St. Angelo was built, lies the cavelike entrance to the tunnels that once housed the galley slaves, and later some of the World War II staff as described. To walk through these tunnels today is to walk with many ghosts.

3. Although the German paratroop invasion of Crete was known about in advance and General Freyberg was fully informed, it would seem that it was not so much an unwillingness to act upon Ultra that prevented a counterattack at the right time as some military mishandling of the information. On the other hand, it was because of forewarning by Ultra of German intentions that no seaborne convoys ever reached the island and that the losses among German paratroopers were so heavy as to be unacceptable.

CHAPTER TEN

1. In addition to that available in official postwar histories, much vivid information about RAF activities during the siege can be gained from *The Air Battle of Malta,* op. cit.

2. In the notes on rationing Joseph Micallef (op. cit.) comments: "Families of five or less were entitled to four boxes of matches; larger families were allowed six. Soap and coffee rations were more complicated: a single person was entitled to one bar of soap [rations were issued on the 6th and 21st of each month]; a family of four or less got two bars; families of five to eight persons got three bars. Families of three or less had a ration of ¼ rotolo of coffee. . . . [A rotolo is an old Maltese measure, still in use in the island, the equivalent of 28 ounces.] In August

1941 lard, margarine and edible oil were also put on the ration card. The tapering scale was also applied to these items."

Kerosene, used for cooking and lighting, was rationed on a weekly basis from May 1941. The kerosene carts that supplied the towns and villages were horse-drawn, and the distribution was under the supervision of the local police. The rationing of kerosene caused more disputes than almost any other item, being particularly susceptible to bribery and black-market operations. Canned tunafish and sardines, a daily fare of the working men, became increasingly scarce and again were bought up by the unscrupulous and sold at black-market prices.

CHAPTER ELEVEN

1. The letter "X" is pronounced "sh" in Maltese. The sirocco is also known as the *Rih Isfel*, the "Wind from below"—from Africa to the south. Seamen's refinements are *Xlokk lvant*—southeast sirocco—and *Xlokk punent*—southwest sirocco. The sirocco is most common in spring and autumn; the latter is the most unpleasant, being warmer and more humid. The respite that the Maltese found from aerial attack during the war when a heavy sirocco blew was also enjoyed by the garrison of Tobruk, where the wind was felt as the desert *khamsin,* which could completely obscure sky and sun with sand. Under this gritty blanket, unpleasant though it was, the soldiers, sailors, and airmen knew at least that they would be spared the routine attention of the Stukas.

2. The identification of Malta and Gozo with Calypso's isles was made by Byron in a poem during a visit in 1809. The game of identifying places mentioned in the wanderings of Odysseus was popular enough in classical times, but the Maltese archipelago does not seem to have been proposed as the home of the goddess Calypso until the eighteenth or nineteenth century, when the identification of places mentioned in classical literature was being pursued all over the Mediterranean, mainly for the edification of rich, classically educated travelers from the north. Modern guides usually show visitors the cave overlooking the sandy bay of Ramla on the northeast coast of Gozo as the home of Calypso, where she detained Odysseus for seven years. All such ascriptions are of course purely imaginative, and as good a case can be made out for a cave above Pwales Valley with its ever-running stream on Malta's northeast coast.

3. Vice Admiral Sir Wilbraham Ford was one of the main pillars of Malta's defense. His work overseeing the dockyard and particularly in getting so great a part of the engineering workshops sited in tunnels and safe from bombs did much to ensure Malta's efficiency in the darkest days of the siege.

4. Commander W. P. Carne was the fleet torpedo officer responsible for suggesting this method for dealing with Malta's magnetic mine problem. He later went on to become captain of H.M.S. *Coventry,* a famous antiaircraft cruiser that saw more action, protecting both fleet and convoys in the Luftwaffe-dominated years to come, than almost any other ship.

CHAPTER TWELVE

1. It has sometimes been suggested that General Freyberg did not make the best use of Ultra during the campaign. There is little evidence one way or the

other. The great error, leading to the loss of Crete, was the failure to send into Maleme Airfield the two New Zealand battalions held in reserve at Canea. That the Royal Navy would never permit any reinforcements to be landed by sea, no matter what the loss to itself, seems to have been something that the general did not understand. Had he had full confidence in the Navy, he would have sent in the reserve battalions and held the airfield. In fact, no seaborne reinforcements reached the invaders until such time as the order to abandon Crete had been given and the last of the Allied survivors were being taken off—an operation that totally engaged all of Cunningham's ships that were still seaworthy.

2. In the postwar years a number of books were written about the Battle of Crete by survivors and others. A novel that gives the bitter taste of those days is the second volume of Evelyn Waugh's "Sword of Honour" trilogy, *Officers and Gentlemen* (Boston: Little, Brown, 1955).

3. Cunningham, op. cit.

4. Ibid. A previous attempt to send the *Glenroy* to Crete with reinforcements on May 22 and 23 had been turned back on Cunningham's express command—in contradiction to orders from the Admiralty. "It appeared to be sheer murder to send her on," he later wrote.

Winston Churchill seems always to have been hypnotized by the Aegean Sea and to have been unlucky there—from the Dardanelles campaign of World War I onward. As late as 1944, for no good reason except perhaps the hope of involving Turkey on the Allied side, he initiated the unfortunate (and usually tacitly ignored) Dodecanese campaign. A number of destroyers were sunk or badly damaged, operating once again in narrow waters without air cover and providing perfect targets for the by then almost obsolete Stuka. The writer was aboard H.M.S. *Glenroy* in the first of these campaigns and in H.M.S. *Exmoor* for the second.

CHAPTER THIRTEEN

1. The city of Valletta and the fortress architecture of Malta has been brilliantly dealt with in words and photographs by Professor J. Quentin Hughes: *Fortress. Architecture and Military History in Malta* (Lund, Humphries, 1969).

2. A typical instance of such a raid is given by Eric Newby, *Love and War in the Apenines* (London: Hodder and Stoughton, 1971). In this case a raid on the aerodrome at Catania was the objective, and the whole atmosphere of such an operation is well portrayed.

3. Donald Macintyre, *The Battle for the Mediterranean* (London: 1964).

CHAPTER FOURTEEN

1. The dramatic story of how the *Sydney Star* managed to reach Malta on her own through every kind of hazard is told in Chapter 5, Cameron, op. cit., a book that recounts the exploits of the major convoys to the island and many of the individual actions that form part of that history.

2. Joseph Attard, op. cit., states that a number of these expeditions were made for reconnaissance purposes and that Commander Moccagatta "who was in charge of the Malta operation . . . said that the Italians had to rely on this type of

reconnaissance because they could not find and they did not have a single spy on Malta."

3. Stewart Perowne, op. cit.

4. The siege of Fort St. Elmo was a principal feature of the Great Siege of 1565, and the length of time that it took the Turkish forces to reduce the fortress was largely responsible for their ultimate defeat.

CHAPTER FIFTEEN

1. George Hogan, op. cit.

2. The quotation comes from "A Chinese Sage" in Lin Yutang, *The Importance of Living* (New York: Reynal & Hitchcock, 1937).

3. Francis Ebejer, op. cit.

4. Whitworth Porter, *The History of the Knights of Malta* (London: Longmans, Green, 1883).

5. Even between the citizens of the two main islands of the archipelago, Gozo and Malta, there exists some rivalry. Malta is basically dependent for its livelihood on the dockyards, shipping repairs, and light industry, while Gozo is the market garden of the islands. Tourism involving both islands has proved something of a leveling influence, but quite recently a Gozitan was still capable of remarking to the writer: "That's the only thing that spoils the view." He was pointing south across the blue strait at Malta, only three miles away.

CHAPTER SIXTEEN

1. *The Air Battle of Malta,* op. cit., and Weldon, op. cit.

2. Captain S. W. Roskill, D.S.C., *The War at Sea* (London: Her Majesty's Stationery Office, 1954–1961).

CHAPTER SEVENTEEN

1. Credit is indeed given in F. H. Hinsley, ed., *British Intelligence in the Second World War,* Vol. III, Part I (London: Her Majesty's Stationery Office, 1984) to the part played by Combined Operations pilotage parties prior to the invasion of Sicily. Even so, one distinguished review of this publication was headlined "Bletchley's Victory."

2. *The Air Battle of Malta,* op. cit., has the following anecdote: "While carrying out, unarmed, a low-level photographic reconnaissance of Bizerta in November 1942, Warburton was attacked and shot up by Me.109s. His aircraft was hit in the engine, oil tank and compass, and he was compelled to land at Bonê. He made his way, via Algiers, to Gibraltar, where he collected a fighter [a Spitfire] which was awaiting delivery to Malta. While flying this machine back he encountered two Ju.88s in the Gulf of Tunis and attacked them. One he shot down, the other managed to escape into cloud. He then returned to his astonished colleagues who had already given him up as missing, having heard nothing of him for four days." Later in the war he was "loaned" to the U.S. Air Force for photographic missions after the big daylight raids over Europe.

In the course of his career Warburton earned two Distinguished Service Orders and three Distinguished Flying Crosses. He disappeared finally under mysterious circumstances, and it is right that his friend Group Captain Spooner should have the last word: "Needless to say, he was flying an aircraft (an American one) that didn't belong to him. . . . Some profess to believe that he is still alive. Just as some believe that Lawrence of Arabia still lives. With such men, and there was much in common between them, anything is possible—anything other than the ordinary."—A. Spooner, D.S.O., D.F.C., *In Full Flight* (London: Macdonald, 1965).

3. Joseph Attard, op. cit.

4. The following table shows quite clearly how, contrary to the general principle that ships are safer in convoy, this was not so in the exceptional circumstances prevailing in the Mediterranean in World War II:

Aug. 1940–Aug. 1942	Sailed for Malta	Sunk	Turned Back	Arrived
In convoy	55	22	11	22
Alone	31	9	1	21

The convoy system that operated so successfully elsewhere did not do so in the context of Malta because the movement of a large convoy was immediately known to the enemy, and in the passage through the Sicilian narrows (dominated by enemy air as well as being mined) the odds were stacked against the convoy. Individual ships, on the other hand, especially if they were old and small and kept close to the edge of French territorial waters along the North African coast, making their final dash for Malta by night, had a good chance of getting through. See Cameron, op. cit.

CHAPTER EIGHTEEN

1. Hughes, op. cit.

2. After the Great Siege of 1565 spies for the Ottomans quite often reported on the state of the island and its defenses, as the sultans succeeding Suleiman the Magnificent did not entirely despair of triumphing where he had failed. Well before the eighteenth century, however, the fortifications of Malta were so massive and so ingenious as to be quite beyond the besieging capability of any armies or navies of the time.

3. Letter quoted extensively in Ernle Bradford, *Mediterranean: Portrait of a Sea* (London: Hodder and Stoughton, 1971).

4. Spooner, op. cit.

5. Macintyre, op. cit. In Chapter 6 the writer deals in detail with some of the worst Axis shipping casualties of this period.

CHAPTER NINETEEN

1. In the Great Siege of 1565 the Turkish commanders first made the mistake of concentrating all their efforts against Fort St. Elmo, failing to observe that Fort St. Angelo and the walled village of Birgu (Vittoriosa) behind it should have been the main objective. They also should have severed the communications between Grand Harbour and the north of the island, including the old capital of Mdina. Unlike Kesselring, Dragut was unable to reverse these tactics for fear of loss of morale among the Ottoman troops. See Ernle Bradford, *The Great Siege,* op. cit.

2. British and Maltese fought side by side at the gun positions. Maltese also

served throughout the war in the Mediterranean fleet. The Royal Malta Artillery received numerous awards for gallantry. From February 1941 there was national service for all males between sixteen and sixty-five in the island and military service for those between eighteen and forty-one. The complaint of the Italian commander in charge of the small-boat raid—that they did not have a single spy on the island—should be borne in mind in this context.

3. Weldon, op. cit.

4. Vice Admiral Sir Wilbraham Ford, who was knighted in 1942, had spent five years in Malta when he was relieved in 1942 by Vice Admiral Sir Ralph Leatham. As Admiral Cunningham rightly said of him: "It is no exaggeration to say that he was one of the mainstays of the defence of Malta."

CHAPTER TWENTY

1. One such prayer to the Virgin Mary, translated from Maltese, reads:

> *O Maiden Lady of Victory,*
> *Queen of Heaven and Earth,*
> *Gather the bombs into your mantle*
> *And deliver us from the attack.*

2. In postwar politics, prior to the island's independence in 1964, some play was made by the Malta Labour party with the argument—in favor of neutrality—that Malta's sufferings in World War II would never have occurred but for her being a British colony. But, particularly given the moral approach of the German and Italian states at the time, is it conceivable that Maltese neutrality would have been respected? Such an ideal harbor, situated in the center of the Mediterranean, would still have been fought over. Malta's geographical importance, which has also given it one of the highest standards of living in the depressed region of the Mediterranean, has always had to be paid for.

3. Hummel E. Siewert, *Il Mediterraneo* (Milan: 1938). Siewert was also one of many who pointed out the proximity of Malta to Sicily, arguing that in the age of the aircraft Malta was untenable. This theory was one often adduced by RAF and Army officers in Britain before the war, leading, despite the Navy's protestations, to the weak and unprepared state of the island when war did finally break out.

4. The whole area abounds in Homeric place names. The long-identified Scylla is the rock on the toe of Italy (opposite the whirlpool Charybdis on the Sicilian side of the Messina Straits) from which the legendary monster seized passing sailors. Italian journalists also sometimes referred to Malta as "Medusa," not inappropriate since the Homeric Medusa turned people who looked upon her to stone. Also, in modern Italian, *medusa* is the word for the poisonous jellyfish.

5. German books and articles dealing with Malta in World War II include: *H. J. Nowarra, Geleitzug-Schlachten im Mittelmeer* (1978); Th. Weber, *Luftschlacht um Malta, Flugwehr un Technik* (1956); O. Möhlenbeck, *Ein Kampf gegan Malta und um Nordafrika* (1966); W. Warlimont, *Insel Malta in der Mittelmeer—Strategie des Zweiten Weltkriegs.* (1958).

6. From a conversation with a Messerschmitt pilot in Mtarfa Hospital re-

corded in the diary of O. Ormrod, a Hurricane pilot who was himself killed over the island in April 1942.

7. Weldon, op. cit.

Chapter Twenty-one

1. Francisco Balbi di Correggio, *The Siege of Malta,* trans. from the Spanish edition of 1568 by Ernle Bradford (London: The Folio Society, 1965).

2. Gray was a brave man, and his on-the-spot reports from Malta are as good as any that survive. George Hogan, op. cit., wrote: "He told the few of us who sometimes congregated near Fort St. Elmo in Valletta of life in England, and brought over to us the feeling of home and the suffering there, too." It was clear that he thought life in Malta and the interminable air raids were even worse—almost unendurable.

3. Hogan, op. cit.

4. Attard, op. cit.

5. Joseph Conrad, *Typhoon* (1903).

6. Cunningham, op. cit.

Chapter Twenty-two

1. About four thousand tons of seed potatoes had normally been imported each year. After the loss of this important cargo, substitute tubers were brought in from Cyprus, but they failed to germinate satisfactorily in Maltese soil.

2. In the postwar years, during the reconstruction and redevelopment of the island, an attempt was made to start a commercial fishing industry using modern trawlers. The venture failed for many reasons, the salient one being that the total unsuitability of the sea area had not been taken into consideration.

3. This story was still current in Kalkara when I lived in the village some years after the war.

Chapter Twenty-three

1. Cunningham, op. cit.

2. Too much should not be made of this. The British destroyers by their mobility and their diversity clearly had many advantages. One of the most surprising things about the day's action is the apparent inactivity of the Italian destroyers.

3. Under the circumstances—wind, difficult weather, heavy sea, heavy fire—this may not appear surprising. The British torpedo-control system, however, as compared with its gunnery control, remained somewhat in the "Jutland era" until late in the war.

4. The Italians certainly built the most beautiful-looking warships of this period, but they were not comparable in sea-keeping qualities and strength to those of the British.

5. The last voyage of the *Breconshire* has been recounted in a number of accounts of the Malta convoys, notably in Cameron, op. cit.

Chapter Twenty-four

1. Perowne, op. cit.

2. T. S. Eliot, O.M., *The Hollow Men* (1925).

3. Paul Cassar, M.D., *Medical History of Malta* (London: Wellcome Historical Medical Library, 1964).

4. Alastair Mars, *Unbroken. The Story of a Submarine* (London: Frederick Muller, 1953). This book and the same author's *British Submarines at War 1939–1945* give a lively personal account of the submariner's life in the idiom of the times.

CHAPTER TWENTY-FIVE

1. Weldon, op. cit.

2. The medal itself was not officially presented until September 13, 1942, when Lord Gort, who had succeeded General Dobbie as governor, handed it over to Sir George Borg, the Chief Justice of Malta, in a formal ceremony on Palace Square in Valletta. The silver cross was later displayed in villages throughout the island so that all citizens could see the tribute that had been paid to their courage in withstanding what Lord Gort termed "the most concentrated bombing in the history of the world." The medal and the citation are now displayed in the Palace in Valletta, and a plaque on the wall outside records the citation.

3. D. Barnham, *One Man's Window* (London: William Kimber, 1956).

4. *The Air Battle of Malta,* op. cit.

CHAPTER TWENTY-SIX

1. Cunningham, op. cit.

2. Lord Gort arrived by Sunderland flying boat during the night of May 7, 1942, touching down off the Kalafrana seaplane base in the south of the island. He and General Dobbie, together with Malta's civic leaders and the service chiefs, met in a bomb-damaged building at the Fleet Air Arm base, where Lord Gort took the oath of office. (May 7 was the Feast of our Lady of Pompeii, usually celebrated by the Maltese with offerings of roses.) During the swearing-in ceremony a stick of bombs dropped near the building where the dignitaries were gathered. The whole situation was somewhat reminiscent of the last days of Pompeii. After the governorship of the island had been formally handed over, General Dobbie and his family boarded the same Sunderland that had brought in his successor and flew off to Gibraltar. The new governor proceeded into the capital through an air raid.

3. *The Air Battle of Malta,* op. cit.

4. Ibid.

5. Micallef, op. cit., presents many details of life under the siege that have escaped the attention of other writers more preoccupied with the war in itself.

CHAPTER TWENTY-SEVEN

1. Calvocoressi, op. cit.

2. "In the period from 26th May to 27th July, Malta-based aircraft made 191 sorties, of which 102 were directed against shipping at sea and sixty-two against ports and bases. With the aid of air superiority Malta was regaining her position as an air/sea offensive base." *The Air Battle of Malta,* op. cit.

3. The *Centurion* certainly did attract the enemy, being the main object of attack and being hit a number of times. A W/T operator who was lent from

H.M.S. *Glenroy* to the *Centurion* for the duration of the convoy provided an illustration of something the writer had hitherto thought to be an old wives' tale: He left the *Glenroy* with a normal crop of dark hair and returned to the ship after the convoy with a snow-white thatch. All conceded that it was most interesting. . . .

4. Both convoys were desperately hard fought—among the worst of all the Malta convoys—involving continuous bombing, submarine attacks, and even the intervention of surface forces. For full accounts see Donald Macintyre, op. cit., and Cameron, op. cit. It is safe to say that if Rear Admiral Vian, in command of the cruiser escort from Alexandria, had been left in sole control, he would have fought as brilliantly as he had previously done in the Battle of Serte. Certainly, *some* of his merchant ships would have got through. The combined command ("remote control") exercised by the Navy and the Air Force from Alexandria proved disastrous.

CHAPTER TWENTY-EIGHT

1. Weldon, op. cit.
2. W. Beck, Reuters correspondent in Malta. Quoted in Micallef, op. cit.
3. Fernand Braudel, *The Mediterranean and the Mediterranean World in the Age of Philip II, trans.* Sian Reynolds (New York: Harper & Row, 1972).
4. Sir Arthur Bryant, *The Turn of the Tide 1939–1943.* A history of the war years based on the diaries of Field Marshal Lord Alanbrooke (New York: Doubleday, 1957). Field Marshal Lord Alanbrooke. Alanbrooke's impressions of the island, which he toured briefly before flying on to Cairo, confirm all the others: "The destruction is inconceivable and reminds me of Ypres, Arras, Lens at their worst during the last war." The salient difference was that a whole civilian population was *living* under these conditions.

CHAPTER TWENTY-NINE

1. *The Air Battle of Malta,* op. cit.
2. Ibid.
3. Elliott, op. cit.

CHAPTER THIRTY

1. The Mediterranean was a notoriously difficult area for the submarine-detection device now called sonar but then known as asdic after the British abbreviated name (it being a British invention). The water's high salinity and varying densities, and the occurrence of curious layers of cold water that deflected the Asdic transmission, were major factors in unreliability. Also, in some parts of the sea whales returned an echo that the nervous operators were likely to accept as submarines. The Mediterranean is not and never has been a whaling sea, but modern information suggests that a certain amount of old bull whales "retire" to its indulgent waters, usually accompanied by a small group of three or four cows. (Some human analogy seems obvious here.)
2. From these beginnings the Germans were later to develop a somewhat similar pilotless glider bomb that was first used effectively from a Junkers 88 against

the Italian battleship *Roma* in September 1943, at the time of the Italian surrender. The *Roma,* on her way to Malta, was a total loss.

3. Apart from Macintyre, op. cit., and Cameron, op. cit., the story of this convoy has been told at length in Peter Shankland and Anthony Hunter, *Malta Convoy,* which relates the saga of the *Ohio* in detail and gives a more accurate picture of just what such a convoy was like for those involved in it than many pages of official war histories.

CHAPTER THIRTY-TWO

1. In June 1943 King George VI visited Malta aboard the cruiser *Aurora,* familiar to the islanders from her days in Force K. He received a tumultuous welcome from the people, which Admiral Cunningham (now back in the Mediterranean as Allied Naval Commander of the Expeditionary Force in North Africa) described in his autobiography (op. cit.): "The dense throngs of loyal Maltese, men, women and children, were wild with enthusiasm. I have never heard such cheering, and all the bells in the many churches started ringing when he landed.... It was the first time a Sovereign had landed in the island since 1911, and the effect on the inhabitants was tremendous. The visit produced one of the most spontaneous and genuine demonstrations of loyalty and affection that I have ever seen."

Malta was chosen as the site of Allied headquarters for the invasion of Sicily (once again demonstrating its outstanding importance as a communications and intelligence center). Among the many other notables who visited over these months were Generals Eisenhower, Alexander, and Montgomery.

On September 8, 1943—the anniversary of the end of the Great Siege of 1565—the Italian fleet set sail to Malta to surrender, the armistice with Italy having been concluded. On September 11, Admiral Cunningham was able to make the historic signal to the Admiralty: "Be pleased to inform their Lordships that the Italian Battlefleet now lies at anchor under the guns of the fortress of Malta."

Early in 1945 Prime Minister Churchill and President Roosevelt both came to Malta, together with the many officers of their respective staffs, on their way through to their fateful meeting with Stalin in the Crimea.

2. The song "Malta of Gold" is quoted in Pernot's edition of Vendôme's *History of Malta and the War between the Knights and the Grand Turk* (Paris: 1910).

3. On October 23, 1942, the Battle of El Alamein began. On November 8 the Anglo-American assault forces landed in North Africa prior to the occupation of French Morocco, Algeria, and Tunisia.

4. Weldon, op. cit.

5. In December 1942 four convoys sailed into Malta without loss, and in this one month some 200,000 tons of stores of all kinds were brought ashore. It took a long time, however, for the physical damage caused by shortage of food and living conditions generally to be made good. The effects of malnutrition and its attendant diseases were further aggravated in November 1942, by a severe epidemic of poliomyelitis that did not bate until the beginning of June the following year.

Index